Beate Wagner-Hasel

The Fabric of Gifts

Culture and Politics of Giving and
Exchange in Archaic Greece

Translated from German by Elena Theodorakopoulos

Revised edition of *Der Stoff der Gaben: Kultur und Politik des
Schenkens und Tauschens im archaischen Griechenland*
(Frankfurt & New York: Campus 2000)

Zea Books
Lincoln, Nebraska
2020

Copyright © 2020 Beate Wagner-Hasel

ISBN: 978-1-60962-173-5

doi 10.32873/unl.dc.zea.1102

Composed in Sitka, New Athena, and Lithos types.

Zea Books are published by the
University of Nebraska–Lincoln Libraries.

Electronic (pdf) edition available online at
https://digitalcommons.unl.edu/zeabook/
Print edition available from
http://www.lulu.com/spotlight/unllib

UNL does not discriminate based upon any protected status.
Please go to https://www.unl.edu/equity/notice-nondiscrimination

Contents

List of Illustrations 5
Preface and Acknowledgements 7
Introduction 9

1. The Circulation of Goods and the Theory of Gifts: A Debate on
   Economy and Morality 19
   1.1. Prehistory of the gift: Discourses of law and economics on gifts
        and exchange 19
        1.1.1. The gift in the debates of the Historical School of political
               economy 20
        1.1.2. The legal-historical debate: From reciprocity to free surrender . . 26
        1.1.3. The sociological debate: The contribution of Marcel Mauss 35
   1.2. Critique of modernity and the idealisation of the gift. 39
   1.3. Return ticket to the South Sea Islands: On the use of ethnological
        comparisons and a critique of reciprocity 53
   1.4. Gift-exchange in the Greek world: The debate over the formation
        of state and *polis* 59
   1.5. Methodological reflections: The sensory world of signs and the
        imagery of Homeric epic 76

2. Guest-Gifts and Relationships in Homer: *Xeinia* and *Phila Dōra* 80
   2.1. *Xeinion* and *dōtinē*: The hospitality of the herdsmen Eumaeus
        and Polyphemus 83
   2.2. Exchanging arms: Glaucus and Diomedes 96
   2.3. Goblets and textiles: *Xeinion* as *keimēlion* and the ritual of
        guest-friendship 112
        2.3.1. Mementoes and tributes: Tripods, goblets, mixing bowls,
               and cloth 113
        2.3.2. The ritual of guest-friendship: Bathing, libation, and dressing . 122
        2.3.3. The terms of hospitality: *Xeinizein, komizein, phileein* 127
   2.4. Woven textiles, sacrifice, and the formation of bonds: *Philotēs*. . . . 133

3. Structures of Reciprocity and the Production of Signs: *Charis* and
   the Charites 144
   3.1. The warrior's service and the gods' favour 146
   3.2. Women's thanks and the weaving of *amphipoloi* and Charites 155
   3.3. Visualizing status: *Charis* in appearance and speech 169

CONTENTS

4. *Timē* and *Geras*: Gifts of Honour and Structures of Power 185
   4.1. Homeric kingship 185
   4.2. The visibility and socioeconomic value of honour: Fighting
        for Agamemnon's *timē* and the *geras* of Achilles 192
        4.2.1. The terminology of social value: τιμή (*timē*), τιμήεις/τιμήεσσα
               (*timēeis/timēessa*), τίμιος (*timios*), and ἄτιμος (*atimos*) 193
        4.2.2. The economic meaning of honour: *Dōtinai, themistes,
               temenos* 200
        4.2.3. Rulership and social control: *Aidōs* 209
        4.2.4. Honouring the *basileus* and the *basileia* 215
        4.2.5. *Themistes* and the sceptre 219
        4.2.6. The distribution of *timē* and the character of Homeric
               kingship 222
   4.3. Penelope's trick and the *geras* of Odysseus: Weaving as a
        symbol of power 232
   4.4. The *geras* of the dead and the process of renewal in the
        death ritual 246

5. The Benefits of Travel and Supraregional Exchange in the Archaic Age . . 266
   5.1. Paying debts of cattle and exchanging pasture lands:
        Prēxis, chreios, and *amoibē* 270
   5.2. *Kerdos* and *ōnos hodaiōn*: Pastoral yields and profits from
        kidnapping 280
        5.2.1. *Kerdos, kerdea, kerdios, kerdaleos* 280
        5.2.2. *Ōnos* and *apoina* 290
   5.3. The quest for the means of living (*biotos*) and other necessary
        goods: Alum, purple, linen, and metals 295
   5.4. Transhumance, supraregional exchange, and the emergence of
        extra-urban sanctuaries 311
        5.4.1. The golden tripod of the Seven Sages 311
        5.4.2. Transhumance and exchange 315
        5.4.3. Sanctuaries at the periphery 320

6. Conclusion: The Sensory World of Gifts: Weaving, Signs, and
   Communication 328

Bibliography 347
Index 412

Illustrations

Figure 1a: The joint coverlet. Red-figure *kylix*. Paris. Louvre G 99.
Photo: Egisto Sani, https://www.flickr.com/photos/69716881@N02/9195936448 140

Figure 1b: Couple sitting on a *klinē* and wrapped in a common mantle. Attic red-figure *kylix* of the Marlay painter, ca 430 BCE. Vienna, Kunsthistorisches Museum 131. After Koch-Harnack 1989: 137, Fig. 7. 140

Figure 2: Wool working at Athens. Attic black-figure *lekythos* of the Amasis painter. 540 BCE. New York, The Metropolitan Museum of Art, Fletcher Fund 1931, 31.11.10
https://www.metmuseum.org/en/art/collection/search/253348 158

Figure 3: The warp-weighted loom. Harlizius-Klück 2004: 103, Fig. 11, cf. also Barber 1991: 270, Fig. 12.3 with modifications. 164

Figure 4: Warp-weighted loom with figured weave.
Ellen Harlizius-Klück 2016: 70, Fig. 5.2. 165

Figure 5: Prothesis. Geometric Attic mixing bowl, ca 750 BCE.
Paris, Louvre A 517. After Kurtz and Boardman 1971: Fig. 7. 166

Figure 6: Indonesian ceremonial cloth. Supplementary weft weave. Sumatra, Lampung, late nineteenth century CE.
After Kahn-Majlis 1991: Fig. 78. 167

Figure 7: The mourning Penelope. Red-figure *skyphos* of the Penelope painter, ca 440 BCE. Chiusi, Museo Nazionale Archaeologico Inv. 1831. After Boardman 1989: Fig. 247 (= J. D. Beazley, *Attic Red-figure Vase-paintings* 1963: 1300, 2 = A. Furtwängler and K. Reichhold, *Griechische Vasenmalerei*, 1904–32). 260

Figure 8: Hermes weighing *eidola*. Attic black-figure *lekythos*, 5th century BCE. London, British Museum B 639.
https://research.britishmuseum.org/research/collection_online/collection_object_details/collection_image_gallery.aspx?partid=1&assetid=1305668001&objectid=459047. 261

ILLUSTRATIONS

Figure 9: Arcesilaus weighing silphium or wool. Laconian *kylix*,
 ca 560 BCE. Bibliothèque Nationale, Cabinet des Médailles 1899.
 http://medaillesetantiques.bnf.fr/ark:/12148/c33gbhc8h 304

Figure 10: Nine women wrapped in a common cloak. Black-figure *kylix*,
 5th century BCE. Berlin, Antikenmuseum F 3993.
 After Koch-Harnack 1989: 111, Fig. 1. 342

Figure 11: A group of women on Sumba wrapped in an Indian cotton
 textile performing a dance prior to the burial of
 King Umbu Nai Wolang of Kapunduk.
 After Kahn-Majlis 1991: Fig. 2. 342

Preface and Acknowledgements

This study, *The Fabric of Gifts: Culture and Politics of Giving and Exchange in Archaic Greece*, is a revised edition of my book *Der Stoff der Gaben: Kultur and Politik des Schenkens und Tauschens im archaischen Griechenland*, a book originally developed as a *Habilitationschrift* in 1995 and published in 2000. Marie-Louise Nosch, the founder of the Centre for Textile Research at the University of Copenhagen, took an interest in my research on textiles as gifts and suggested a translation of my study into English to make it accessible to a wider academic readership. In 2013 a cooperation between the Copenhagen Centre of Textile Research and the Historical Seminar (*Historisches Seminar*) of the *Leibniz Universität Hannover* was established, thanks to the generous support from the Alexander von Humboldt-Stiftung and the Anneliese Maier Award. The results of this cooperation were presented at a conference in Hannover in 2016; the papers on *Waren, Gaben und Tribute: Stoffkreisläufe und antike Textilökonomie* were published in 2019. The interest our cooperation has raised, current interest in economic history,[1] and recent research in the cultural history of material objects, especially in the historical investigation of sensory experiences,[2] encouraged me to take up Marie-Louise Nosch's suggestion and work on the English translation.

In recent years, practices of giving in the ancient world have become the subject of many publications and conferences.[3] Yet little attention is being paid to the symbolism of the materiality of gifts. It is this symbolism that is at the core of my argument. I am also confident that my study *The Fabric of Gifts* offers some answers to the new debate on the character of archaic aristocracy, in which the circulation of goods forms a key factor for understanding elite competition.[4] Parts of the first chapter of my book,

---

1. Drexhage, Konen and Ruffing 2002; Mattingly and Salmon 2001; Eich 2006; Morley 2007; Klinkott et al. 2007; Bresson 2008; Burns 2010; Wagner-Hasel 2011: 315-340; Droß-Krüpe and Nosch 2016.
2. See now Grand-Clément 2011; Hamilakis 2012; Bradley 2015; Squire 2016; Purves 2018; Canevaro 2018.
3. See Algazi, Groebner and Jussen 2003; Satlow 2012; Lyons 2012; Carlà and Gori 2014.
4. See Duplouy 2006; Fisher and van Wees 2015; Domingo Gygax 2016; Meister 2020.

those dealing with the relationship between gift theory and the critique of modernity,[5] were published in English in 2003 and 2005.[6] Some considerations on the exchange of gifts between couples, discussed in the third chapter, can be found in my publications in English on the *Charites and colour-weaving*[7] and on the Solonian regulation of the dowry in ancient Athens.[8] As part of the translation, some footnotes have been revised and some additions made to the bibliography. The final chapter of the original book, that on the role played by Delphi as the centre of a supraregional network of transhumant relationships, has been omitted from this English version. Instead, I have added a new section on *Transhumance, supraregional exchange, and central sanctuaries* to the fifth chapter, dealing with the terminology of exchange. Translations from the Greek are by Elena Theodorakopoulos unless otherwise acknowledged. Abbreviations follow *The Oxford Classical Dictionary*.

I thank Elena Theodorakopoulos for her careful translation. Particular thanks are due to Claire Taylor and Liselotte Glage for reading and helpful comments. My warmest thanks go to Marie-Louise Nosch and her generosity in supporting the English publication. I would like to thank, once again, those colleagues and friends who supported the German version of this book with their valuable comments and hints, especially Okko Behrends, Hinnerk Bruhns, Justus Cobet, Hans-Joachim Gehrke, Susanne Gödde, Ruth E. Harder, Elke Hartmann, Hans-Jürgen Hildebrandt, Ludolf Kuchenbuch, Jochen Martin, Astrid Möller, Wilfried Nippel, Évelyne Scheid-Tissinier, Pauline Schmitt Pantel, Michael Stahl, Katharina Waldner, and Anja Wieber. Last but not least I would like to thank Paul Royster and Linnea Fredrickson from the University of Nebraska–Lincoln Libraries for their efficient and kind help with the final editing. The University of Nebraska and the Leibniz University of Hannover are partner universities. This book is therefore a result not only of the cooperation between Copenhagen and Hannover, but also between Europe and the United States.

Hannover, February 2020

---

5. See now Azoulay 2012, who took up my argument.
6. Wagner-Hasel 2003; 2005.
7. Wagner-Hasel 2002. The ideas I developed there were used by McNeil 2005.
8. Wagner-Hasel 2012.

Introduction

In Plutarch's *Life of Solon*, the circulation of the tripod among the Seven Sages is said to have 'contributed still further to their standing and fame' as it was handed around 'with honourable good will' (Plutarch, *Sol.* 4.1).[1] Barely a century ago a similar circulation of objects undertaken for the sake of honour could be observed in the South Pacific. The father of modern anthropology, Bronislaw Malinowski, describes the circulation and exchange of prestige goods, called the *Kula* or *Kula* ring, in his famous 1922 book *Argonauts of the Western Pacific*. This title involved reference to ancient practices—not to the tale of the circulation of the golden tripod but to the myth of the first seafarers, the Argonauts, and their search for the Golden Fleece. Shortly afterwards Marcel Mauss would develop crucial elements of his theory of the gift with reference to the *Kula*.[2] In his famous *Essai sur le don: Forme et raison de l'échange dans les sociétés archaiques*, published in 1923/24 in the journal *L'Année sociologique*,[3] Mauss undertook to grasp both the social and the ethical dimensions of the exchange of objects observed in the Trobriand Islands and elsewhere in the world. The flow of goods in the Trobriand system of exchange does not imply a transfer of ownership, but it does involve forms of compensation, which means that it cannot legally be defined as a form of goods-exchange or trade, nor is it simple gift-giving. Thus, this new form of exchange was defined as gift-exchange, or more simply as reciprocity.[4]

The results from this early ethnographic research, and of the sociological theorisation that built on it, have made a lasting impact on anthropology and on sociology, even if they have been subject to numerous modifications and critical reviews.[5] Our own disciplines saw the *Return of the Argonauts from the South Pacific*—to cite the programmatic title of a 1982 study of the

---

1. For further detail see ch. 5.4.
2. For the influence of Malinowski on Mauss see Firth 1963: 222.
3. Mauss's *Essai sur le don* was translated into English as *The Gift* in 1954 by Ian Cunnison, in 1990 by W. D. Halls, and in 2016 by Jane Guyer.
4. The concept of reciprocity ('Gegenseitigkeit') goes back to Richard Thurnwald, who, like Malinowski, conducted his ethnographic research in the South Pacific. For further detail see ch. 1.
5. For an overview of the anthropological debate see Gregory 1982; Godelier 1996: 19–53.

influence of economic anthropology on the field of ancient history—around fifty years after Malinowski's and Mauss's first contributions.[6] Since the beginning of the 1980s there has been a marked increase in the influence of gift theory in classics and ancient history,[7] as demonstrated by titles such as *Reciprocities in Homer*,[8] *The Treasury at Persepolis: Gift-Giving at the City of the Persians*,[9] *Gift and Commodity in Archaic Greece*,[10] *Gifts to the Gods*,[11] and *Reciprocity and Ritual*.[12] Such scholarship is no longer limited only to the analysis of the Homeric world, which was the focus of Moses Finley's 1954 book *The World of Odysseus*—often thought of as the first work to apply Mauss's research to the analysis of ancient evidence.[13] These days, the rule of Roman imperial families is as likely to be analysed in terms of gift-exchange[14] as the practices of early Greek tyrants or the politicians of classical Athens.[15] Not only Homer and other Greek authors such as Pindar, Aeschylus, Euripides, and Herodotus[16] but also Roman writers like Seneca or Martial are thought now to bear witness to the widespread ancient practice of establishing networks of obligation and reciprocity through the exchange of gifts.[17]

A large number of early publications were concerned with the debate about the character of ancient rulership and the development of the *polis* and/or the state in ancient Greece. Here, the focus is primarily on rituals of generosity and on competitive forms of giving, which are interpreted

6. Nippel 1982: 1–39; for a modified reprint see Nippel 1990: 124–51.
7. In France, Louis Gernet, a sometime collaborator of Marcel Mauss, contributed the earlier and more sustained influence of Maussian theory on ancient historians and classicists. See Humphreys 1983: 175–79.
8. Donlan 1982.
9. Cahill 1985.
10. Morris 1986.
11. Linders and Nordquist 1987.
12. Seaford 1994.
13. Cf. e.g. Donlan 1989: 2 and Qviller 1981: 112, who praises the revolutionary character of Finley's discovery. In the first edition of the *World of Odysseus*, Finley refers only to Malinowski and to Karl Polanyi; it was only in the revised edition, published in 1978, that he named Marcel Mauss. For the discussion of the scientific background of Finley's research, see Shaw and Saller 1981; Nafissi 2005; Scheid-Tissinier 2005.
14. Cf. Flaig 1993: 289–305; Martin 1994: 106; Grüner 2007; Zuiderhoek 2009; Beyeler 2011.
15. Herman 1987; 2006; Satlow 2012; Carlà and Gori 2014; Domingo Gygax 2016; Maehle 2018.
16. Campagner 1988: 77–93; Gould 1991; Seaford 1994; Gill, Postlethwaite and Seaford 1998; Mueller 2001; Lyons 2012.
17. Spisak 1998; Griffin 2003; Grüner 2007: 460; Zuiderhoek 2009; Coffee 2017; Hildebrandt 2019; Wieber 2019.

INTRODUCTION 11

as evidence for the lack of institutionalisation in early Greek systems of rulership,[18] and the creation of bonds through guest-friendship.[19] Prehistorians are especially interested in the debate around the relationship between trade and goods-exchange and guest-friendship.[20] Other aspects of religious or social practices of gift-giving such as sacrifice, votive offering,[21] or the giving of gifts in the contexts of marriage[22] or pederasty, are increasingly examined.[23]

Theoretical concepts are no longer limited to the influence of Mauss and Malinowski but remain indebted to social and economic anthropology. The work of the Hungarian-American historian and economist Karl Polanyi is of considerable significance here. In the 1940s Polanyi differentiated between forms of exchange such as 'reciprocity', 'distribution', and 'market exchange', developing categories that were further refined and modified by his students and colleagues.[24] Of these developments, the most significant for classical scholarship were Marshall Sahlins's distinction between generalised, balanced, and negative reciprocity and Paul Bohannan's recognition of the separation between the routes of circulation of subsistence and prestige goods.[25] The differentiation between short-term and long-term transactional orders made by Maurice Bloch and Milman Parry is now widely accepted.[26] Notwithstanding some variations in theoretical frameworks, most scholars accept the Maussian notion that gifts create a relationship of obligation between the giver and the receiver.[27] Originally, these forms of exchange had been thought of as belonging to separate historical eras, but since ethnographic observations suggest the contemporaneous presence of practices of gift-exchange and market exchange, recent scholarship postulates a similar contemporaneity for antiquity.[28] Therefore, economic

18. See esp. Qviller 1981: 109–155; Donlan 1982: 1–15; 1989: 5–29. Cf. also Stahl 1987: 87, 141; Stein-Hölkeskamp 1989: 50–54 in reference to rituals of demonstrative consumption.
19. Herman 1987; Mitchell 1997; Zuiderhoek 2009; Grüner 2007.
20. Kromer 1982: 21–30; Bradley 1982: 108–22; 1985: 692–704; Coldstream 1983: 201–207; Rowlands, Larsen and Kristiansen 1987; Shortman 1989: 52–65.
21. von Straten 1981: 65–151, 283–311; Linders and Nordquist 1987; Bartoloni, Colonna and Grottanelli 1989–90; Silber 2002; Patera 2012; Brøns 2017.
22. Finley 1955; Scheid 1979; Wagner-Hasel 1988; 2009; 2012; Mueller 2001; Lyons 2003, 2012; McNeil 2005; Wieber 2019.
23. Koch-Harnack 1983; von Reden 1995: 195–216.
24. Polanyi 1957a: 243–270.
25. Sahlins 1974: 185–275 and Bohannan 1955; 1968. Donlan 1982 uses both concepts.
26. Cf. e.g. von Reden 1995; Foxhall 2007: 30; Widzisz 2012.
27. Von Reden 1995; Domingo Gygax 2016: 29; Grüner 2007: 459.
28. Cf. e.g. Morris 1986 who refers to the anthropological research of Gregory 1982.

concepts, such as game theory and rational choice theory, developed for the interpretation of economic behaviour in modern societies, are now used to interpret ancient practices of reciprocity.[29]

The close links between classical scholarship on gift-exchange and ethnographical theory account also for the delayed reception of the Maussian concept of the gift by ancient historians. It is not surprising that Malinowski chose to refer to an ancient myth in the title of his book. The long history of the reception of classical myth in Europe meant that whenever explorers set out towards the rest of the world, they could take comfortable recourse in projecting their experiences onto the 'closest other'. The projection of the Greek myth of the Argonauts onto the *Kula*-traders in the Western Pacific may serve to assimilate or familiarise the foreign culture into a Western discourse. Conversely, however, it has an alienating effect too. Through association with the gift-exchange practices of the Trobriands, the Greeks, cultural heroes of the Western world, are moved into the realm of what—not so long ago—was thought of as the 'savage' or 'uncivilised' world. Even Finley refers to the Trobriand islanders as 'primitive' and is keen to emphasise the cultural superiority of the Greeks: 'The Greeks of Homer were not primitive men, like Malinowski's Trobriands; they lived in what is often called, by convention, an archaic society. And the Greeks of the succeeding centuries were remarkably civilised people.'[30]

The homage paid here by Finley to the belief in the greatness of ancient civilisation may sound anachronistic today, but it is entirely in keeping with the ethos of classical scholarship in Europe in the decades after World War II.[31] In our now 'inter-connected, polyphonous world', 'in which all demand to be heard by all', as the classical archaeologist Tonio Hölscher put it several years ago in his plea for an alienated view of ancient art, the old Eurocentric position threatens to lock classical scholarship into an ivory tower.[32] Christian Meier is right when he demands

---

29. Cf. e.g. Herman 1998; 2006; Low 2007: 43–54; Tracy 2014. For discussions in recent economic theory see Rehbinder 2012.
30. Finley 2002: 5 (NYRB edition).
31. Cf. e.g. Dodds 1973: 26–27, who praises ancient cultures as a source of moral and intellectual values of the western European culture. Alexander Rüstow warned of the dangers of 'unbridled relativism' that would result from any departure from this 'humanist point of view' (1952: 12).
32. Hölscher 1989: 5.

INTRODUCTION   13

that we acknowledge the changed position of Europe in the world and abandon the privileging of ancient and western history in order to redefine the place of antiquity in the history of the world.[33] As he notes, 'it will become clear that statements about Greek distinctiveness that do not take into account a rounded view of other cultures, will no longer be up to scholarly standards'.[34]

Taking proper account of the reality of our interconnected 'one world'[35] means that communication with disciplines such as anthropology that are able to give us access to knowledge of non-European cultures is a matter of urgency. Indeed, it is quite likely that such interdisciplinary communication has been responsible for the increasing interest of ancient historians in the practices of gift-exchange over the past thirty years. Comparative approaches are, however, no recent discovery. The progressive Enlightenment scholars of the eighteenth century and the adherents to evolutionary theory of late nineteenth-century legal history were already perfectly happy to compare the Greeks to the 'primitive' peoples of America or the South Seas.[36] And when we look at the history of the debate on gift-giving we will see that many of the positions now represented with reference to Mauss and Finley can be found—illustrated with examples from ancient, medieval, and non-European contexts—in the writings of evolutionist historical and economic historians of the nineteenth century. This is true for the obligatory and obliging character of gifts that Mauss was so keen to emphasise, as much as for the reciprocal nature of premodern gift-giving. Many of these works of legal and economic history have found their way into ancient history quite independently of Mauss. Both Mauss and Finley thus stand at the beginning and at the end of a tradition of studying archaic forms of communication. This tradition has its origins not only in the Historical School's critique of the universal validity of Adam Smith's classical liberal theory but also looks back to the legal historians' debate over the nature of premodern gift-giving. This prehistory, well known to Mauss himself, has fallen into

---

33. Meier 1989: 22 and 15. See also Settis 2005.
34. Meier 1989: 24.
35. See Wolf 1982: 23.
36. See Moravia [1970] 1989: 137–44. For the practice of comparative research in classical scholarship history see Finley 1975: 102–20; Humphreys 1983: 15–30; Hunter 1981: 144–55; Ampolo 1986: 127–31; Nippel 1988: 300–18; 1990; Settis 2005; Payen and Scheid-Tissinier 2012.

oblivion as a consequence of the paradigm shift from evolutionism to cultural relativism and structuralism. *Essai sur le don* stands at the pivot of this change—a context which has been barely considered to date.[37]

I do not wish to diminish Finley's contribution to the study of gift-exchange in antiquity. But the claim that it was he who introduced Mauss's theory into classical scholarship has more to do with scholarly hero-worship than it does with the facts of the history of scholarship.[38] The long interval between the publication of *The World of Odysseus* in 1954 and the beginning of the gift-exchange debate in classical scholarship in the early 1980s argues against such linear genealogy.

It was no coincidence that the debate began at a time when the creation of the 'one world', which had begun with the explorers of the early modern age, entered a new stage with the industrialisation of Europe. In their attempts to make theoretical sense of this new stage, evolutionist scholars could look to the ethnographical reports of these explorers. The latter had themselves made practical use of the phenomenon idealised in ethnographic research by using gifts to create obligation. During the same period, the new legal definition of donation as an altruistic act that enriches only the receiver was developed in the centres of the old world.[39] With this, the distance between the reciprocal customs of gift-giving common in peripheral cultures and the new European conceptions of altruistic gift-giving increased. Theorising about the practice of gift-exchange should also be understood as going hand in hand with the process of structural transformation undergone by the western industrialised societies of the nineteenth and twentieth centuries. The idealising tendencies that can be observed, especially in Mauss but also in Malinowski, make sense as an aspect of theoretical reappropriation such as is often prominent in times of crisis. Like many other new concepts that emerge as forms of a critique of modernity, and in which the strangeness and difference of antiquity are underlined, the theory of the gift also contains a kind of reversal of the present.[40]

---

37. For the forerunners of Malinowski see Köcke 1979: 119–67. Maffi 1979: 33–62 discusses the development after Mauss. See also Geary 2003, who stresses the influence of American anthropologists on Mauss, and Wagner-Hasel (2011: 289–95 and 2014: 51–69) on the influence of the German Historical School of political economy.
38. See n. 13.
39. See ch. 1.
40. See e.g. the concept of matriarchy as a kind of critique of modernity. Gossman 1987; Wagner-Hasel 1992: 295–373.

INTRODUCTION   15

My first chapter pursues the economic and ethical ramifications of the theory of the gift before subsequent chapters turn to the material content and to the interpretation of ancient evidence. My goal is to gain insight into the structures of communication in archaic Greece and to contribute to the history of the formation of the *polis* through the analysis of the semantics and circulation of gifts. The object of this historical investigation is not a concrete historical place but a body of texts, the Homeric epics. My starting point is the conceptual analysis of a selection of terms used for giving in Homer.[41] The aim is to examine the messages conveyed by the material and concrete form of gifts. Starting from their material form, conclusions can be drawn about the symbolic and practical meaning these gifts have with respect to the relationships in which they are put to use. These are the types of gifts which have considerable significance for the reconstruction of social structures of communication.

The investigation of the term for guest-gifts, ξεινήιον/ξεινίον (*xeinēion/xeinion*), in chapter 2 takes into account the whole range of circulating objects and the different relationships into which strangers (*xenoi*) are temporarily or permanently integrated. The term χάρις (*charis*), discussed in chapter 3, gives an insight into the inner workings of such relationships. *Charis* denotes the material as well as the abstract effects of services or favours, and of gifts; this alignment of the concrete with the abstract imbues the term with the highest symbolic charge. The potential for conflict inherent in the structures of exchange we are considering becomes apparent in the discussion of the terms for gifts of honour, τιμή (*timē*), and γέρας (*geras*) in chapter 4. With the analysis of the terminology of trade and exchange in chapter five—πρῆξις (*prēxis*), χρεῖος (*chreios*), κέρδος (*kerdos*), ὦνος (*ōnos*), and ἀμοιβή (*amoibē*), usually rendered as 'business', 'debt', 'profit', 'price', and 'exchange'—we return to the question of the function of guest-gifts within reciprocal relationships.

Research into gift-exchange has often disregarded the issue of narrative consistency that is so important for both analytical and unitarian approaches to Homeric epic.[42] Understanding the circulation of gifts depends to some extent on the logic and consistency of epic narration, especially since the narrative action so often focusses precisely on those occasions when the flow of gifts and counter-gifts becomes susceptible to disturbance or breakdown. So, the *Iliad* opens with Achilles's anger about the loss of his gift of honour

---

41. For a philological study of all terms of giving in the epics see Scheid-Tissinier 1994.
42. Cf. e.g. Hölscher 1990.

(*geras*), Brisëis, and it depicts the consequences of the dishonoured hero's refusal of service in battle (*charis*) for Agamemnon. The *Odyssey* deals with Penelope's refusal to complete her weaving task, which in turn maintains for Odysseus the possibility of attaining gifts of honour. If we do not acknowledge narrative sequence, individual acts of giving may appear functional, even when in the context of the narrative itself they are not. Conversely, the refusal of gifts may appear dysfunctional in isolation, while the narrative context will show the intrinsic logic of such refusal. As an example, one may consider the exchange of arms between Glaucus and Diomedes in *Iliad* 6. Scholarship tends to present this as an ideal example of gift-exchange, but I will show further along that the narrative context reveals that this exchange is a reversal of the usual norms of reciprocal giving.

Alongside the question of narrative consistency stands the question of historicity and place. For a long time, archaeological research had pointed to Mycenaean Greece of the second millennium as the historical context for heroic epic. With the oral theory research of the 1930s, dating of the epics has shifted towards the eighth and seventh century as the time when they were fixed as written texts after the spread of the Phoenician alphabet.[43] This turn reflects both the limited historical depth of oral memory and the role of audiences in the reception of oral poetry.[44] It suggests also that the poems must have satisfied the interest of those who are said to have commissioned the creation of a written text and organised the recitation of the Homeric poems during the Great Panathenaic festival: the Athenian tyrant Peisistratus and his sons.[45] Indeed, some scholars think that the epics represent historical realities from as late as the sixth century BCE.[46] Scholars concerned with Homeric gift-exchange tended rather to backdate the social and historical conditions represented in the epics to the ninth century BCE, claiming that the poems reconstruct a 'pre-state' reality.[47]

---

43. See Patzek 1992; Latacz 1979; 1989; Raaflaub 1991: 205–56; Ulf 2002; Rengakos and Zimmermann 2011.
44. This is stressed by Svenbro 1976: 16–35; Jensen 1980: 164; Boyd 1995. See also Thomas 1992; Bakker and Kahane 1997.
45. On the sources of the so-called 'Peisistratean Recension' see Merkelbach 1952 and Boyd 1995. In his account of the 'Peisistratean Recension', Boyd concludes that the story of the organisation and editing of the texts of the *Iliad* and *Odyssey* must be understood as the product of 'a literate age, even while hoping that we can free ourselves to imagine a world before fixed texts' (1995: 45). Svenbro 1976: 106–7 interprets Hipparchos's and Peisistratus's interest in Homer as an attempt to gain control over the tradition.
46. See Jensen 1980: 167–71; Boyd 1995.
47. This is the case for Finley [1954] 1967 and Donlan 1989. For more detail see ch. 1.4.

INTRODUCTION   17

My preferred method, which is to work from the text itself, allows me to reopen the question of the historical era represented in the poems.

Despite the focus on the terminology of giving, this is not strictly a philological study aimed only at establishing the semantic field of individual technical terms. Rather it is intended as a historical study. The analysis of terminology and concepts forms the methodology through which to determine the social symbolism of gifts within early Greek structures of communication. The research context within which I would like to place this investigation is the debate about the formation of regional and supraregional centres that has been invigorated by the works of François de Polignac, *La naissance de la cité grecque: Cultes, espace et sociétés VIIIe-VIIe siècles avant J.C.* (1984, 1995), and Catherine Morgan, *Athletes and Oracles: The Transformation of Olympia und Delphi in the Eight Century B.C.* (1990).[48] With these studies we see attention paid not merely to the inner workings of individual communities or settlements and to conclusions about the formation of state structures. Rather, the formation of the *polis* is now seen as a process of spatial integration and of the increased density of spatial communication. This formation can be observed through the placement of temples on the peripheries of *poleis* and in the establishment of heroic tombs or shrines.[49] The communicative patterns underlying the distribution of gifts are of considerable significance for an understanding of this process; the epics provide the best literary example of an idealised depiction of such patterns of communication through gifts. Often seen as a repository of cultural knowledge,[50] the epics have been linked to the spread of hero-cults practised at the heroic tombs and thus to the evolution of the *polis*.[51] The supraregional level on which the pattern of gift-exchange appears to operate in the poems suggests, as we shall see, that its sociohistorical context is rooted in the interregional communications of the eighth to sixth centuries. This conclusion is also suggested by the placing of the tripod of the Seven Sages, noted at the beginning of this chapter, in supraregional temples.[52]

Current scholarship on gift-exchange has caused the objects themselves to fade into mere abstractions or symbols of power; a key aim of this study

---

48. See also Alcock and Osborne 1994; Rowlands, Larsen and Kristiansen 1987: 1–11.
49. See de Polignac 1996; Wagner-Hasel 2002; McInerney 2006: 33–59; Cole 2004.
50. Havelock 1978: 10–12. Thomas 1992: 116 understands the poet as 'administrator' of the cultural heritage. For more detail see ch. 1.5.
51. Cf. e.g. Coldstream 1979: 341–356; Bérard 1982: 89–105; Snodgrass 1982: 107–19; de Polignac 1984: 42–49; Whitley 1988: 173–82; Patzek 1992: 121–43.
52. See ch. 5.4.

is to recover the sensory, material content of these objects. My approach has certainly been influenced by the interest in cultural history taken by historians since the 1990s.[53] However, in this study, cultural interpretation of history focusses not only on mentality and on the imaginary. It is also built on the interest in material objects themselves that in recent years has been gaining much attention.[54] By analysing the 'sensory content' of gifts, my aim is to illuminate social structures of communication. The title, *The Fabric of Gifts* (*Der Stoff der Gaben*), refers to textile gifts that are just as important in the epics as the metal gifts. While metal gifts may be understood to carry more spatial symbolism, textile gifts are more strongly connected to time than to space and to the internal workings of society. What both types of object have in common is their semiotic power, which is as readable as the language that is used to speak about them.

My approach is also linked to an interest in interdisciplinary communication. At its beginning, research into gift-exchange brought together a range of different disciplines so that the theory of the gift is the result of communication between legal history, political economics, and classical scholarship; once it enters firmly into the realms of sociology and economic anthropology, however, this interdisciplinarity came to an end. It was not only classical scholarship that withdrew from interdisciplinary dialogue;[55] sociology and economic anthropology also pursued new paths, putting aside the ancient world as a field of enquiry into the effects of the gift.[56] The contribution that can now be made by an ancient historical study to the debate on the gift is to recall the roots of that debate, and in particular to recall the critique of modernity which so markedly characterised early discourse on the gift. Thinking about gifts was never only an attempt to approach archaic and forgotten practices. It has always and quite specially been an attempt to understand the relationship between economics and morality—an attempt that may also result in utopian thinking.

---

53. Cf. Daniel 1993: 69–99; Neidhardt 1986: 10–12; Oexle 1995. For a critique see Kaschuba 1995: 27–46.
54. See Grand-Clément 2011; Wagner-Hasel 2015; Canevaro 2018.
55. In German scholarship, the work of the economic historian Bernhard Laum in the 1920s on the development of money in the ancient world forms a turning point in appealing to 'Stammesverwandtschaft' and 'Nachbarschaft', with reference to Eduard Meyer's position, as preconditions for comparative methodologies. Laum 1924: 5–6. In anglophone and French scholarship, the comparative approach is and was much more accepted. See Humphreys 1983; Wittenburg 2012.
56. In the meantime, anthropologists and philosophers are also venturing into classical scholarship. See Beidelman 1989; Hénaff 2002.

CHAPTER 1

The Circulation of Goods and the Theory of Gifts: A Debate on Economy and Morality

1.1. Prehistory of the gift: Discourses of law and economics on gifts and exchange

The history of the debate on gift-exchange is a history of the relationship between economics and ethics within modern societies. The 'founding fathers' of these theoretical discussions leave no doubt about this connection. In his *Argonauts of the Western Pacific* (1922) Bronislaw Malinowski described a form of exchange of goods which was meaningless when viewed from the 'perspective of the imperial market-economy of Europe'.[1] In *Essai sur le don* (1925) Marcel Mauss made use of Malinowski's account to launch an attack on the principles of modern 'rationalism' and 'mercantilism', which were responsible for the increasing value of 'profit and the individual'. He concluded that retaining these principles would harm the 'purpose of the whole, the rhythm of our work and our pleasures, and finally each of us'.[2] Mauss's message is unambiguously critical of, even hostile to, modernity: he advocates the reunification of economics and morality, of social and economic practice, and the subordination of the individual to the needs of the community.[3] In contrast to modern market-economics, Mauss saw in gift-exchange what he described as a 'system of total prestations' ('le système des prestations totales') in which 'the market is but one element and the circulation of wealth but one part of a wide and enduring contract.' The most significant items exchanged in the Maussian system are 'courtesies, entertainments, ritual, military assistance, women, children, dances and feasts', and these exchanges 'take place under a voluntary guise', although 'they are in essence obligatory, and their sanction is private or open warfare'. The three constitutive elements of this form

---

1. See Kramer in Malinowski 1979: 557 and 570.
2. Mauss 1990: 76.
3. See Godelier 1996: 7–12; Berking 1996: 246–55.

of contract, which is not one between individuals but between groups, are giving ('donner'), receiving ('reçevoir'), and returning ('rendre'). Mauss views the alliance of pairs of phratries in Australian and North American tribes as the best representation of this archaic form of contract. In its most evolved form, it can be found in the agonistic exchange ceremonies ('prestation totale de type agonistique'), known as *potlatch*, and practised by the Kwakiutl, Tlingit, and Haida on the northwestern coast of America.[4]

With this critique of modernity, Mauss is part of a tradition reaching back through Émile Durkheim (1858-1917) to the Historical School of political economy ('Historische Schule der Nationalökonomie'). In France, any critique of individualism such as the one Mauss undertook implied a critique of the ideals of the French Revolution.[5] In this, Mauss followed his teacher and uncle, Émile Durkheim, who had argued that the kernel of the development of moral discipline lay in group formation.[6] Durkheim's belief in the collective, often criticised in sociological research, is also informed by a critique of modernity.[7] In the preface to the second edition in 1902 of his study *De la division du travail social* (1893), in which he had laid out the concept of the advance from mechanical to organic solidarity, Durkheim is no less critical than Mauss of the loss of the connection between economics and morality in modern societies. Durkheim suggests here that the dominance of the market over 'military, administrative and religious functions' forms 'a notable source of general demoralization.'[8] As a solution he imagines tying the individual back into the collective sphere through the creation of guilds or similar organisations, which would help to rein in individual egoisms and create feelings of solidarity; for Durkheim this would be synonymous with morality.[9]

1.1.1. The gift in the debates of the Historical School of political economy

A key factor in the formation of Durkheim's belief in the collective emerged during his studies under the psychologist Wilhelm Wundt (1832-1920)

---

4. Mauss 1990: 4.
5. See Giddens 1976: 710.
6. Cf. Lévy-Bruhl 1948/49: 1-4; Hollier 1972: 55-61; Gane 1992; Cefaï and Mahé 1998: 209-28.
7. Cf. Hofmann 1973: 16-30; Adorno 1984: 7-44; Hauck 1984: 106-9. Hauck criticises the moralism of Durkheim, whereas Giddens (1976: 708-14) underlines the social aspects of Durkheim's concept. See also Borlandi 1998: 27-65.
8. Durkheim 1964: 4.
9. Durkheim 1964: 26-31.

and the political economist Gustav von Schmoller (1838–1917) towards the end of the nineteenth century in Germany. Durkheim had drawn his ideas from the Historical School's critique of the neoclassical notion of *homo oeconomicus*. The *Methodenstreit*, the dispute between the Historical School of political economy (of which von Schmoller was a leading exponent at the time) and the adherents of neoclassical liberal economic theory around Adam Smith, e.g. Carl Menger (1840–1921),[10] taking place in the 1880s and 1890s, was therefore a decisive factor in the development of the theory of gift-exchange.

The Historical School had evolved in the wake of historicism and remained essentially limited to German-speaking areas, and within these circles a strictly ethical conception of the economy dominated. The economy was understood, in a neo-romantic sense, as a socio-organic life process subject to continuous change.[11] This, in turn, cast doubt upon the universal applicability of modern economic categories. The Historical School's critique was thus directed against the moral implications of the concept of exchange which had become canonical with the emergence of liberal economic theory, and which presented exchange as an act of self-interest aimed at attaining economic advantage. This critique, therefore, developed into a questioning of the universality of such an understanding of exchange. The legal concept of making a gift ('Schenkung') as an altruistic act undertaken for the benefit of another functioned here as a counter-model, a concept of giving associated with a collective economy. Special emphasis was given, however, to the aspect of mutuality ('Wechselseitigkeit') or reciprocity ('Gegenseitigkeit'), so that in the course of time the concept of 'gift-exchange' was established as the accepted designation for this alternative form of interaction. This concept itself was influenced by legal historians, whose reflections on the character of premodern gifting formed the second root of the theory of gift-exchange.

This association between collective economic systems and altruistic forms of human interaction could already be found among exponents of the older Historical School of political economy, such as Adolph Wagner

10. The Austrian economist Carl Menger, using the deductive approach of classical economics, aimed to develop universal principles of economics, while Gustav von Schmoller proceeded with a primarily inductive approach to relativize the economic theorems of neoclassicists. See Winkel 1977: 138–50; Schmölders 1988: 109–121; Starbatty 1989: 97–134; vom Bruch 1988: 219–38. The debate between representatives of formalist and substantive approaches to the economy continued in the 1960s within anthropology. Cf. Röpke 1969: 101–34.
11. Winkel 1977: 82–89.

(1835–1917). In his book *Allgemeine und theoretische Volkswirtschaftslehre* (1876) Wagner argued that 'mutual solidarity in granting goods and services' was a typical feature of communal economic systems.[12] Drawing on this tradition, which was supposed to have made altruism, or rather public spirit, 'an impulse equal in value to that of acquisition',[13] Gustav von Schmoller distinguished between altruistic domestic economy ('Hauswirtschaft') and egoistic exchange economy ('Tauschwirtschaft'). Schmoller argued that within the former, an individual could be compelled to 'service and assistance', but 'could also receive services and assistance free of charge'. The exchange economy, by contrast, was said to be based on 'the free play of interests with the continual aim at service in return.'[14] In any case simple market and exchange relations were still based, according to Schmoller, 'upon a feeling of a certain solidarity' and 'mutual trust'.[15] In his *Volkswirtschaftslehre* of 1900, Schmoller explained that this change in perspective on perceptions of exchange had arisen through contemporary crises:

> The optimistic glorification of the individual's egoistic striving for acquisition and wealth had to give room to a more pessimistic view, when free competition, world-economic crises, and the progress of technology caused the numbers of the poor and the unemployed to rise, inequality of wealth to increase, and the power of the rich to show itself from a less favourable side. Noble humanitarians began to discuss the disadvantages of the new economic order, and in particular of free competition.[16]

Schmoller's younger colleague Karl Bücher (1847–1930) is even more explicit in distancing himself from the notion that exchange was part of the origins of human society. He dismissed this idea as a 'rationalist construct', first in *Die Entstehung der Volkswirtschaft* (1893)[17] and more clearly still in *Schenkung, Leihe und Bittarbeit* (1918).[18] Instead, he assumed for the earliest days of history a form of 'unpaid surrender where goods and services transition from one household to another'.[19] He counted loan

---

12. Wagner 1876: 164.
13. Schmoller 1900: 33.
14. Schmoller 1900: 2.
15. Schmoller 1900: 37.
16. Schmoller 1900: 93.
17. Bücher 1893: 39.
18. Bücher 1918: 3.
19. Bücher 1918: 4.

('Leihe') and boon-work ('Bittarbeit'), as well as gift-exchange, among such nonpaid forms of giving, and considered taxes, duties, and tributes to have developed from these over time. Bücher considered all these forms of unpaid giving to be altruistic in character, but underlined the necessity of reciprocation, while denying the need for exact equivalence in value that characterised modern exchange. 'In all of these cases, it is not a matter of attaining service in return, but rather of affirming devotion with the purpose of attaining something different, the amount of which, to a certain degree, one was able to determine'.[20] As an economist with prior training in ancient history,[21] Bücher especially emphasised reciprocity with respect to borrowing, referring back to Hesiod in support of this.[22] Other forms of unpaid giving, such as gifts handed over to guests or bridal gifts, also demanded reciprocation according to Bücher, since the acceptance of gifts created obligation: 'To refuse them would be a serious insult to the giver; their acceptance obligates the receiver absolutely, and the gift-giving is only concluded when the gift-giver has declared himself satisfied with the counter-gift. Up until that point the initial gift can be recalled'.[23] All these forms of mutual gift-giving, in Bücher's opinion, benefitted the interests of single households, and belonged to the developmental phase of what he termed a 'closed domestic economy' in his *Entstehung der Volkswirtschaft*.[24]

Bücher was also concerned with the connections between ethics and economics. Thus, his representation of unpaid forms of exchange concludes as a plea for the consideration of ethics in market-economics:

> Boon-work alone has remained unchanged in rural economies. Indeed, it has even become ennobled, since in situations when a family is lacking a bread-winner, neighbours will often undertake urgent field-labour in a form of voluntary mass-labour.

20. Bücher 1918: 4.
21. See Schefold 1988: 239–68; Wagner-Hasel 2011: 31–37; 2014.
22. Bücher 1918: 12.
23. Bücher 1918: 6–7. This concept was widely accepted in the economic and social anthropology of these years. Cf. e.g. Post 1895: 681: 'Schenkungen scheinen bei uncivilisierten Völkern stets auf Gegenseitigkeit zu beruhen'. Similar Berolsheimer 1907: 222–27.
24. The second edition of the book was translated into English and French. While at first Bücher had assumed that an exchange of goods at the stage of the closed household economy occurred only in terms of voluntary gifts or theft, he emphasized the reciprocity of giving in the second edition. See the English translation of S. Morley Wickett: *Industrial Evolution* 1901: 111–12.

Here we see the kindness of the human heart shine through; we can assume its effectiveness for all three forms of unpaid giving in ancient times to a far greater degree than may appear at first sight to be the case. Ethics is still a force in economic life, and it would be a dire thing for our future if it were to be eclipsed entirely.[25]

At the beginning of the twentieth century, however, critics of *homo oeconomicus* were not alone in arguing for reciprocity when it came to gift-giving. In his *Güterverkehr in der Urgesellschaft* (*The Circulation of Goods in Primitive Society*) from 1909, Felix Somló (1873–1920) defined the primitive form of interaction he called 'gift-exchange' as a 'clearly defined legal transaction completed according to specific rules, which is the original form of our own gift-giving and exchange'. He considered 'gift-exchange' ('Geschenktausch') to be similar to gift-giving in so far 'as it is originally a one-sided gift which corresponds to a one-sided acceptance, and as the size of the gift and the actual fact of giving itself, originate from a one-sided decision made by the giver. It also resembles exchange insofar as the act of giving occurs with the expectation of a return gift, and usually strictly obligates the receiver to offer such. The value of the gift and the value of the return gift are governed by strict customs'.[26] Unlike Bücher, who regarded gift-exchange as complementary to household economies, Somló, in line with neo-classical liberal theory, sees it as guaranteeing the cohesion of economic groups. Such groups consisted, in Somló's view, even at the lowest level, of mutually dependent individuals and smaller economic units.[27]

Richard C. Thurnwald (1869–1954), a follower of Bücher's work, is similarly placed between the neo-classical and the Historical School of political economy.[28] In a letter to Bücher from Sarajevo on January 21, 1898, Thurnwald introduced himself 'as one of those German political economists [...] to whom you express the wish in your *Entstehung der Volkswirtschaft* that they observe "those contemporary peoples who are primitive and lacking in culture according to the economic side of their lives".'[29] Because of the connotations of altruism and gift-giving,

---

25. Bücher 1918: 24.
26. Somló 1909: 156–57.
27. Somló 1909: 177.
28. Köcke 1979: 119–67.
29. Leipzig University Library, Nachlass 181, Karl Bücher. Tr. T. Lambert.

HISTORICAL SCHOOL OF POLITICAL ECONOMY

Thurnwald avoided the term 'gift-exchange', preferring to refer to 'reciprocity' instead, and integrating this term within a theory of sociation, or *Gesellung*.[30] Thurnwald considered the practice of exchange to be both universal and very ancient. In this he differed from his teacher Ferdinand Tönnies, who distinguished in the 1880s between *Gemeinschaft* (community) and *Gesellschaft* (society); in this sequential model reciprocity is a feature of community, but exchange and contracts between individuals only arise with the development of *Gesellschaft* or society.[31] However—and in this Thurnwald followed the ideas of the Historical School of political economy—he did not believe that exchange is invariably aimed at gaining economic advantage, nor that it is always governed by self-interest. Instead he recognised its social uses, especially in early societies. For instance, he considered exchange acts in 'primitive' communities to be acts of compensation between individuals or families, very unlike the rational impersonal transactions of modern-day societies.[32] In Thurnwald's account, transactions involving gifts and feasting served to knit a tightly woven fabric of friendship and mutual obligations, while reciprocity forged emotional rather than purely economic bonds.[33] These bonds are horizontal as well as vertical and can be seen in the relationships between generations and genders, among relatives and within male groups, between the living and the dead. Indeed, according to Thurnwald the obligation of reciprocity affects even the most powerful.[34] When it came to the question of equivalence, he distinguished between gifts that were identical in type and number, and exchanged like for like, and those that were similar in worth, and where the measure of their worth was to be read as deeply embedded in societal norms and values. Thurnwald suggests that money developed from the use of tokens, which served as reminders and symbols to help maintain reciprocal obligations.[35]

Within the traditions of the Historical School, Bronislaw Malinowski (1884–1942), like Thurnwald, assumed the universality of exchange, although in his assessment profit and self-interest were not always under-

---

30. Thurnwald 1936: 275–97 (this article is a synthesis of former studies on the subject). See Thurnwald 1911: 422, where he writes: 'Jede Gabe heischt ihre Gegengabe' ('Every gift demands a gift in return'). Similar Thurnwald 1912; 1921; 1932.
31. Tönnies [1887] 1991: 10, 24, 35. On the problematic nature of the opposition between *Gemeinschaft* and *Gesellschaft* see Oexle 1994: 118–25.
32. Thurnwald 1936: 282.
33. Thurnwald 1936: 283.
34. Thurnwald 1936: 289.
35. Thurnwald 1936: 284.

lying motivations in all exchange transactions.[36] For this he earned high praise from his mentor James G. Frazer. In the preface to *Argonauts of the Western Pacific*, Frazer wrote that Malinowski had provided proof that individual striving for profit and cost-benefit analysis had not always determined the traffic of goods everywhere. In Frazer's view, Malinowski instead demonstrated that 'the curious circulation of valuables', which took place 'between the inhabitants of the Trobriand and other islands, while it is accompanied by ordinary trade', was 'by no means itself a purely commercial transaction.' Malinowski rather showed that this circulation of valuables was 'not based on a simple calculation of utility, of profit and loss', but that it satisfied 'emotional and aesthetic needs of a higher order than the mere gratification of animal wants.'[37]

1.1.2. The legal-historical debate: From reciprocity to free surrender

An alternative to the egoistical model of exchange came through the work of German legal historians concerned with modern legal definitions of gift-giving, and it was they who introduced the term 'gift-exchange' ('Geschenktausch') to the debate. Their reflections were a response to the legal redefinition of gift-giving which had come to a conclusion in the 1890s. On 1 January 1900, the groundbreaking new German Civil Code (*Bürgerliches Gesetzbuch = BGB*) came into effect,[38] defining gifting, assuming that both parties are agreed that there will be no compensation, as an 'allocation through which one person enriches another with his property'. The legal definition, therefore, excluded the possibility of a gift given in expectation of receipt of any equivalent (such cases would be defined as barter or purchase). In modern legal thought, gifting is essentially defined as a one-sided donation. Any obligation is on the side of the giver, and the transfer of property does not aim to place any obligation on the receiver of the gift. This one-sidedness, both economic and ethical, distinguishes modern gift-giving from its ancient predecessors.

---

36. Malinowski [1922] 1999: 85. Malinowski acknowledged Bücher's pioneering work in the area of economic ethnology: 'The best analysis of the problem of the savage economy is to be found in, in spite of its many shortcomings, in K. Bücher's "Industrial Evolution", English Translation 1901.' But he criticises Bücher's view of primitive trade. For the influence of Bücher on Malinowski see Köcke 1979: 152–59; Firth 1972: 467; 1963: 209–27, where he criticises Malinowki's concept of economy. Cf. also Spittler 2008: 197–217.
37. Frazer in Malinowski [1922] 1999: X.
38. Wesel 1988: 94–97.

THE LEGAL-HISTORICAL DEBATE

By contrast, the Prussian *Allgemeines Landrecht* of 1794 had no such unified notion of gift-giving, requiring 140 paragraphs to regulate different kinds of gifting, which could be one-sided or reciprocal, or remunerative, and which also included ethical elements.[39] The social and ethical implications of gift-giving played a significant role in the debates leading up to the new definition formulated for the Civil Code. There was discussion for instance about whether gifting should presuppose that the giver approaches the transaction voluntarily and with selflessness. There was also debate about the need for regulation when it came to gifts given as part of social interactions, such as at weddings or birthdays. Finally, it was decided that the only gifts deemed relevant in terms of the code were those that affected property. The focus on property is an expression of the sharp dividing line between law and ethics on which lawmakers such as Hugo Burckhard (1854–1912) insisted.[40] Legal handbooks, by contrast, frequently referred to older German law according to which a gift was not binding in the absence of any form of return gift or service.[41] In his study of German civil law of 1917, Otto Gierke (1841–1921) showed that the new definition of gifting in the German Civil Code of 1900 formed the conclusion of a gradual evolution from a reciprocal to a one-sided definition of gift-giving.[42]

39. See §§ 1037–1177, as well as §§ 893–900 (ed. Hattenhauer 1970). According to this legal code, making a gift could be one-sided but could equally be of a mutual and paid nature, thus allowing for moral elements in gift-giving as well. Paragraph 1037 defined gift-making as 'contracts through which one person is obligated to surrender to another person the property of an object without requital'. Mutual gifting required two contracts (§ 105). The following was written about 'rewarded giving' in § 1169: 'If a laudable act or an important service completed is repaid, then this is called a rewarded gift'. § 1041 guaranteed the legal claim to services which arose from the obligation to charity: 'Where a special personal obligation exists, even if it is not fundamentally binding, then it is assumed that this has been given without any reservations in the intention of giving'. Relatives, siblings, married couples, poor people, charities for the poor, and foundations are all named here as examples (§§ 1042–1045). Cf. Gierke 1917: 430–32, n. 73.
40. Burckhard 1899: 130–31; Mauss 1990: 4, n. 4 refers to the publication, but said he was not able to consult it. For a moral argumentation see Meyerfeld 1835. For the evolution of the modern concept of giving see now Sorge 2012.
41. Cf. Kiekebusch 1928: 286. Ogris 1990: 1382 also states that older German law insists that gifts are binding only when counter-gifts have been given, and that to avoid the possibility of a gift being recalled, it was necessary to disguise the gift as a transaction involving either genuine or apparent compensation. Hattenhauer 1992: 13–14 argues that there was no such thing as a gift without the expectation of compensation in older legal cultures that were founded on the principle of *do ut des*.
42. Gierke 1917: 432.

This process of standardising the legal definition of gift-giving and focussing it entirely on the economic dimension of the unpaid transfer of assets also occurred in a similar way in other countries, crystallizing the distance from past European practices as well as from forms of interaction observed in the colonies.[43] It created an awareness that it was necessary to rethink those forms of human interaction which could neither be classified as market exchange nor as gift-giving in the sense of the German Civil Code. It is thus no coincidence that the concept of gift-exchange appeared for the first time in legal-historical literature of the 1880s and 1890s, although descriptions of the phenomena are clearly older.[44] With this new concept, a third category was created in addition to paid giving (barter, purchase) and unpaid giving ('pure' gifting), a category which combined elements of both forms of giving.

The concept of gift-exchange was first introduced by historians of German law working on premodern forms of gift-giving. The beginning of this research is found in Jacob Grimm's (1785–1863) etymologically oriented study *Ueber Schenken und Geben* (*On Presenting and Giving*, 1848).[45] Among subsequent studies, Karl von Amira's two-volume study *Nordgermanisches Obligationenrecht* (*The North Germanic Law of Obligations*), published between 1882 and 1885, was of particular importance.[46] Von Amira (1848–1930) distinguished conceptually between gifts in the Old-Swedish/West-Nordic Middle Ages and modern gifts. In the former, there

---

43. In France the process found its conclusion in the *Code Civil*. See Siebert 1938: 144–59. On practices of giving in premodern France see Davis 2000. On reciprocal gifting in premodern Italy see Arru 1998.
44. Cf. e.g. Pallas [1776] 1980: 105, who reported that the Kalmuks 'share everything which can be enjoyed and keep nothing for themselves […] However, this generosity extends primarily to things that can be consumed. They do not gladly give away property and livestock, except in the hope of a gift in return or as a token of appreciation'. I would like to thank Hans-Heinrich Nolte for this reference. At the same time, the generosity of North American Indians was mentioned by Adam Ferguson [1767] 1986: 212. He draws a parallel between the giving practices of the ancient Germans and the North American Indians in his *Essay on the History of Civil Society*, published in 1767.
45. Grimm [1848] 1865: 173–210.
46. The pioneering character of Amira's work was emphasised by Max Pappenheim 1933: 35–88. Pappenheim posed the same question as Marcel Mauss ten years previously but did not consult *Essai sur le don*. For the German debate on premodern gift-giving see Gierke 1917: 420, n. 22; Hattenhauer 1992: 13–15. In studies on the Middle Ages the interest in the subject has been growing since the 1990s: see Hannig 1988: 11–37; Clavero 1996; Groebner 2000; Algazi, Groebner and Jussen 2003; Grünbart 2011; Münkler, Sablotny and Standke 2015.

was no transfer of assets, which represented, for von Amira, 'marks of favour' that invited gratitude and thus were rewarded with counter-gifts: 'Favour for favour! The receiver must pay for the gift [...]. A gift demands a counter-gift [...]. [This is] a legal tenet which has been definitively confirmed [...]. One gives either because one expects a gift in return, or because the gift itself is supposed to demonstrate the giver's gratitude for favours received or promised'.[47] Von Amira includes land, payment for healing services, and wedding gifts among such gifts,[48] as well as guest-gifts and market rights or tithes.[49] In the first volume von Amira defines this form of giving, which is motivated by reciprocity, as 'obligatory business' ('obligatorisches Geschäft'), 'gift-contract' ('Schenkungsvertrag'), and as the 'prototype of the actual contract ('Urbild des Realvertrages')'.[50] In the second volume he uses the term 'Gabentausch' ('gift-exchange'), which he views as based on the equivalence ('Gleichwerthigkeit') of gifts.[51]

A few years later the Germanist Richard M. Meyer (1860–1914), in his work *Zur Geschichte des Schenkens* (*On the History of Gift-Giving*), made a first attempt at a synthetic analysis of premodern forms of gift-giving; here he claimed that a new understanding of property accounted for the change from reciprocal to one-sided gift-giving.[52] In premodern times (no further temporal definition is given), Meyer assumes that property was tied to communities and that this prevented its transfer without reciprocation: 'According to natural law all things are communal and any individual's possessions are only owned subject to the obligation of handing them on'.[53] He distinguished between different types of giving, such as giving subject to recall, loaning ('Leihe'), giving with the expectation of return, e.g. sacrifice ('Opfer'), and obligatory sharing ('pflichtmäßiges Austeilen'). The latter also includes the largesse of kings and heads of households as well as public services such as the liturgies that wealthy Athenians were obliged to finance. 'All giving in ancient times', Meyer sums up, 'is either subject to recall, or relies on the obligation of one of the parties involved.'[54] Although he considered gift-giving and gift-exchange to be the earliest form of trade, he did not assume that gifts were precisely equivalent, but instead

---

47. Amira 1882: I, 506–8.
48. Amira 1882: I, 509.
49. Amira 1882: II, 611–12.
50. Amira 1882: I, 510, 516, 619.
51. Amira 1882: II, 615 and 620.
52. Meyer 1898: 18–29.
53. Meyer 1898: 27.
54. Meyer 1898: 19.

that values were freely estimated and that usually a counter-gift's value would be greater than the value of the initial gift.[55] Meyer did not take an entirely positive view of this development, as his concluding critique of individualism suggests:

> Our modern concept of gift-giving is based on the notion of freely disposable property, which does not apply to earlier times (especially not in Germany), and it also presupposes a lack of restrictions in relations between giver and receiver that is not in keeping with the restrictive ethics of earlier eras. Thus, free giving is an achievement of a new worldview and its individualism. This should not therefore be regarded as progress in every respect.[56]

Late nineteenth-century historians of Roman law also demonstrated awareness of ancient obligations of reciprocity, but they did not employ the term 'gift-exchange', nor did they engage in any critique of individualism or individual contracts. The concept of reciprocity, or mutuality, was most prominent in the scholarship of Roman law, although this was initially used in a purely legal sense. There, reciprocity was a concept connected to contract ethics (lawyers, for example, explained the legal efficacy of unpaid surrender in ancient times through the reciprocity of giving). It was only through its reception by political economists that reciprocity became a socio-economically significant concept. According to Hugo Burckhard, who drew on Roman law in order to establish the modern concept of giving, older forms of law had recognised reciprocal gift-giving. He argued that 'will only becomes legal will once a counter-gift has been given', and that 'only by presenting non-remunerated business in the form of remunerated business would the parties involved become aware that they were no longer dealing with a service that was entirely dependent on the giver's say-so, but rather with a service under the protection of the law. Only now is the giver legally bound to his stated desire and only now does the receiver have a legal guarantee of

---

55. Meyer 1898: 26.
56. Meyer 1898: 29. Cf. also Gierke [1902] 1962: 113. Gierke tied a change in the concept of giving to a critique of individualism and praise for the ideal of community. In doing so, he relied on Fichte, Wundt, and the Historical Legal School ('Historische Rechtsschule') as well as on folk psychology ('Völkerpsychologie'). On Gierke's ideas on community see Oexle 1988: 193–217. In his *Völkerpsychologie* (vol. 8/1: 138–40) Wilhelm Wundt defines gifting and exchange as the earliest forms of communication. Presumably Wundt took up the ideas of Karl Bücher, his colleague at the university of Leipzig. See Wagner-Hasel 2011: 154–56.

retaining the gift.'⁵⁷ According to Burckhard, this practice of presenting unremunerated gifts in the form of remunerated giving was also valid in Islamic law, in the *launegild* business of the Langobards, and in the *giwa* of the Northern Germans, as well as in the *manicipatio nummo uno donationis causa* of Roman law.⁵⁸

The work of the constitutional law scholar Lothar von Dargun (1853–1983), *Egoismus und Altruismus in der Nationalökonomie* (1885), forms a significant intervention in the *Methodenstreit* between legal historians and political economists.⁵⁹ Von Dargun drew on the position of the Historical Legal School ('Historische Rechtsschule'), represented by Rudolf von Jhering (1818–1892), whose study *Der Zweck im Recht* (*Law as a Means to an End*, 1887) he considered to be essential for the 'doctrine of mutualism' ('Lehre vom Mutualismus'). He distinguished between acts driven by economic self-interest within the framework of the free flow of goods, and altruistic acts which were especially relevant within the framework of 'collective economies', in associations, families, and, above all, in states. He defined state taxation as a 'grand system of giving of gifts by the individual to the community and of gifts by the community to the individual as well as to smaller communities,' a system in which the opposition between egoism and altruism was transcended by a third form: mutualism.⁶⁰ He explained this through the concept of society or partnership ('Societät') which was developed by von Jhering as a fusion of self-interested acts of exchange and acts of giving based on altruism and self-denial:

> In the contract of exchange, the will desires its own interest at the expense of the other person's (egoism); in gift the will desires the other's interest at the expense of its own (self-denial); in association it desires its own interest *in* the other's by furthering its

---

57. Burckhard 1899: 39; 1891.
58. Burckhard 1899: 39-42. On reciprocal, remunerative giving in Roman law, see also Pernice 1882: 37 (*donatio reciproca*) and Kaser 1971: 399 (§ 265: Die Schenkung). For the social implications of gifts in Roman law see Michel 1962: 434-43 and 596-601, who underlines the obligatory character of gifts. Michel differentiates between two systems of generosity. The first, connected to the terms *gratis, gratuitus*, and *gratuito*, makes the recipient a debtor, while in the other system (e.g. *donationis causa, fideicommis*) generosity serves the recipient. For the current discussion of Roman terms of giving see Verboven 2002 and García Morcillo 2014.
59. Lothar von Dargun was professor of the *history of constitutional law and German law* (*Geschichte des Staatsrechts und Deutsches Recht*) at the University of Krakow from 1888 to 1893. He belongs to the forgotten founding fathers of sociology. See Wagner-Hasel 2011: 221.
60. Von Dargun 1885: 71.

own interest in the other's and the other's in its own: partnership equalises all opposition between its own interest and the other's person.[61]

Despite the lack of remuneration, von Jhering thought that Roman giving was characterised by 'the familiar principle of egoism', since gifts were made as a means to an end (even if that end was not material in character). He considers this egoism to be subordinated to a higher social interest, since in Rome 'gratuitous services covered the essential needs of society and the state'.[62]

This emphasis on the 'egoism of the community', or 'communal egoism', can also be found in von Jhering's study of ancient hospitality. Von Jhering rejected the humanist-idealist view of hospitality as anchored in individual ethics that was common in classical scholarship at the time, and insisted instead on the idea that hospitality was instrumentally motivated.[63] He pointed to a justified selfish interest in the development of hospitality, not on the part of individuals but on the part of communities, and thus developed the idea that the germ or seed of international law, which itself made trade and commerce possible, can be found in ancient hospitality.[64] The integrated approach discernible in von Jhering's interpretation of the institutions of hospitality is also characteristic of Mauss's understanding of gift-exchange. Mauss claimed that 'all kinds of institutions are given expression at one and the same time—religious, juridical, and moral, which relate to both politics and the family; likewise economic ones, which suppose special forms of production and consumption, or rather, of performing total services [prestation] and of distribution. This is not to take into account the aesthetic phenomena, to which these facts lead, and the [morphological] contours of the phenomena that these institutions manifest.'[65] Von Jhering wrote in very similar terms about the institution of hospitality which for

---

61. Von Jhering [1877] 1970: I, 217.
62. Von Jhering [1877] 1970: I, 84 and 83.
63. Thus, von Jhering criticises the idealistic view of hospitality in Leopold Schmidt's *Ethik der Griechen* (1882: 336). Schmidt characterised the hospitality of the Greeks as one of the 'most charming aspects' of their 'emotional life'. Denis (1856: 420) took the view that ancient hospitality demonstrated the spirit of humanity, selflessness and egalitarianism of the ancient world. Similar Curtius 1892: 212.
64. Von Jhering 1887: 378. On social utilitarianism and von Jhering's opposition to romantic-idealistic notions, which were not entirely absent in the Historical Legal School, see Helfer 1970: 79–88; Zweigert 1970: 240–51; Viehweg 1970: 211–16; Wieacker 1973: 63–92.
65. Mauss 1990: 3.

THE LEGAL-HISTORICAL DEBATE   33

him contained 'the signature of an entire cultural era of humanity [...] a juncture at which law, ethics, religion, trade and culture—all of which have nothing to do with hospitality today—joined together.'[66]

Von Jhering also used the concept of 'prestation' ('Prästation') by which he means the obligation to perform (economic) services that 'custom imposes on certain relationships'. The obligation to provide such gifts (e.g. wedding-gifts, tips, hospitality, etc.) is social rather than moral for von Jhering as it is for Mauss. Nonetheless von Jhering's investigation of this issue, pursued in volume 2 of *Der Zweck im Recht*, does not conclude that the obligation to perform services has any social purpose.[67] Rather, he explains this obligation by comparison to the obligatory generosity imposed upon wealthy citizens of ancient Rome, who were required to provide unpaid services for the community. For von Jhering the obligation to generosity forms part of an ancient system of favours:

> There were times when one got services for nothing which now one can get only for money, and that too not only in cases where there were special personal relations but in general and with no limitation. At this time then, favor actually constituted *a factor in the life of commerce* and exercised a *function* therein. Similar conditions are still to be found among uncivilized peoples of today in reference to hospitality; and in regions thinly populated they are found among civilized peoples also.[68]

By contrast with Mauss there is no tone of regret in von Jhering's account of the loss of the practice of generosity in the present. Von Jhering's evaluation of such phenomena started from an evolutionary perspective and was based on a clear belief in progress; thus he views the coincidence of the phenomena in a single institution as irreversible, and a return to the past as undesirable.[69] Despite his notion of association ('Societät') von

66. Von Jhering 1887: 359.
67. Von Jhering [1883] 1970: II, 220-26. Von Jhering already pointed here to the term 'total prestation' which Mauss went on to explore. According to Firth (1963: 222, n. 1) the concept of 'total prestation' was introduced by W. Robertson Smith and taken up by Bronislaw Malinowski.
68. Von Jhering [1877] 1970: I, 79-82. Von Jhering explicated his notion through the example of Roman practices, distinguishing between unpaid and paid services. He conceived of the former as gratuitous contracts and the latter as business contracts. The reward for services given free of charge (*munus*), he suggested, consisted in *honores* or *honorarium*. Italics in the translation. Translation from the 1913 edition.
69. Von Jhering 1887: 361-63. See also ch. 2.1.

Jhering viewed the individual, whose lack of connectedness had so irked his Germanist colleagues, as the ultimate winner in this development.[70]

This social view of the gift also influenced the views of legal and economic anthropologists, who adopted the concepts of gift-exchange and reciprocal giving at the beginning of the twentieth century, using them to describe acts of exchange within non-European cultures. Here, however, the moral evaluation of such practices was often reversed, with the original gift viewed as motivated by egoism rather than altruism. 'The legal concept of "giving"', wrote Wilhelm Gaul (1869–1921) in his study *Das Geschenk nach Form und Inhalt im besonderen untersucht an afrikanischen Völkern* (1914), 'is clearly only formed long after that of "purchasing". In ancient times it differs from our concept of giving and the free gift, as well as from anything arising from altruistic feelings. In the object-oriented, sensuous thinking of "primitive people", it is impossible to give with the right hand without the left hand knowing. Rather, when one gives with the right hand, one puts the left hand out to receive a gift in return. One-sided giving and one-sided taking are thus alien to the native.'[71] Despite the lack of evidence of altruistic tendencies, Gaul initially excluded the existence of 'calculated thinking' among non-European natives, considering the measurement of value to be a later development. As examples of this reciprocal giving, which he also designated as 'Geschenktausch' ('gift-exchange'), Gaul pointed to the exchange of hospitality gifts between strangers, the services of tribute and the gifts to kings and

---

70. Whereas von Jhering's evolutionary thinking was branded as social Darwinism in the 1970s (see Wieacker 1973: 63–73), those same elements have been relativized in the contemporary reception by legal historians of Jhering's evolutionary theory. These historians see von Jhering as the main representative of a realist, cultural-anthropological final phase of the Historical Legal School, one who, far removed 'from all romantic notions of alienation', regarded the individual 'as the great winner of the social world'. Behrends 1991: 290–310.
71. Gaul 1914: 225. This lack of altruism was also confirmed by Waclaw von Brun 1912: 60–61. He wrote of the Maori: 'Apart from this hospitality, which has very deep roots in the Maori, their so highly celebrated generosity also had its darker side. They were egoistical to a great degree, and gratitude was for them a completely foreign emotion. Even the well-known student and great friend and admirer of the Maori, Wilhelm Colenso, concedes this fully, reporting that one Maori never does a favour for another or gives anything without having his eye chiefly set upon his own advantage; everyone knew this and everyone responded with something equivalent. We have already seen that a tribute or a reward for work was always offered as a "gift". Other forms of "generosity" were probably also dealt with in a similar fashion. They gave "gifts", but expected, for this, gifts in return. And they gave gladly, for according to the firmly established custom, the return gift must be greater than the original one'.

chiefs who were obligated to generosity. Unlike the Germanists and the Roman legal historians who had emphasized the contractual character of gifts and the legal efficacy of reciprocal gift-giving, Gaul, in keeping with other anthropologists, emphasized the social purpose of reciprocal gift-giving.[72] Even if such gifts did ultimately enable trade, Gaul viewed gifts exchanged between strangers as primarily social in function, in that they created ties between people. They were a 'magic formula that binds two people closely together'.[73] According to Gaul, duty and trade developed from guest-gifts, at which point the 'original purpose of gift-giving—to enable peaceful relationships with strangers' began to recede.[74] Gaul assumed that tributes and gifts to chiefs and kings formed the origin of taxation.[75] Like Meyer, Gaul also attributed this change to the easing of social ties and to the increasing availability of property which could be disposed of without limit.[76]

1.1.3. The sociological debate: The contribution of Marcel Mauss

This, by no means exhaustive, survey of the beginnings of the scholarly debate on gift-exchange demonstrates the degree to which the definition of the concept had advanced by the time Mauss formulated his theory of the gift in the 1920s.[77] This is true of the reciprocal character of pre-modern giving, which had become accepted among legal historians and legal anthropologists as well as economic historians and economic anthropologists by the beginning of the twentieth century; it is also true of the obligating and binding character of gifts, frequently referred to

---

72. Cf. e.g. Heinrich Schurtz (1898: 65–66) who stresses the connection between trade and gift-giving while interpreting gifts as tokens of friendship rather than commodities.
73. Gaul 1914: 236.
74. Gaul 1914: 235.
75. Gaul 1914: 245–46.
76. Gaul 1914: 275: 'Was uns bei dem "modernen" Geschenk gleich ins Auge fällt, ist der viel freiere Verkehr zwischen Schenker und Beschenkten, eine "nur lose Beziehung zwischen einem Geschenk und einem etwaigen Gegengeschenk", die begründet ist in dem viel freieren Verkehr der einzelnen untereinander und einer unbegrenzten Verfügung über das Eigentum. Beides ist dem knechtenden Zwang sittlicher wie wirtschaftlicher Anschauungen der älteren Zeiten gleich fremd'.
77. See Geary 2003: 132–35. Here he makes clear which of Mauss's own earlier works—going back to 1910—could have been used in his *Essai sur le don*. These earlier works deal primarily with the *potlatch* as well as with Polynesian practices. Mauss never engaged in any fieldwork himself.

by economic anthropologists. While legal scholars emphasized the legal dimension of such ties, economic anthropologists and early sociologists, including Thurnwald,[78] reinforced the view that social relations were produced through gifts. The example of von Jhering has demonstrated that the notion of the gift as a 'total phenomenon' was not completely new either.

Mauss himself was well aware of many of his forerunners. Although he distanced himself rather from Bücher's evolutionary interpretation, he praised the works of Meyer, Somló, and Thurnwald.[79] Another follower of Bücher's theses from the Durkheim school of thought, François Simiand, was particularly struck by Bücher's suggestion that the gift preceded exchange.[80] Thus Mauss's *Essai sur le don* represents a combination of different approaches to the problem, to which Mauss himself then added his own specific accent by subsuming a multiplicity of phenomena related to gift-exchange under the single concept of the gift, and by simultaneously sharpening the political economists' and Germanists' critique of modern individualism and economic liberalism. In defining the gift as a contract consisting of three elements (giving, receiving, and giving in return), Mauss worked within the framework of a legal concept of giving, according to which giving became legally binding through acceptance by the receiver and, in premodern law, through reciprocation.[81] Mauss was more emphatic than his predecessors, however, in construing premodern giving as a counter-model to modern practice by endowing early forms of giving with moral qualities which had been lost during the course of

---

78. Cf. also Simmel [1901] 1989: 86 stressing the reciprocity of giving in traditional law and hinting at boon-work as an intermediate form between the subjective forms of transfer of ownership represented by robbery and gift, and the objectivity of exchange.
79. Mauss 1990: 153, n. 3. Durkheim and Mauss were editors of the journal *L'Année sociologique*, first published in 1896–97, which provides ample evidence of Mauss's close knowledge of German scholarship in economic history and anthropology. Mauss himself reviewed works in the fields of psychology and history of religion, such as Wundt's *Völkerpsychologie* of 1907-9 (*L'Année sociologique* 11, 1906–1909, 53–69). Mauss's Alsatian origins favoured the intensive treatment of German-language scholarship in the journal. See the biography of Mauss by Fournier 2006: 9–12, 56–63.
80. François Simiand mainly reviewed works of economic history such as the second edition in 1898 of Bücher's *Entstehung der Volkswirtschaft* and Bücher's studies on primitive economy: *Der wirtschaftliche Urzustand; Die Wirtschaft der Naturvölker*, 1897 (*L'Année sociologique* 2, 1899, 440–48 and 456–57). In these reviews, Simiand emphasized the significance of gift-exchange for Bücher's concept of early household economies.
81. Mauss 1990: 33–43, 47–49.

its standardisation within modern law. Like the political economists who had critiqued the notion of *homo oeconomicus*, Mauss based his theory of giving not on contractual law but on the authority of the collective. In interpreting gift-exchange as a collective contract, Mauss rejected the idea of the primacy of contracts between individuals as well as the presumption of an evolution from a distant or prehistoric past lacking in rules and law.[82] In reaching this conceptual goal Mauss, in fact, reversed the process of standardisation that the modern concept of giving had undergone. He was especially successful in doing this because he tied his model of giving to societies located beyond his own world and experience, and which were at once concrete and utopian, such as the *Kula* ring, a network of exchange on the Trobriand islands, or the *potlatch* practised by North American indigenous people.[83] While Mauss' legally oriented predecessors assumed that the functioning of exchange was owed to reciprocity, albeit a reciprocity interpreted according to modern contract law as a legally binding force,[84] Mauss himself preferred a religious explanation. He argued that archaic societies had a specific moral contract which bound personal law and property law together. From this identity of person and property, Mauss explained the power of gifts to create social bonds as noted by Gaul, Thurnwald, and others. Here he relied upon the idea of the animated nature of objects, developed by the Maori in New Zealand according to his friend Robert Hertz.[85] Mauss rejected internal or moral motivations for gift-giving as well as external factors such as trade or the requirements of collective economies; for Mauss the key motivating factor is in the essence or spirit of things. He traced the circulation of gifts back to what the Maori call *hau*, a spirit inherent in the gift, which compels its

---

82. Mauss follows the concept formulated by his colleague Georges Davy, who explains in his study *La foi jurée: La formation du lien social* (1922: 374): 'La reaction solidariste qui est venue plus en plus limiter, aux XIX siècle, les excès de l'individualisme de notre doctrine classique et de notre Code civile s'éclaire d'un jour singulier lorsqu'on la rapporte aux origines de notre institution'.
83. Cf. n. 130.
84. See the argumentation of Burckhard 1899. According to Henry S. Maine's *Ancient Law* ([15]1894: 348–49) contract law is based on 'complete reciprocity' and is associated with rights and obligations. In his study of Roman hospitality Theodor Mommsen ([1864] 1962: 330) linked permanence with reciprocity when he noted the following for ancient Rome: 'Moreover, the actual guest contract is that which leads to a lasting relationship, as through this real reciprocity is first made possible'. Von Jhering's study of hospitality relied on Mommsen's view of hospitality in antiquity (von Jhering 1887: 370).
85. Mauss 1990: 10–13.

return.[86] In this he was content to follow the explanations given by the Maori themselves, who had developed the idea in order to legitimise the share which priests received from the hunter's game. Mauss was criticised by Marshall Sahlins for taking such explanations at face value instead of tracing them back to the social necessity which had led the Maori to construct the concept.[87] Thus for Mauss, the final authority is magic, while the jurists who preceded him viewed society as held together by the law and its ultimate guarantor, the state. With his metaphysical interpretation of gift-exchange, Mauss indirectly completed the very process of depersonalization and objectivization of human relations which he himself had lamented. According to Mauss, social interaction was originally regulated by the things themselves, inextricably bound to humans. Mauss thus mystified the social context at just that point in history, in the years following the First World War, when traditional forces of integration in Europe were losing their power.

Thus, the additions Mauss made to the theory of gift-exchange, namely his interpretation of the gift as a collective contract and his grounding of the obligation to reciprocate in magic, are also the most problematic aspects of his theory of giving. Mauss summarized findings which, until that point, had been scattered throughout scholarly journals. But he idealized and standardized those findings to such a degree that historical practice became occluded by abstract concepts. Mauss extracted a purely formal sediment from the concrete social practices under discussion.[88] Emptied of content, this sediment was then condensed into a general theory of the gift, a theory which could be understood as valid beyond time and space and which could stand in opposition to modern practice.

---

86. Mauss 1990: 16: 'the legal tie, a tie occurring through things is one between souls, because the thing itself possesses a soul [...] the thing given is not inactive. Invested with life, often possessing individuality, it seeks to return to what Hertz called its "place of origin", or to produce, on behalf of the clan and the native soil from which it sprang, and equivalent to replace it'.
87. Sahlins 1984: 157-62. This part of his theory has frequently been criticised by subsequent researchers as a mystification of the gift. Cf. Firth 1963: 222; McCormack 1982: 286-93; McCall 1982: 303-19; Laughlin Jr., 1986: 156-76; Cathercole 1978: 324-40; Godelier 1996: 19-39.
88. See the critique of Leacock 1954: 68 and Vogt 1981: 276-97. Vogt stresses the mystifying and idealistic tendencies in Mauss's theory of gifts and attributes these to the neglect of historical and economic aspects of giving. Cf. also the critical remarks of Müller 1981: 312-14.

1.2. The critique of modernity and the idealisation of the gift

These very different reflections on premodern gift-giving, which ultimately resulted in a notion of the gift as possessing the power to integrate, have one common point of reference: the process of the modernisation of society and its social differentiation, and the development of independent subsystems and spheres of action that were described by Max Weber at the beginning of the century as a process of bureaucratization and rationalization.[89] With respect to practices of gift-exchange, this process was rolled back and the connection between the different spheres re-discovered as 'other'. This is true not only of the convergence of phenomena in a single institution, as exemplified by von Jhering and Mauss, but also for the theory, upheld by Thurnwald and the Hungarian anthropologist Karl Polanyi, that in ancient societies economics was embedded in sociopolitical life.[90]

In scholarship a reversal of this form of integration took place with the development of the discipline of sociology, founded by just those scholars who insisted on the social and integrating function of gifts, and thus with a new focus on social relationships and interactions.[91] The founders of classical liberal economics, who, like Adam Smith, had developed their theories during the age of colonialism, had, in any case, not perceived the dissonance between economics and ethics. In fact, thinkers of the eighteenth-century Enlightenment endowed trade with just those moral characteristics attributed to noncommercial forms of exchange in theories of gift-giving. For Adam Smith, trade was the source of the wealth of nations, of the security and liberty of their citizens, and brought about the end of internal and external states of war.[92] In *The Spirit of Laws* the French Enlightenment thinker Montesquieu argued that 'the spirit of trade produces in the mind of man a certain sense of exact justice [...]. The total privation of trade, on the contrary, produces robbery, which Aristotle ranks in the number of means of acquiring; yet it is not at all inconsistent with certain moral virtues. Hospitality, for instance, is most

---

89. Cf. Münch 1984; Luhmann 1988.
90. Thurnwald 1932: 45; Polanyi [1944] 2001: 45–58. Firth 1972: 468, n. 1 refers to Thurnwald.
91. Wolf 1982: 7–23. Cf. also Groh 1988: 132. Dahme 1988: 222–74 shows how early sociologists responded to modernisation.
92. For the moral dimension of the liberal theory of Adam Smith see Macfie [1957] 1985: 131–57; Medick 1973: 206–21; Bürgin 1996: 366–90.

rare in trading countries, while it is found in the most admirable perfection among nations of vagabonds.'[93]

Thus the idea of a convergence of the spheres of justice, ethics, politics, and economics does not only apply to some kind of imagined prehistory. Instead, such fluid circumstances are characteristic of types of individual power and labour relations that were still in place in the nineteenth century.[94] Unlike ancient practices of gift-exchange, however, these more recent examples were unsuited to idealisation by critics of modernity.[95]

It is not surprising that studies of past gift-exchange practices were already tinged with nostalgia around the turn of the century and that they then culminated in Mauss's fundamental critique of civilisation. Critiques of modernity go hand in hand with the process of modernisation, but they became especially strident at times of upheaval when new and changed conditions upset traditional patterns of behaviour, as will have been the case during the years following the end of the First World War. Individualism, rationalism, utilitarianism, and materialism all came under attack from a critique of civilisation that ultimately contributed to the demise of evolutionism.[96] While evolutionists were bent on determining a place on the ladder of civilisation for each of the cultures they were studying, cultural relativists, who were critical of the idea of progress, insisted the practices of any alien culture observed in the field should be judged by its own criteria. The drawback of this process, for which Malinowski's work is key, is that the field of enquiry becomes de-historicised, while the cultures under examination become mere frozen relics of the 'archaic'.

Malinowski's perceptiveness, praised by Frazer in the preface to *Argonauts of the South Seas*, was the sharpened vision of a politically homeless aristocratic intellectual affected by the collapse of the Austro-Hungarian empire and looking for security through his writing.[97] It was only a matter

---

93. *The Spirit of Law* II, 20, 2, 3-4; translation taken from Thomas Nugent (1752) published by Batoche Books 2001.
94. Cf. Wehler 1987: 221, 589-605, who stresses the embeddedness of work into social life in preindustrial Germany. The connectivity of the economy and social life can be studied in nineteenth-century Basle. See Sarasin 1990 and Wagner-Hasel 1998: 33-63.
95. See Bücher 1918: 29 who knew boon-work from personal experience. According to von Dargun 1885: 46-48, the household-economy of his own time gives an ideal image of altruistic economy.
96. Cf. Sontheimer 1978: 41-62; Kiesel 1989: 497-521; Beßlich 2000.
97. For the social and intellectual background of Malinowski see Urry 1992: 181-82, who underlines the 'aristocratic' attitude of his observations of the world of the Trobriands. Malinowski is characterized by Gellner 1985: 5-7 as an 'ahistorical holist'. His role as founding hero is discussed by Fardon 1990: 569-87 and Stagl 1991: 91-105. Cf. also Spittler 2008: 221-42.

of a couple of generations, according to Malinowski, before the Trobriand Islanders, whom he had observed between 1915 and 1918 from the distance of a nearby mission station,[98] would be caught up by the progress of civilisation.[99] The experience of the loss of his own culture was reflected in Malinowski's vision of the imminent demise of Trobriand culture and thus endowed the practices he examined there with an appearance of originality and authenticity that did not fail to affect his contemporaries.

This explains how Malinowski and Mauss came to be credited with the discovery of gift-exchange, even though the concept had already been largely developed by jurists and economists, as we have seen. Their version of gift-exchange unfettered by utilitarianism and interest in profit appeared to offer the promise of an alternative world that was free from the tension between individual and society, between ethics and economics.

But such alternative worlds always also reflect the real world. Mauss could not have known that his idea of a collective held together by magic would be realised fatally in the form of National Socialism with its programme of a return to an idealised past, stage-managed by magical spectacle.[100] He was hurt by later accusations that the Durkheim school's naive belief in the collective had prepared the ground for Fascist ideology.[101] In a letter responding to an article by Svend Ranulf on the scholarly forerunners of Fascism in 1939, Mauss expressed dismay over the role of magic in the political stagings of the Fascist movement: 'That large, modern societies could be hypnotised [*suggestionées*] as the Australians are by their dances [...] is a thing that basically we had not expected. That return to the primitive had not been the object of our reflections.'[102] This statement is not without tragic irony: after the occupation of France the National Socialists' archaizing spectacles would pose an immediate threat to Mauss as a scholar of Jewish descent, while other students of Durkheim, including Maurice Halbwachs, lost their lives in concentration camps.[103]

---

98. This is underlined by Kramer 1981: 82. See Young 1984: 1–26 on Malinowski's choice of location and on his knowledge of the region.
99. Malinowski [1922] 1999: xvi.
100. Whether this process of modernisation was intended, or an unintended consequence, is open to debate. For discussion see Barkai 1988: 68–102; Peukert 1989: 81–83; Frei 1993: 363–87.
101. Mauss 1939: 16–34.
102. Citation after Vogt 1981: 290, 296, n. 34. The extent to which French observers perceived the National Socialists' cult of the *Führer* as ritual celebration can be seen in diary entries by Denis de Rougement 1998: 62 (11th March: a holy ceremony).
103. Cf. König 1972: 636.

The debate on gift-exchange yields further, more explicit links between National Socialist ideas and the Durkheim school's belief in the collective.[104] While Durkheim's collective is cooperative and viewed by critics as leaning towards Socialism,[105] the National Socialist idea of Universalism is markedly more 'statist' in character and developed out of concepts introduced by the Historical School.[106] This difference is relevant to the work of the classically trained economic historian Bernhard Laum, whose 1924 study *Heiliges Geld* (*Sacred Money*) focussed on Greek antiquity and is influenced by the concept of gift-exchange. Laum traces the development of Greek coinage back to sacrificial rituals, viewing the state as the creator of a sacred rule of law and defining money as a creature of this system.[107] He refers to sacrificial ritual as a 'trade transaction',[108] in which the sacrificed animal is a remuneration for favour granted by the gods; but he also considers this transaction in terms of an exchange of gifts.[109] He also stressed the interconnectedness of economic life with other aspects of life,[110] whose loss he regretted in a later work. In his study *Die geschlossene Wirtschaft* (1933) his focus is on the present; here, like Mauss in *Essai sur le don*, Laum complains about the independence of the economy and demands a return to an 'organic whole' and the rejection of the 'individualist quest for profit'.[111] He considers the economic crisis of his time to be part of a process of a 'loss of the soul of economic life' and seeks the solutions to this crisis in the state, idealising the latter as the realisation of the idea of justice.[112] This critique,

---

104. It is significant that during the years of National Socialist rule, von Jehring's focus of social utilitarianism on the interests of the individual is viewed as the main flaw in his work. See Wieacker 1942: 55–58.
105. See Chiozzi 1983: 631–54. Cf. Birnbaum 1972: 41–54; Hollier 1972: 55–61. Giddens 1976: 712 situates the Durkheim school between conservatism and socialism. For the influence of Durkheim on social and historical theory see Borlandi 1998: 27–65; Oexle 1994: 128–32.
106. Barkai 1988: 68–102.
107. Laum 1924: 160.
108. Laum 1924: 32. Some of Laum's ideas are taken up by Seaford 2004.
109. Laum 1924: 32: 'Die Gabe oder das Opfer an die Götter ist kein Geschenk in unserem Sinne; jedes δῶρον erfordert vielmehr ein ἀντίδωρον'. He views Homeric exchanges such as the Greeks' purchase of wine at Troy in a similar sense not as trade but as exchange of guest-gifts, based on the assumption that guest-friendship creates the proper conditions for the peaceful acquisition of goods abroad. Laum refers to Bücher's work for his notion of gift-exchange as the origin of trade. Ibid. 13–14.
110. Laum 1924: 161.
111. Laum 1933: 479 and 458.
112. Laum 1933: 15. Besides this Laum notes rationalism, exaggerated specialisation, and unbounded eccentricity as symptoms of the crisis.

published in 1933 (and repeated more moderately in his 1960 work *Schenkende Wirtschaft*) is linked to a clear commitment to the National Socialist idea of totality: 'The return to primitiveness and totality, the organic renewal of the people through separation from the outside world, which National Socialism demands, is necessary for the sake of the preservation of life itself. In short: the inner truth of the leading idea of National Socialism rests on the fact that it corresponds to biological necessity.'[113] Although Laum did not repeat this praise after 1945 for obvious reasons, a rejection of individualism remains characteristic of his later work as well. In *Schenkende Wirtschaft*, where he first engages with Mauss's work,[114] he borrows the core of Mauss's theory, namely the idea that the obligation to reciprocity originates from the spirit of things: 'Since the giver gives away a piece of his soul with his gift, a magical coercion forces the receiver to reciprocate.'[115] Laum's criticism of his own times is primarily directed at what he considered to be the emergence of individualist tendencies that commercialized 'a primal human instinct for giving'.[116] This convergence with National Socialist ideologies at least partly explains why modern scholarship is keen to look elsewhere for the founding fathers of gift-theory.

Unlike Laum and Mauss, Karl Polanyi, a major contributor to economic theories of premodern gift-exchange,[117] was clearly aware of the ways in which totalising ideologies served to cover up estrangement or alienation, and he warned of the potential dangers emerging from this way of thinking.[118] Nor was Polanyi sympathetic to the anti-individualism espoused by the totalizers.[119] His utopian aim is not the unity of individual and community but the reintegration of the economy into society and the subordination

---

113. Laum 1933: 488.
114. In his earlier study on *Sacred Money* Laum did not refer to Marcel Mauss. See Wittenburg 1995: 270.
115. Laum 1960: 119.
116. Laum 1960: 460.
117. For Polanyi's position see Zeisel 1968: 172-74; Humphreys 1983: 31-75; Maucourant 2000; 2005.
118. Polanyi 1935; [1947] 1968: 59: 'Behind the fading fabric of competitive capitalism there looms the portent of an industrial civilization, with its paralyzing division of labor, standardization of life, supremacy of mechanism over organism, and organization over spontaneity'.
119. He considered anti-individualism to be the guiding principle of all fascist ideologies, which reify social phenomena, deny the existence of alienation, and propagate the idea of a return to a preconscious social organism (Polanyi 1935). R. M. MacIver's preface to Polanyi (1944) highlights the importance of individual freedom in Polanyi's thinking. In the new edition, of 2001, MacIver's introduction is replaced with a foreword by Joseph E. Stiglitz and an introduction by Fred Block.

of economic activity to the needs of society. In his work *The Great Transformation* (1944) he argues that the crises of the twenties and thirties were caused by the increasing independence of a self-regulating market economy, which began with industrialisation and led to economic activity being entirely separate from the fabric of society. His vision of premodern and preindustrial societies takes a view of economics in keeping with previous critics of rampant acquisitiveness.[120] Unlike classical economic theorists, Polanyi considered ancient economic activity as a form of human cooperation driven by the needs of society. In his view economic activity driven by markets and prices, and oriented towards meeting potentially limitless requirements with a limited supply of means, is characteristic of market-driven systems typical of industrialised societies.[121] Polanyi suggested that other forms of exchange, such as reciprocity or redistribution, govern the distribution of goods in societies that lack self-regulating markets. These forms of exchange are linked to social structures, with reciprocity linked to symmetrically organised groups such as family-groups, and redistribution linked to central entities through which the traffic of goods flows. Polanyi agreed with Mauss and Malinowski that an absence of individual profit-seeking is the distinguishing feature of the principle of reciprocity.[122] Recalling the work of Malinowski, Thurnwald, and Firth, he writes:

> The performance of acts of exchange by way of free gifts that are expected to be reciprocated though not necessarily by the same individuals—a procedure minutely articulated and perfectly safeguarded by the establishment of 'dualities' in which groups are linked in mutual obligations—should in itself explain the absence of the notion of gain or even of wealth other than that consisting of objects traditionally enhancing social prestige.[123]

This moderate critique of modernity forms a link between nostalgic interpretations of the gift in the 1920s and contemporary idealising tendencies that are no longer influenced by the spirit of anti-individualism and nostalgia for a primitive past. Modernisation has long since reached the places and cultures where Malinowski and other anthropologists had

---

120. See Schmoller 1900: 2 and Dargun 1885: 12. For discussion see Röpke 1984: 101–34.
121. Polanyi [1944] 2001: 45–47; 1957: 243–44. For Polanyi's concept of economy see Humphreys 1983: 39–73.
122. Mauss 2016: 184–85; Malinowski 1999: 175.
123. Polanyi [1944] 2001: 49.

CRITIQUE OF MODERNITY

made their observations. Economic anthropologists setting out to conduct further studies into gift-exchange after the Second World War did so less to preserve ancient practice than to contribute towards a careful adaptation to modernisation.[124] Contrary to their expectations, the cultures in question had not abandoned gift-exchange in favour of market economies only but instead developed manifold, mixed forms of exchange.[125] Thus, today the question is no longer one of a return to an idealised 'whole', symbolised by supposedly primitive cultures, but rather one of looking for the contemporary presence of the gift. The notion of gifts is now complementary to the notion of goods, and gift-exchange viewed as an ethically clad version of the exchange of commodities, not only in developing countries but especially in western industrialised countries.[126] What Mauss had imagined as the 'total social fact' of the gift has become 'universal fact'.

Mauss's successor to the chair in Sociology at the Collège de France, Claude Lévi-Strauss, led the way towards the universalising of the gift.[127] In his 1949 work *Les structures élémentaires de la parenté* (*The Elementary Structures of Kinship*) Strauss developed the idea that the exchange of women was a universal, original form of reciprocal exchange, while also emphasising the significance of gifts for building social alliance. His concept is akin to the modern myths of origin dismantled by ethnologists since the 1970s.[128] For Lévi-Strauss gift-exchange is not only an original form of exchange but also a living practice in modern societies. He describes the ritual of dinner invitations and the exchange of Christmas presents as a giant *potlatch*, which also includes the collective destruction of wealth as seen in the practices of the indigenous people of the North American northwest coast. He views the acquisition of honour, prestige, respect, and power as the essential core of the practice of gift-exchange: 'Goods are not only economic commodities, but vehicles and instruments for realities of another order, such as power, influence, status and emotion; and the skilful game of exchange [...] consists in a complex totality of conscious

---

124. See the remarks of Dalton 1961: 21: 'Western economic theory has proved a powerful tool for making industrialized market systems grow. But primitive economies are neither industrialized nor market systems. One must start from ethno-economic analysis—with Malinowski, not Ricardo—in order to choose those transformation paths to industrialization which entail only the unavoidable social costs'.
125. Cf. Gregory 1980: 626-52; Bloch and Parry 1989.
126. Elwert 1991: 159-77.
127. Cf. Charle and Teklès 1988: 167-68.
128. Cf. e.g. Weiner 1976. Maurice Godelier, who worked as Lévi-Strauss's assistant, also refers to Weiner in his own study on gifts (*L'enigme du don* 1996).

or unconscious manoeuvres in order to gain security and to guard oneself against risks brought about by alliances and rivalries.'[129]

Unfortunately, in his search for universal structures, Lévi-Strauss appears to have ignored the fact that the *potlatch* developed the specific competitive and excessive features he describes only as a consequence of the Kwakiutl tribe's interaction with Europe through the fur trade.[130] Thus, while it is true that Lévi-Strauss's critique of the idea of the 'spirit of the gift' contributed to the demystification of Mauss's concept of gift-exchange,[131] he does share Mauss's tendency to universalize and de-historicize the idea of the gift.

In *The Gift Economy* (1988) the American sociologist David Cheal is wary of the dangers of nostalgia inherent in Lévi-Strauss's view of 'gift-giving as natural economy'.[132] In his view the practice of gift-exchange represents a system of 'redundant transactions within a moral economy [...] which makes possible the extended reproduction of social relations.'[133] According to Cheal this applies especially to western industrialised societies, within which it is particularly women who, through 'gift-giving', safeguard the reproduction of social relations.[134]

A similar definition of the gift as social bond can be found in a 1991 essay in the *Revue de Mauss* by Alain Caillé and Jacques Godbout, in which the two sociologists answer the rhetorical question *'Le don existe-t-il (encore)?'* with an unequivocal 'yes'. According to them, the gift exists indeed, as a form of primary socialisation taking place within families, neighbourhoods

---

129. Lévi-Strauss 1967: 54.
130. More recent research has established that the *potlatch* forms part of an alternative economy only to a limited extent. In the region of Fort Rupert, where a number of different families of an Indian confederation were competing for influence in the fur trade, the change towards excess and competition was especially pronounced. Here, traditional gift-exchange ceremonies, which served to determine a chieftain and assemble his followers, became especially excessive in the context of competition for fur trade. Success in the ceremonies did also determine greater profit in trade with Western companies, since the followers or entourage gained through the ceremony were also a source of sea otter furs for trading. For a summary of the research see Wolf 1982: 182-92. Cf. also Drucker 1967: 481-93; Codere 1950; Kan 1986: 191-212; Mauzé 1986: 21-63.
131. See Godelier 1996: 27-44.
132. Cheal 1988: 12.
133. Cheal 1988: 19.
134. Cheal 1988: 2-9. Cf. also Hyde 1983: 108, who writes: 'to labor with gifts [...] remains a mark of female gender.' Similar Bloch and Boisson 1991: 54-71; Berking 1996: 40.

CRITIQUE OF MODERNITY 47

and groups of friends, and accompanied by secondary socialisation in the shape of the market.[135] In his contribution on the subject of market exchange and gift-exchange, the anthropologist Gerald Berthout proposes a similar model of two forms of social bond, which are complementary and overlapping.[136] These authors are not concerned to offer a positive evaluation of relations established through gifts, and indeed Caillé and Godbout reject as totalitarian fantasies any attempts to reform modern societies according to archaic structures.[137] Nonetheless, they warn of the loss of humanity and sociality that might occur if the gift were not taken seriously in the context of market exchange, as Berthoud suggests in reminding us of the '*leçon de sagesse*' to be drawn from Mauss.[138]

The difference between such approaches and Mauss's own critique of modernity lies primarily in the location of the archaic. Today's archaic is no longer to be found in the premodern economies of ancient and alien cultures but is instead concealed behind the facade of goods exchange in industrialised western societies. According to the sociologist Georg Elwert, the promise of an economy beyond individualist capitalism that inheres in Mauss's work has been replaced since the 1980s with talk of a 'patina' of moral economy imposed on relationships based on commodity. As he puts it in an essay of 1991, *Gabe, Reziprozität und Warentausch*:

> Where the generalised reciprocity of informal services governs everyday life in offices and workplaces the interface of interaction between colleagues and within workplace hierarchies is no longer ruled by the contract of salaried employment. Given the dominance of such informal relations, the moral-economic exchange of information, services and presents understood as gifts takes precedence over the formal or contractual working relationships. Informal relations and exchanges cloak the world of work (and it should be

---

135. Godbout and Caillé 1991: 26. They finish their study with the following remarks: 'La seule hypothèse qu'il soit nécessaire de nous accorder à cette étape est qu'il existe dans la société moderne comme dans la société archaïque ou traditionnelle un mode de circulation des biens qui diffère intrinsèquement du mode analysé par les économistes [...] Qualifions de don toute prestation du bien ou de service effectuée sans garantie de retour, en vue de créer, nourrir et recréer le lien social entre personnes. Nous nous proposons de déterminer la manière dont le don, ainsi caractérisé comme mode de circulation des biens au service du lien social, forme le système social primaire des relations de personne à personne' (32).
136. Berthout 1991: 86 and 12; 1991: 79–96.
137. Godbout and Caillé 1991: 29.
138. Godbout and Caillé 1991: 94.

noted that they also make working together more pleasant). We recognise generalised reciprocity as a distinctive feature of modern industrialised society, even though it was first spoken about in connection with pre-industrial societies.[139]

Thus gift-exchange continues even today to function as a counter-model to market exchange.

While the gift is viewed as complementary to market exchange and the exchange of goods in western industrialised societies, it seems to some sociologists outside the western world to function as an alternative to the imported economy of industrial centres. In his 1988 article 'Modernity, Identity, and Utopia in Latin America', the Peruvian sociologist Anibal Quijano presents reciprocity as a specifically Latin American form of rationality that unites individualism and solidarity. He suggests 'that in the very center of Latin American cities, the masses of the dominated are building new social practices founded on reciprocity, on an assumption of equality, on collective solidarity, and at the same time on the freedom of individual choice and on a democracy of collectively made decisions, against all external impositions'.[140] Such new social practices based on reciprocity are shaped, according to Quijano, 'outside or against the state and private capital and their respective bureaucracies' as alternatives against the instrumental rationalism of the West.[141] The opposing forces of individualism and collective thought that had governed the beginnings of the debate on gift-exchange are united in Quijano's reception.

The idealising gaze eventually reached classical scholarship too. Since Bücher, the concept of gift-exchange had been debated from the perspectives of political economy and legal history without any links to the critiques of modernity we see in other fields.[142] It should be noted, however,

---

139. Elwert 1991: 163; 1985: 509–13.
140. Quijano 1993: 154.
141. Quijano 1993: 155. Quijano's argument is based on the critique of reason by Horkheimer and Adorno. In *Minima Moralia* (1951) Adorno himself objected to the universalising of the principle of gift-exchange and of the transformation of gifts into goods. In his view gift-giving presents itself as unalienated action par excellence: 'Every undistorted relationship, perhaps indeed the conciliation that is part of organic life itself, is a gift' (quoted from the English translation by E. F. N. Jephcott, first published 1974. Verso edition 2005: 43).
142. Besides Laum 1924 see especially Bolkestein 1939: 156–58. According to him, social life in ancient Greece was based on the principle of reciprocity and gifts were given in hope of receiving a counter-gift. Bolkestein's view is based on Bücher and Mauss (see p. 165 and 220–22). Köstler 1950: 23 stands in the tradition of

CRITIQUE OF MODERNITY 49

that among economic historians the concept of gift-exchange was predominantly used by representatives of a 'primitivist' position who assumed that ancient and modern economies were not comparable.[143] Within this 'primitivist' tradition the work of ancient historian Moses I. Finley stands out, as he is credited with first bringing Mauss's findings to bear on illuminating ancient evidence.[144] Finley insisted on the difference between ancient and modern economies (and implicitly criticised modernity) when he argues in *The World of Odysseus* (1954) that Homeric exchange, by contrast to modern market trading, was not led by the pursuit of profit.[145] Significantly, Finley refers to the observations of Malinowski who had considered lack of profit-seeking as a distinctive feature of primitive economy.[146]

Only recently have such reflections become consolidated to form a counterpoint to modernity. These debates are governed by the opposition between altruism and egoism that had long been recognised by economists. In a 1990 work, *Ma'at: Gerechtigkeit und Unsterblichkeit im Alten Ägypten*, the Egyptologist Jan Assmann refers to the theories of Durkheim, Mauss,

---

    Bücher and Laum when he argues that in early Greece transactions were usually organised as gift-giving and exchange was developed in later times. 'Schenkung auf Gegenschenkung' was considered as the original form of exchange also by Bruck 1926: 61. For the use of the theory of gift-giving by legal scholars see Maffi 1979: 33–62.

143. This is true of Bolkestein whose work *Economic Life in Greece's Golden Age* (1958) belongs to the primitivists' school of thought that refused to employ modern categories to analyse ancient economies. Karl Bücher is foundational to this too, although Eduard Meyer's polemical rejection of Bücher's theses meant that his views were slow to gain attention among German scholars. On the Bücher-Meyer controversy and its reception see Will 1954b: 7–22; Austin and Vidal-Naquet [1972] 1977, ch. 1; Andreau and Etienne 1984: 55–83; Andreau 1995; Schneider 1990: 417–45; Wagner-Hasel 2011: 198–214; 2014: 51–69.

144. See ch. 1.4.

145. Finley [1954] 1967: 66: 'Behind the market lies the profit motive, and if there was one thing that was taboo in Homeric exchanges it was gain in the exchange. Whether in trade or in any other mutual relationship, the abiding principle was equality and mutual benefit'. For a similar view today see e.g. Seaford 2004: 23: 'Precise equivalence of value and enforceable immediacy of return have no place in the exchange of gifts'.

146. Finley 1967: 61–62: 'An exchange mechanism was then the only alternative [to violence], and the basic one was gift-exchange. This was no Greek invention. On the contrary, it is the basic organizing mechanism among many primitive peoples, as in the Trobriand Islands, where "most if not all economic acts are found to belong to some chain of reciprocal gifts and counter-gifts." Here Finley cites Malinowski, *Crime and Custom in Savage Society*, New York 1952: 40.

and Marshall Sahlins in his discussion of the concept of 'Ma'at' as a principle of integration through which community, justice, and reciprocity are established between a pharaoh and his people. Assmann sees in 'Ma'at' the realisation of the central virtues connected with solidarity and social justice, namely altruism and the protection of the weak, which are 'disempowered in contemporary economic ideology'. Egyptian 'Ma'at', as a form of vertical solidarity, shows, according to Assmann, that the Egyptians had already constructed 'an alternative [...] to economic liberalism'.[147]

The classicist and scholar of religion Walter Burkert views 'giving' as a universal and timeless behavioural pattern, a survival strategy rehearsed in religious practices. According to Burkert early Greek economic life was especially dominated by gift-exchange, and like others he also emphasises the gulf between ancient and modern economies: 'Modern economy is definitely different, with strategies that aim at immediate profit and ruthless exploitation, ending of course in diminishing return.'[148]

A conference at the University of Exeter in 1993 on the subject of ancient reciprocity saw participants debating whether gift-giving was motivated by altruism or utilitarianism.[149] The debate at the time focussed primarily on the interpretation of the Attic liturgy system,[150] which Richard Meyer had already studied from the point of view of gift-exchange in 1898.[151] But the conflict between altruistic and utilitarian views of the gift has become increasingly relevant to the interpretation of sacrifice. In the mid-twentieth century, Laum had tended towards a utilitarian position in interpreting sacrifice as a means of requital in the reciprocal traffic between men and gods.[152] More recently, the opposite view has tended to dominate. Thus Christiano Grottanelli, referring back to theories of Gerardus van der Leuuw,[153] understands sacrifice as the repayment of a

---

147. Assmann 1990: 278. Assmann primarily refers to Marcel Mauss to whom he attributes the achievement of having demonstrated, through the example of the potlatch, the communicative significance of exchange (68).
148. Burkert 1987: 50; 1984: 26. Here Burkert argues that the universal act of giving originates in the distribution of meat after the hunt.
149. Gill, Postlethwaite and Seaford 1998.
150. Whereas Gabriel Herman (1998; 2006) interprets the liturgies as altruistic services, Paul Millett (1998) stresses the idea of reciprocity. See now Liddell 2007 and Christ 2012 (who follow the debate opened by Bolkestein 1939 and Hands 1968) and Domingo Gygax 2016 for the connection of reciprocity and euergetism.
151. See n. 54.
152. Laum 1924: 20.
153. van der Leeuw 1920–21: 241–53.

CRITIQUE OF MODERNITY

debt and the fulfilment of moral obligation towards the gods.[154] Sitta von Reden's work on ancient Greek gift-exchange focusses on its metaphysical dimensions. She understands the gift-exchange and market exchange practices described in poetic and historical texts as providing insight into Greek world views and into competing, negative and positive, models of the *polis* and its order.[155]

Contemporary research into gift-exchange is not short of voices warning against its idealisation, and it is unpersuaded of the moral qualities ascribed to this form of giving by the scholars cited here. Objections are made especially by ethnologists, while the idealising tendencies are mostly found in sociological literature. Thus Maurice Bloch and Jonathan Parry argue in *Money and Morality* (1989) against the imagined high moral value associated with gift-giving and characterise this as the inversion of the values of economic rationalism and utilitarianism into their opposite.[156] The sociologist Pierre Bourdieu had highlighted the interested nature of giving, and introduced the notion of 'symbolic capital' in his examination of the Kabyle people in the 1970s. He proposed that the rituals of giving he observed were a matter of continuously transforming economic capital into symbolic capital, and thereby concealing naked self-interest.[157]

The more recent idealisations of the gift as a more altruistic, morally more laudable form of transaction, have their origin, once again, in discontent with modernity, and in a loss of trust in traditional paradigms and strategies. Caillé and Godbout for instance claim that the impetus for their reflections on the presence of the gift came from the failure of Marxist, utilitarian, and structuralist interpretative paradigms, which led them to

---

154. Grottanelli 1989–1990: 45–54. See also Bodei Giglioni 1989–1990: 55–64, who follows a similar idea regarding the position of Aristotle and Theophrastus. For a discussion of the reciprocal character of sacrifice in the epics see Hitch 2009: 93–140.
155. Von Reden 1995: 18.
156. Bloch and Parry 1989: 9. Sitta von Reden 1995: 7 and 171–75 made use of this critique for her metaphysical interpretation of coinage. See also Kurke 1999.
157. Bourdieu [1972] 1977: 171. See also Appadurai 1986: 12 who follows Bourdieu. The classicist Marcel Widzisz (2012) has recently made use of Pierre Bourdieu to analyse Homeric gift-giving from this perspective. Cf. also van Wees 1992: 230, who stresses the utilitarian motivations underlying Homeric gift-giving in *xeinos*-relationships and the profit-orientation of the heroes in nearly every context. His 1998 summary of anthropological research begins with a quote from Thomas Hobbes (*Léviathan* 1651: 1.15) saying that no one gives something or anything without expecting to benefit from it (Van Wees 1998: 13).

search for a new key to solving the world's problems.[158] For Maurice Godelier, reasons for recalling the practice of gift-giving are found in the crisis of the Western welfare state, systemic unemployment, and an increasingly threadbare social safety net (*tissu social*). The gift can fill the gap, and assume a mediating function between state and market or between impersonal law and cold calculation.[159] The German sociologist Helmut Berking is convinced that the dominance of utilitarian profit-seeking has allowed society's moral consensus to evaporate. In the practice of gift-exchange he sees, therefore, the potential for social integration.[160] In an essay published in 1990, in a commemorative volume for Karl Polanyi, the economist Björn Hettne argues for a revival of the principle of reciprocity, after the failure of neoliberalism to cope with global recession, structural unemployment, and crises in political trust. In his opinion, reciprocal practices are still alive in the informal economic sector of Western industrial societies and also in those of developing countries.[161]

In the 1920s early idealisations of the gift were led, as we have seen, by a disenchantment with modernity, which ultimately transformed into nostalgia for a return to total unity between individual and society that characterised fascist ideology. We must therefore ask whether contemporary idealisations of the gift as a primary social practice and counterweight to modern capitalist society are not, themselves, expressions of similar misapprehensions. Within the field of management consultancy, there are discussions concerning the replacement of ethical morality with economic morality and arguments that the moral effects of economic actions should be included in any cost-benefit calculations.[162] This raises the suspicion that we are now negotiating a further step on the way into modernity. Conversely, fields that until now were not market-dominated are also becoming subject to the laws of the market. In this case, conjuring up the presence of the gift would simply be nothing but a reaction to its absence and to the social disintegration caused by the globalisation of markets.[163]

---

158. Godbout and Caillé 1991: 11–12. Cf. also Godbout 1992.
159. Godelier 1996: 12.
160. Berking 1996: 9–12.
161. Hettne 1990: 208–20.
162. Cf. Lay 1991; 1990. For a discussion of the benefits of reciprocal and altruistic behaviour in the field of economy see Grant 2014; Singer 2015; Frevert 2019. For a critique of the integration of social life into the market-economy see Siemons 1993: 66–79; Sandel 2012.
163. See Forrester 1996.

1.3. Return ticket to the South Sea Islands: On the use of ethnological comparisons and a critique of reciprocity

What remains of the theory of the gift? Is this conception of gift-exchange simply the reverse image of modern economy, a counter-model to economic liberalism, a utopia? Certainly not. Discussions at the end of the nineteenth century about the standardization and the reconception of giving clearly indicate that the development of the theory of the gift was, in fact, accompanied by changes in the practices of giving, changes that required conceptual formulation. Yet it has become just as clear that these premodern practices cannot be subsumed under a single concept of giving. The British social historian Edward P. Thompson, who developed the concept of a 'moral economy', has noted correctly that there can be no 'constant "act of giving" with constant features, which may be isolated from particular social contexts', since the structure of giving always emerges within the historical peculiarity of the ensemble of social relations 'and not in a particular ritual or form isolated from these'.[164]

Recent anthropological and sociological work has built on the work of Mauss and Malinowski and resulted in more differentiated interpretations of the concept of the gift. They are most frequently indebted to Polanyi's system of categorisation. For example, his students Paul and Laura Bohannan distinguished between different spheres of circulation for subsistence goods and prestige goods.[165] More famous is Marshall Sahlins's differentiation between generalised, balanced, and negative types of reciprocity.[166] The organising principle underlying his typology is social distance, with altruism and egoism or self-interest forming the two opposing poles. According to Sahlins, generalised reciprocity refers to transactions that take place within neighbourly or family networks and refers primarily to giving without (immediately) taking. Balanced reciprocity subsumes trade and gift-exchange, while negative reciprocity refers to profit-orientated exchange and also includes theft. Sahlins has, however, been accused of differentiating reciprocity to such an extent as to have deprived it of its key element—that of mutuality.[167]

In the field of social anthropology, the problematic definition of reciprocity has led to renewed attempts to distinguish between gift-exchange and

---

164. Thompson 1977: 258.
165. Bohannan 1955; 1968.
166. Sahlins 1984: 184–275.
167. Ganzer 1981: 23–41. MacCormack 1976: 89–103 and criticises this lack of clarity.

the exchange of goods, in which the type of relationship that underlies the transaction is taken to be the distinguishing criterion. Thus Chris Gregory describes gift-exchange as a 'debt economy' which is not concerned with exchanging commodities but with establishing obligations.[168] In the field of ancient history Ian Morris especially has taken up this model.[169] Bloch and Parry distinguish between long-term and short-term transactions in a model applied to early Greece by Sitta von Reden in her analysis of gift and goods exchange.[170] Ancient historians nonetheless overwhelmingly work with Sahlins's typology and with the Maussian concept of the gift as a form of social integration to interpret evidence from antiquity.[171] Émile Benveniste's study of the Indo-European vocabulary of gift-exchange is based on an understanding of the socially integrative function of gifts, but in the search for linguistic origins it tends, like other such studies, to lose sight of the historical and social contexts of the terms under investigation.[172] By contrast, Évelyne Scheid-Tissinier pays proper attention to the historical and social contexts of Homeric terminologies of giving and exchanging, but the interpretative range is limited by her acceptance of the Maussian and Lévi-Straussian positions which view all gifts as means of establishing alliances and obligations.[173] Scheid-Tissinier analyses the process of giving and taking by starting with the use of the term *didōmi* (to give), its derivations *dōron*, *dosis*, and *dōtinē* (gift), and a series of synonyms (*porēn*, *tithēmi*, *pherō*, *teleō*, etc). She considers the process within the frameworks of marriage, guest-friendship, safe passage, and rulership and interprets gifts (especially bridal and guest-gifts) as means of forging alliances and

---

168. Gregory 1982: 18 follows Mauss when he argues that things and persons are not separated in a 'gift-economy'. He characterises gift-economy as 'debt-economy' whose aim it was to create bonds of obligations. According to Gregory, commodity-exchange and gift-exchange exist side by side and complement each other. Cf. also Godelier 1969: 5–37, who argues that the salt-money of the Baruya people of Papua New Guinea served both as a gift and as a commodity. This idea is not new. Cf. Schurtz 1898: 170, who notes that salt functioned as a gift within the society of the Baruya but was used as money outside it. While this exchange of goods could not be defined as an exchange of equivalence, the Baruya people took payment in return for their monopoly on the specialised knowledge required for the production of salt. For similar emphasis on the porous boundaries between gift and commodity see also Appadurai 1986: 11–16; Elwert 1991: 159–77. For the relationship between money and gift in ancient Rome see now Coffee 2017.
169. Morris 1986: 1–17.
170. Von Reden 1995: 3.
171. Cf. e.g. von Reden 1995: 3 and 79–81.
172. Benveniste 1951: 7–20, reprint 1966: 313–26; 1969: 65–101.
173. Scheid-Tissinier 1994: XII, 158.

relationships between different communities. The most important area in which she sees the ethics of the gift and its two obligations (generosity and reciprocity) unfold most clearly is in the warrior community assembled at the feast.[174] Drawing on Sahlins, Walter Donlan's typology of reciprocities in Homer seems to run entirely counter to ancient Greek concepts, raising some doubt as to its usefulness. Thus he places terms for debt (*chreios*), payments of penalties and ransoms (*poinē, apoina, ōnos*), and bridal and guest-gifts (*dōra, hedna, xeinia*) in the category of balanced reciprocity, even though their social contexts are fundamentally different.[175]

In order to regain a different perspective that allows us to appreciate the many facets and meanings of gifts in premodern societies, I propose to follow quite a different strand of thinking, one that calls for a complete departure from the concept of reciprocity.[176] This will allow us to return to a key turning point in the debate, namely to the *Argonauts of the Western Pacific*, and to pick up once more the threads which Malinowski wove to connect the world of the Greeks with the world of the 'savages'.

In the 1970s, the American sociologist Annette B. Weiner examined the classical sites of gift-exchange in the Southern Pacific, the Trobriand Islands, and Samoa and reanalysed Malinowski's material in light of her own field work.[177] The result of her research is a revision of the concept of reciprocity and a new perspective on the question of the value of gifts. She suggested that traditional concepts such as 'balanced reciprocity', 'pure gift', or 'generosity' reduced the complexity of the processes of exchange, which should not be divided into linear sequences of giving, receiving, and returning. What appears superficially as a pure gift, without any compulsion to give in return, may in fact be the start of a long-term process of mutual obligation that may 'switch back and forth between giver and receiver through time'.[178] Weiner starts from the fundamental supposition that gifts may be reciprocated or retracted, although she rejects the widespread assumption that the expectation of a counter-gift is undefined.[179] In her view,

---

174. Scheid-Tissinier 1994: 251–84.
175. Donlan 1982: 137–74. In his article 'Scale, Value, and Their Function in the Homeric Economy', he uses Bohannan's concept and differentiates between gifts of food for the poor and gifts of precious objects circulating amongst the warrior elite. Donlan 1981: 101–17.
176. Weiner 1980: 72.
177. Weiner 1976.
178. Weiner 1980: 73.
179. On equivalence between gifts and counter-gifts cf. Racine 1987: 97–118, who distinguishes between elementary and complex forms of reciprocity.

the expectation tied to a gift is clearly defined and is expressed through the form of the objects which are given. She proposes that the materiality of the object itself conveys the message with regard to future expectations, which may not always be articulated openly in words.[180] The crucial point for Weiner is that exchange is a long-term process regulated by a process of social reproduction.[181] She observes that in the society of the Trobriands it is the funeral ritual that sets in motion the process for the compensation of wealth and the renewal of social relations through gifts.[182]

Weiner demonstrates that Malinowski's classification of the different types of gifts among the Trobriand islanders according to their relation to equivalence, distinguishing between pure gifts, which compelled little or no reciprocation, and gifts which more or less aimed at equal value,[183] is misleading. For example, Malinowski designated as pure gifts those allocations which a father made to his son, such as the right to trees in village groves and in garden lots belonging to the matrilineage of the father. However, with the death of the father, these 'pure gifts' were demanded back from the son through gifts (*sagali*) given by the members of the father's matrilineage because according to the matrilineal ideology of the Trobriand people, the son belonged to the matrilineage of his mother. Bundles of banana leaves and fibrous skirts, which in older literature also had been seen to act as a limited currency, symbolized these claims for the return of 'pure' gifts.[184] The bundles and skirts were produced by the deceased's matrilineal descendants or exchanged with other women for food, preferably yams, which they received from their brothers. Such 'textile' gifts for the dead are distributed during funeral celebrations to all those who had received or given valuable objects or obligations to the deceased during their lifetime. Weiner proposes that women guarantee the return of resources into their own familial groups through the production of funeral gifts. They also renew alliances forged between different familial groups, which are otherwise threatened with dissolution by the death of one of

---

180. Weiner 1980: 76.
181. Cf. also Bloch and Parry 1990: 23–25, who differentiate between short-term and long-term transactional orders, an approach now used by many scholars. See e.g. von Reden 1995: 3; Foxhall 2007; Widzisz 2012: 154.
182. Weiner 1989: 63.
183. Malinowski [1922] 1999: 177–91. Malinowski revised his ideas about the pure gift after noting Marcel Mauss's work on the gift. See Malinowski's *Crime and Custom in Savage Society* (London 1926: 41). Mauss 1966: 71 (see n. 2) had criticized Malinowski on this point.
184. Schurtz 1898: 127–33. See also Ella 1899: 165–70; Krämer 1902.

their members. A large proportion of the gifts is handed to the deceased's spouse and to his or her father, in order to replace the provision made for them (referred to as *mapula*) by the deceased during their lifetime. When sons wish to enter into their father's matrilineal group and share in its resources, they need, according to Weiner, to bring gifts of food to the funeral celebration organised by the head of the deceased father's matrilineage and by his sisters.[185]

The compensatory or return gifts of banana leaf bundles and skirts occasioned by a death have great symbolic character. They stand for material resources as well as for the social network of a matrilineage. Weiner describes them as a kind of currency that represents circulating wealth. This wealth is not, however, permanent. Weiner emphasises the levelling effect of the rituals of redistribution that take place during funeral rites as a 'replacement process'. According to her observations, this process effects both an inflow and an outflow of matrilinear resources, since the distribution of the gifts for the dead (*sagali*) is preceded by a continuous process of transformation in which other forms of wealth (from agriculture and craftwork, which are the domain of men) are converted into the textile wealth produced by women (an individual woman needs 1,000 banana leaf bundles and twenty or thirty skirts for one funeral). Weiner shows that it is the women's textile wealth that renews social relations between clans. Mauss had been interested in just these groups when he made use of Malinowski's research into the *Kula* ring for his concept of the gift as a collective treaty. According to Weiner, the goods exchanged in the ring are employed by men to make claims on the resources of the father's matrilineage, but they establish personal obligations and lend social prestige only to individuals. The position of 'chief' does give a man the right to distribute the resources of a matrilineage, but these must be reclaimed through women's textile wealth. Thus, textile wealth represents the inalienability of a group's identity and the social and economic power of matrilineage.[186]

Weiner offers a second, quite different, example to illustrate the unsuitability of the concept of reciprocity for explaining exchange processes in premodern societies. While the Trobriand symbols of the social and economic power of matrilineage cannot be converted into permanent power, she suggests that in Samoa the possession of such symbolic goods (finely woven mats made from pandanus leaves) is tied to actual means

185. Weiner 1989: 38-42.
186. Weiner 1980: 76; 1983: 147-70.

of power. The difference is made by the objects themselves, as Weiner indicates: 'Samoan cloth has much greater longevity, giving it a measure of inalienability and historical authority, which can support more formal levels of rank'.[187] This means that fine mats tend to be stored up rather than exchanged. In Samoa the mats are circulated at occasions such as births, marriages, funerals, and enthronements but also as compensation gifts in cases of murder. Like the Trobriand banana bundles and skirts, the distribution of these fine mats serves to renew social relationships and to support the cohesion of splintered family groups. Distribution is organised by the highest-ranking titleholder in a descent group and by his oldest sister, who herself may be a titleholder. It is she who, with the wife of the highest-ranking titleholder, organises the manufacture of the mats when these are made by groups rather than by individuals. The mats are viewed as the property of the descent group, but they are kept by the women (who may work on one mat for as long as a year), and handed over, albeit with a right of refusal, on demand from the highest-ranking titleholder, or in support of a husband or brother. According to Weiner the collaboration of titleholders and their sisters reflects the branches of descent groups whose members trace themselves back to either the founding father of their line, or the mother, with the two thought of as siblings. Both the titleholder and his sister may collect mats from relatives in both branches of the descent group in order to distribute them at weddings and funerals according to criteria of rank and status. Weiner clarifies how rank and power are visualized in this way. The finest and oldest mats—heirlooms that contain the history of past relationships and are passed on only under special circumstances—are especially expressive with respect to rank and power. Weiner tells us that they are sometimes given names and function as a 'material archive'.[188]

Both types of cloth—banana leaf bundles and pandanus mats—are also linked to their society's conceptions of time in that they absorb time and give it visual form.[189] In both societies time is conceived as duration and is manifested in the durability of objects. Thus, we find that Trobriand exchange processes are tied to life cycles, and that the role of the textile bundles featured in the funeral rituals does not reach beyond the ceremony itself. By contrast, in Samoa there is a constant striving to transcend the individual's lifespan so that the textiles involved in distribution ceremonies

187. Weiner 1989: 70.
188. Weiner 1989.
189. Weiner 1989: 71.

have longevity and are stored for generations. Genealogical memory is structured accordingly in each society: while in Trobriand matrilineal genealogy, the ancestor (or their spirit) returns directly into the body of a woman without building a long chain of ancestry, Samoan descent groups have considerable genealogical depth, often tracing themselves back as far as fifteen generations.[190]

I will now return from the South Pacific to the ancient Mediterranean world. My aim is not to compare Trobriands and Samoans to Greeks and Romans but to make use of Weiner's methodological and analytical framework, which I think is applicable. What is particularly inspiring is her attempt at symbolic interpretation of the materiality of gifts and her concern to understand individual exchange transactions in relation to the social structures in which they take place as well as in relation to symbolic and material production. Of course, contextualising transactions of exchange within their social context is a widely accepted principle within our field of research, but Weiner's focus on reproduction and on the question of the replacement and regeneration of material and immaterial values is especially valuable. By discarding the perspective of the giving and taking individuals, Weiner's study reveals relationships between apparently discrete exchange transactions and renders modern classifications of types of reciprocity obsolete. Reciprocity is a characteristic of the exchange relations she describes, but it is recognised in long-term relationships and relates to structural unities. In view of Weiner's work, a historical analysis needs to take seriously the material character of gifts, and to seek to understand the message that is expressed through their materiality. Most importantly, however, her method suggests that it is important to consider exchange transactions not as discrete acts but to look for relationships between them. This means that any question about the function of gifts in antiquity must always entail a social analysis.

1.4. *Gift-exchange in the Greek world: The debate over the formation of state and polis*

The interpretation of gifts as a form of social integration means that gift theory has some bearing on the discussion over the emergence of the state which, at its beginning, was concerned with the question of the

---

190. Weiner 1989: 40–45, 56–62.

subordination of individual interests under a central power.[191] Sahlins drew an analogy between the Maussian concept of gift-exchange and Thomas Hobbes's concepts of the 'commonwealth' and 'common power', to which individuals surrender their self-interest in the interest of social and political peace. He concedes that the gift in Mauss does not structure society in a corporate sense but only in a segmentary sense and that this would not involve surrender to a central authority as in Hobbes. Instead the individual surrenders to an irrational power, the spirit of the gift.[192] In Sahlins's interpretation Mauss joins the social contract theorists[193] who distinguish between a primitive anarchy and a state of civilisation created through agreement and contract. The more recent debate about the origins of the state is more prominently marked by conflict theory. Here, the formation of the state is a matter of overcoming internal and external social conflicts. Recent theories stress consensus rather than conflict, in contrast to both Marxist theories of class-struggle (the state viewed as a means for enforcing the interests of the ruling class) and conquest theories (the state is formed through the conquest of agricultural cultures by nomadic tribes) that gained in influence towards the end of the nineteenth century.[194] The key question here is 'how personal power become[s] depersonalized power' and how 'an egalitarian, segmental society become[s] an hierarchical society with permanently ascribed differential ranks of high and low statuses'.[195] Elman Service argues that institutionalised leadership emerges through the fulfilment of administrative functions that serve the maintenance of the community.[196] Gift-exchange is, therefore, important to Service's argument in two ways. On the one hand he suggests that reciprocal exchanges play a vital role in the creation of status hierarchies; on the other hand, he stresses the role of gifts in the creation of external alliances which may also strengthen the status of officials.[197]

---

191. For an understanding of the state as centralised power, a concept which was developed by Thomas Hobbes, cf. van Creveld 1999: 195-218 and Hölscher 1979: 60-69, who discusses the invention of the term 'state' in the seventeenth century. Different definitions of the state are discussed by Stagl 1974: 311-22 and Service 1975: 43-46.
192. Sahlins 1984: 167-80.
193. For another view see Giddens 1976: 706-14.
194. For an overview see Service 1975: 21-46.
195. Service 1975: 71-72.
196. Service 1975: 8. Similar Stahl 2003: I, 110-13.
197. Service 1975: 60-63, 73-75.

GIFT-EXCHANGE IN THE GREEK WORLD

Moses Finley's 1954 work *The World of Odysseus* plays a key role in the application of theories of gift-exchange to understanding the formation of the state in antiquity. While previous ancient historians, working with a concept of reciprocal gift-giving within the tradition dominated by Bücher, had assumed the existence of a state from the beginning of written accounts,[198] Finley considered the social circumstances of the *Iliad* and *Odyssey* to belong to a pre-state era: 'a large measure of informality, of fluidity and flexibility, marked all the political institutions of the age', Finley argued.[199] He exemplifies this through the uncertain position of the king, who was not able to rely upon regular taxes or tributes and had to secure his position through warfare and external alliances.[200] In Finley's view, Homeric society was structured around *oikoi*, individual households that came together to collaborate for communal good only in times of crisis.[201] He viewed gift-exchange as a key means for the formation of alliances between different households and leaders:

> No single detail in the life of the heroes receives so much attention in the *Iliad* and the *Odyssey* as gift-giving, and always there is frank reference to adequacy, appropriateness, recompense [...] There was scarcely a limit to the situations in which gift-giving was operative. More precisely, the word "gift" was a cover-all for a great variety of actions and transactions which later became differentiated and acquired their own appellations. There were payments for services rendered, desired, or anticipated; what we would call fees, rewards, prizes, and sometimes bribes [...] The whole of what we would call foreign relations and diplomacy, in their peaceful manifestations, was conducted by gift-exchange.[202]

Finley illustrates the relationship-building functions of gifts especially through examples of bridal gifts and gifts of hospitality.[203] Unlike Rudolf Köstler, who had interpreted reciprocal gifts in Homeric marriage

---

198. Cf. also Laum 1924: 160 and Köstler 1950: 7-25. Both are consulted by Finley. According to Köstler the description of the world of the Cyclops gives an idea of a pre-state-reality, characterised as based on primitive tribal law (11: 'urtümliche Sippenrechtsordnung auf natur und vernunftrechtlicher Grundlage').
199. Finley [1954] 1967: 84.
200. Finley [1954] 1967: 100-3.
201. Finley [1954] 1967: 103.
202. Finley [1954] 1967: 63-64.
203. Cf. Finley 1955: 167-94.

laws and politics in terms of legal history as forms of contract,[204] Finley views gifts of guest-friendship in particular as predecessors of contractual agreements: 'What other firm proof could there have been, in that unlettered world, that a relationship had been established, creating obligations and responsibilities'?[205] According to Finley, these archaic forms of agreement were formed between individuals rather than groups, as Maussian theory would suggest. This stress on personal relationships distinguishes Homeric alliances from agreements made in classical Greece: 'Croesus exchanged oaths of guest-friendship with the Spartans but Homer knows of no such tie between Argives and Lycians or Taphians and Ithacans—only between individuals, Diomedes and Glaucus, "Mentes" and Telemachus.'[206]

Indeed, Finley did not refer to Mauss in *The World of Odysseus* but instead to the tradition founded by Bücher, which in ethnology had been continued by Malinowski and had been taken up in the field of ancient history by legal historians such as Rudolf Köstler. It is only in his 1974 appendix *The World of Odysseus Revisited* that Finley referred to Mauss's research: 'Fifty years ago the French sociologist Marcel Mauss published his famous account of the integral role of gift-giving in a large range of societies. Twenty years ago I showed that gift-giving in the Homeric poems is consistent, I might even say absolutely consistent, with the analysis made by Mauss (who, curiously, ignored the ancient Greeks in his study)'.[207] Finley thus joined this line of tradition rather belatedly—although he was well aware of the significance of the work of Louis Gernet, which stood at its beginning.

Gernet, a student of Durkheim just like Mauss himself, had taken on the task of collating the evidence on gift-exchange in ancient Greece, which Mauss had largely left untouched—with the exception of a brief study on the *potlatch* in Thrace[208] and on the Roman *nexum*.[209] There is, therefore, nothing strange about the absence of ancient Greece from Mauss's work.[210] Mauss had assumed that already in antiquity there had been a division

---

204. Köstler 1950: 22–23.
205. Finley [1954] 1967: 133.
206. Finley [1954] 1967: 105.
207. Finley [1954] 1978: 151.
208. Mauss 1921: 388–97.
209. Mauss [1923/4] 2016: 146–56.
210. Cf. Ulf 1990: 212 arguing that Mauss neglected the ancient Greek world because he could not find in it a system of 'prestations totales', which the French scholar considered as the basis for complete material reciprocity.

between contract and moral obligation, and that trade was independent of gift-exchange.[211] Gernet is less inclined than Mauss to modernising interpretations of ancient practices and laws, preferring to assume that there is no division between law and religion in early Greece. Gernet recognises allusions to the practice of gift-exchange, especially in the mythical tradition, interpreting this as competitive much as Mauss had argued for the Tlingit and Haida *potlatch*.[212] Above all, Gernet highlights the role of gifts in forging alliances in Greek international relations ('*l'ordre international*').[213] Finley too refers to this in his article 'Marriage, Sale and Gift in the Homeric World', which appeared a year after *The World of Odysseus* and in which he highlights the significance of gifts and counter-gifts in Greek social and political relations. Finley, however, does not agree with Gernet on the competitive character of gift-giving, and he also takes a more 'primitivist' position on the subject of rulership.[214]

Moses Finley may appear today as the founding father of ancient historical gift-exchange debate, but the debate's prehistory is in fact far more complex.[215] Not unlike Malinowski, Finley sketches out the picture of a homogeneous society (albeit a fictional one) which he locates in the tenth and ninth centuries BCE.[216] In doing so, Finley rejected the then widely accepted consensus that located Homeric society in the Mycenaean age and viewed Homeric rulership as based on feudal models or on sacred kingship.[217] Finley's colleague George D. Thomson had attempted to build support for James Frazer's concept of sacred kingship only a few years earlier in his *Prehistoric Aegean* (1949), about which Finley maintains a studious silence.[218] Having adopted a school of thought founded by Henry Morgan and Friedrich Engels according to which the state was an instrument for securing the rule of one social class, Thomson saw the development of

---

211. Mauss [1923/24] 2016: 157.
212. Gernet 1948: 415–62.
213. Gernet 1951: 21–119, reprint 1982: 17.
214. Finley 1955: 179, n. 35.
215. This is the argument of Qviller 1981: 112, who praises the revolutionary character of Finley's discovery, and of Donlan 1989: 2.
216. For this he is criticised early on. Cf. Snodgrass 1974: 114–25; Whitley 1991: 35–37; Raaflaub 1998: 169–93.
217. For more detail see ch. 4.
218. The opposition against Thomson can be derived from his critique of 'a repressed memory of ancient matriarchy [...] reflected in some verses' of the poem. He does not name any of his opponents: 'Some scholars have seen in it [i.e. Penelope's and Arete's power] a confused vestige of a mother-right system that prevailed among the Greeks centuries before.' Finley [1954] 1967: 92–93.

private property as the decisive catalyst for the emergence of the state in antiquity. He was working with the evolutionary model designed by Morgan in which primitive society is matriarchal and characterised by communal property and group marriage, while the final stage sees a class structure characterised by private property and patriarchal family structures. He thought that this final stage was reached by the Greek *polis*. Thomson interpreted the system depicted in Homeric epic as a primitive ancestral monarchy with elements of sacred kingship inherited from the Minoan and Mycenaean era; he too located it in the Dark Ages, the tenth to ninth centuries BCE.[219]

Thomson is on the side of the conflict theorists who explained the emergence of the state from inner and outer contradictions,[220] while Finley clearly shows more affinity with contract theorists. For instance, Finley explains the necessary forging of obligations through gift-giving or marriage through an ongoing state of war, although the causes of this are not made clear.[221] Despite the peace-making function he ascribes to ancient gift-giving, Finley does not arrive at a picture of the Homeric world as a positive antithesis to modernity. This is because of his opposition to Thomson's model, which embodies most clearly such a prehistoric utopia.[222] Thomson describes the history of human civilization as a story of decline from a matriarchal paradise of communal property, whose return was promised by Socialism. Finley rejects both the evolutionary theory that underlies this concept and the description of the ancient Greek world as a tribal society.[223] For him, the key criterion for

---

219. Thomson [¹1949] ⁴1978: 416–32.
220. Thomson 1978: 430 combines the Marxist theory of class-struggle with the concept of invasion: 'Behind the work of the humane poets who composed the *Iliad* and the *Odyssey*', he argued, 'lies an age of brutality and violence, in which the bold pioneers of private property had ransacked the opulent, hieratic, sophisticated civilisation of the Minoan matriarchate'. For a critique of the concept see Wagner-Hasel 1992: 320–21.
221. Finley [1954] 1967: 103.
222. See Wagner-Hasel 1992: 320–23.
223. Cf. Finley 1985: 90–93, arguing against the traditional evolutionary view of a regular evolution from an early 'tribal' organization of society, based on kinship groups, to a political, territorial organization, and Finley 1983: 44–45. Whereas in the 1970s the concept of tribal societies was deconstructed by Felix Bourriot (1976) and Denis Roussel (1976), current research is beginning to reevaluate the role of kinship-relations. See Dmitriev 2018 who stresses a strong connection between kinship and democracy in Solonian Athens. Duplouy 2006 discusses the role of genealogical prestige in archaic and classical Athens. For an overview of the debate see Varto 2017.

distinguishing between state and pre-state is the binding implementation of decisions.[224]

In contrast to *The World of Odysseus*, research into early Greek gift-exchange in the 1980s and 1990s makes explicit reference to evolutionary theory.[225] It favours various typologies of stages in the emergence of states (such as 'bands, tribes, chiefdoms, states'; 'egalitarian, ranking, stratified society'; and 'kinship society' and 'stratified society') developed by Elman Service, Morton Fried, and Jonathan Friedman.[226] The Homeric world is usually assigned a position between 'ranking society' and 'stratified society', a stage somewhere between chiefdom, clan society, and state. Along with this change in perspective, we also find a renewed interest in the competitive aspect of gift-giving underlined by Mauss and Gernet as well as in the Marxist theory of class-struggle.

In a 1981 essay, 'The Dynamics of Homeric Society', Bjørn Qviller argued that the disappearance of Homeric kingship and the emergence of the aristocratic *polis* were caused by the Homeric leaders' competitive displays of wealth. In his view, '(t)he importance of redistribution and gift-giving in the activities of a Homeric king places him between the big-man and a chieftain in a continuum of political leadership'.[227] In contrast to Finley, Qviller stresses the role of kinship in social organisation and sketches out the image of a society consisting of 'small groups based on kinship' and a

---

224. Finley 1983: 51–52: 'Three distinctions seem to me be necessary. [...] The second is between states in which decisions are binding and enforceable and pre-state structures in which they are not'.
225. Cf. Qviller 1981: 145, who talks of a 'multi-linear evolution'. Donlan 1981: 2 describes the Homeric world as 'simple societies in evolution'. Cf. also Morris 1986: 4; Ulf 1990: 230–31.
226. Service 1975: 80; Fried 1967: 182–84; 224–26; Friedman 1975: 161–202.
227. Qviller 1981: 120. His view is based on the observations made by Jonathan Friedman with the Kachin in upper Burma (now Myanmar) during a similar transition from 'kinship society' to state (111–12). According to Friedman, kinship structures are broken up when one of the lineages manages to make a surplus which is distributed at feasts, in return for which they may require other, lower-ranking, lineages to provide surplus labour. This stimulates local population growth, which exceeds what the region is able to sustain, and thus leads to territorial expansion and in turn to conflicts with other expanding populations. The search for internal solutions such as intensive land cultivation and reduced fallow periods results in exhausted soils and indebtedness of the poorer lineages. The dependence of the indebted, lower ranking lineages provokes internal conflicts and revolts, which result in the reestablishment of the former conditions. This is the situation Qviller claimed for the Homeric world which he located at the end of the ninth or the beginning of the eighth century (113–45).

system of ranking 'based on generosity'.[228] He views generosity at feasts and the distribution of gifts as means for the creation of obligations and the recruitment of followers. Qviller argues that the competition for followers created pressure on the king to keep on generating new wealth—be it through seizing wealth from others or through claiming it from his people—which led to internal and external instability. Among the destabilising factors are 'revolts caused by exploiting kings', when population growth is stimulated beyond the capacity of the area by the king's competitive activities, which in turn leads to conflict over territorial expansion with neighbouring communities, weakening the king's position. This ultimately contributes to the replacement of structurally weak kings through the emergence of an aristocratic order.[229]

Walter Donlan similarly assigns Homeric society to the historical stage of chieftain societies,[230] although he also recognises elements of the *polis*, and thus the state, in Homeric epic.[231] Donlan is primarily interested in institutional aspects of state formation rather than the question of social inequalities that Qviller stresses. It is in the development of formal administrative and military structures, and in the formalising of political bodies such as the assembly and council, that Donlan sees the state emerging—although it is still overlaid with personal forms of rule in Homeric society.[232]

Since Qviller and Donlan's work of the early 1980s a series of further contributions have similarly considered gift-exchange within the framework of a minimal degree of institutionalisation in Homeric society. In his 1986 study *Individual and Community: The Rise of the Polis, 800–500 BC*, Chester G. Starr assumed strong personal leadership, an unstructured political system lacking taxation, and an effective assembly were key features of these communities. Starr too speaks of an 'age of chieftains' and refers to anthropological studies on the emergence of institutionalised leadership. But he limits the role of gift-exchange to relationships between leaders only, and he stresses the role played by profit-oriented thought, especially in the *Odyssey*.[233]

---

228. Qviller 1981: 112.
229. Qviller 1981: 113, 126-27. The assumed agonistic character is stressed by Beidelman 1989: 250 who also claims that Finley underestimated this aspect of Homeric gift rituals.
230. Donlan 1982: 2; 1981: 137-38.
231. Donlan 1989: 5-29.
232. Donlan 1989: 13. See also Whitley 1991: 39-45, 198, who underlines the diversity of institutions and practices that were part of poetic reflection.
233. Starr 1986: 17-32. See also von Reden 1995: 58-76.

In contrast to Starr, Michael Stahl emphasises the importance of the rules of reciprocity for establishing peaceful external alliances in goods exchange and marriage. Internal conflict was, according to Stahl, the responsibility of individuals with high social status. Based on this, he argues that the manner in which such societies maintain cohesion is personal rather than institutionalised, but that it nonetheless creates binding and therefore effective obligations.[234] He assumes various elements of statehood, such as the establishment of anonymous political roles, the celebration of state identity through festivals, the maintenance of political stability through a state judiciary, and—connected to this—the concentration of power, during the age of tyranny.[235] Following Stahl, Karl-Wilhelm Welwei also argued in his 1992 monograph that Homeric Greece did not yet have institutionalised forms of office holding and decision-making and thus no state, although he rejected the characterisation of Homeric rulership as a 'chiefdom'.[236]

In a 1990 study of Homeric society, Christoph Ulf saw the world of Odysseus placed between an egalitarian-segmental society and an organised state marked by central political institutions. Signs of this intermediate status include 'the emergence of status-roles, and the beginnings of institutionalised leadership including privileged access to basic resources and prestige goods'.[237] Ulf rejected the political character of guest-friendship proposed by Finley and Donlan and refused to speak of a 'gift-giving society' since, in his view, there is no competitive aspect to Homeric gift-giving and no connection between a person's status and their giving. But he did consider the Homeric leader's obligation to generosity to be an essential feature of Homeric rulership.[238] This demonstrates the extent to which the *potlatch*, represented by Mauss as the most highly developed form of a system of total services, had become synonymous with gift-exchange itself—despite the fact that from a modern perspective it should be considered atypical.[239]

---

234. Stahl 1987: 141.
235. Stahl 1987: 141-42, 181; 2003: I, 201-51. Linking on to Stahl, recent research has come to use the term 'citizen state' ('Bürgerstaatlichkeit') and to study practices of being a citizen, e.g. athletic contests, common meals, civic feasts. See Walter 1993; Blösel et al. 2014; Seelentag 2015.
236. Welwei 1992: 78-80 with n. 9.
237. Ulf 1990: 230.
238. Ulf 1990: 206, n. 73; 211; 195-96. See also Ulf 2011: 302. Here he uses the term 'Gabenökonomie' to characterise Dark Age-societies.
239. Cf. ch. 1.1.

While the majority of studies cited above consider practices of gift-exchange in close connection with the pre-state organisation of the Homeric age, there is a tendency in more recent scholarship to recognise similar informal practices in later sources too. According to Gabriel Herman's research in *Ritualised Friendship* (1987), guest-gifts continued to play a role in building external alliances in classical Greece beyond the frontiers of one's own *polis*.[240] Also, relations of friendship and of patronage have been gaining attention.[241] Earlier views of a strong connection between reciprocity and statelessness have been abandoned.[242] Ian Morris distinguishes between 'clan-society' and 'state communities' and characterises the *poleis* of early Greece as 'nascent state communities'; he also assumes that gift-exchange continues into post-Homeric times. Like Thomson, Morris sees early Greek society as marked by slavery, private property, and the descriptive terminology of kinship. In keeping with Finley's antimodernist position, Morris also sees elements of a clan-society manifested in gift-exchange rituals which he argues were a means of establishing social hierarchy. In Morris's view, gift-exchange and commodity-exchange exist in parallel in archaic Greece, although the fact that land is not yet a commodity at this time supports the idea that the society depicted in Homeric epic evokes a transitional phase between clan-society and state.[243]

For most of the research discussed here, Homeric epic forms the primary evidentiary basis for reflections on the emergence of the state in ancient Greece, although Morris also draws on archaeological findings, such as forms of burial, the spread of ceramics, and other artefacts. While the distribution of Attic and other Greek pottery or metal vessels (bronze tripods, cauldrons, bowls) was considered as evidence of trade in the past, Morris

---

240. Herman ²1989; 2006. Cf. also Mitchell 1997; Low 2007: 37.
241. Cf. Mann 2007: 98–123; Domingo Gygax 2016; Maehle 2018.
242. For a connection of reciprocity and statehood see van Wees 1998: 13–49.
243. Morris 1986: 4. His point of reference is not Thomson, but Karl Marx, Claude Lévi-Strauss, and the ethnological study of Chris Gregory on the society of Papua New Guinea (*Gifts and Commodities* 1982). Cf. also Morris 1987: 475 and Sakellariou 1989. Sakellariou uses the Marxist theory of class struggle (see Breuer 1990: 7–16) but also the three-elements theory, i.e. unity of people, power, and territory ('Staatsvolk', 'Staatsmacht', 'Staatsgebiet'). See also Hansen 1998. For a Marxist approach see now Rose 2012: 11–17 who criticises former research for its lack of interest in exploitation and the neglect of the productive role of women. For current debates on statehood in ancient Greece see Stahl 2003: I, 94–116; Fraß 2014; Lundgreen 2020.

and others now view such distribution as indicative of a wide network of guest-friendships and aristocratic exchange of prestige goods.[244]

Instead of continuing to outline this research, I will draw attention to an opposing view. In a 1991 essay Fritz Gschnitzer points to a whole range of institutions in the Homeric world that indicate the existence of the public rule of law and, thus, a state. Refuting the notion of Homeric Greece as a pre-state community, Gschnitzer refers to examples such as the council ('Ratsversammlung'), compensation for expenses incurred through hospitality that can be demanded from the community, the existence of personified justice (*Themis*), of penalties (θoή) imposed by the community on individuals, the liability of communities for the debts of their members, and, finally, alliances forged by oaths of obligation. In commenting on Nestor's warning to the Greek army not to desert Agamemnon and the war for Troy, he states: 'This is a matter of the validity and permanence of obligations entered upon. They have sworn oaths and have confirmed these through shaking hands and through ritual and sacred celebrations; the respective partners rely on all this; if it were suddenly to become invalid the entire world would collapse.'[245]

Underlying Gschnitzer's critique is a concept of statehood that goes back to Eduard Meyer and which implies that the existence of a legal system effectively equals the existence of a state.[246] In his own time, Meyer too had been reacting against assumptions of an original pre-state phase, by inferring that where rules for communal living existed, there is statelike organisation; in effect, Meyer's view equated state with society.[247] This ahistoric concept of statehood that gained influence during the nineteenth century is a flaw in Gschnitzer's work too. Nevertheless, the significance of the law for archaic Greece should not be denied.[248] Gschnitzer's argument sheds some light on the oath as a means of obligation that serves precisely the purpose assigned by Mauss to the gift, namely the forging of peaceful alliances between different communities. Medievalists are well aware of the importance of oaths for the creation of obligations between

---

244. Cf. e.g. Coldstream 1979: 334–8; 1983: 201–6; Whitley 1991: 9–10; Langdon 1987: 107–13.
245. Gschnitzer 1991: 197.
246. Meyer 1910: 11–15. On Meyer see Nippel 1990b. Even Köstler (1950: 15–16) understood the Homeric state as 'Rechtsgemeinschaft', but also underlined the supplementary role played by religion.
247. For a critique see Stahl 2003: I, 104–9; Nippel 1990: 311–28.
248. Cf. Stahl 2003: I, 213–19; von Ungern-Sternberg 1998: 85–107; Hölkeskamp 1992: 87–117; 1999.

nonfamilial groups. But the existence of oaths does not necessarily prove the existence of a state.[249] In *Promise-Giving and Treaty Making*, Peter Karavites demonstrates the role played by agreements or treaties described as *horkia* in making peace between enemy camps. Karavites acknowledged fully the informal, although nonetheless binding, nature of such treaties while also presupposing the existence of sovereign states in the Homeric era.[250] By contrast, the medieval historian Gerd Althoff took the forging of alliances via such treaties (be they between communities or between leaders) to indicate an absence of statehood and of centralised state power.[251]

Little attention has been paid, however, to these kinds of pre-state alliances in the context of scholarship on gift-exchange. Herman does acknowledge oaths alongside gift-exchange as a part of the rituals of politically motivated hospitality.[252] But since hospitality is thought of as making alliances between individuals rather than between communities, it occupies a separate realm from that of treaties and alliances. Thus, informal treaties forged between communities are not acknowledged as independent forms of alliance alongside individual guest-friendships. This is the case, despite the fact that forming obligations by oaths is an essential characteristic of personal forms of rule, which in turn are acknowledged as characteristic of the pre-state era in Greece. Such oaths rely on a concept of personal rulership that is based on reciprocal obligation between ruler and subjects. In the Early Modern Period, individual subjects offered personal oaths of allegiance on the occasion of installing a new king in the form of a 'Huldigungsumritt' ('or royal progress').[253] Gift-giving formed part of this ritual of personal obligation to the individual ruler up until the seventeenth and eighteenth centuries when such gifts became monetised and were transformed into taxation, as Richard Meyer and Karl Bücher have stressed.[254] The ruler received gifts, foodstuffs, textiles, and tableware but also carried the cost of providing hospitality for the citizens whose homage he

---

249. See Althoff 1990: 119–33. According to Raaflaub (1997: 1–27), Finley had underestimated alliances between societies.
250. Karavites 1992: 8. Baltrusch 1994 understands alliances created by oaths as forerunners of international treaties.
251. Althoff 1990: 217. The concepts go back to Max Weber. Cf. Oexle 1994: 154–56. According to Hattenhauer (1992: 2–15), in ancient law the oath was, next to the gift, one of the most important means for the creation of obligations.
252. Herman 1987: 49. Cf. also Low 2007; Sommerstein and Torrance 2014.
253. Holenstein 1991: 433–85. Cf. also Prodi 1997.
254. Holenstein 1991: 460–72. For the *Ancien Régime* see Guery 1984: 1241–69; 1997: 154–62.

received.²⁵⁵ From the seventeenth century onwards, this reciprocity-based concept of rulership began gradually to be replaced by a more abstract idea of sovereignty, which went hand in hand with a more defined sense of territorial rule.²⁵⁶ This is also the period during which the concept of *homo oeconomicus* arose, as Werner Plumpe has shown.²⁵⁷ During this time of change from personal to abstract rule, we also find the emergence of the term 'state' that eventually replaced the ancient term *res publica*. The new term defined the state in the sense we see in the arguments of Eduard Meyer and Fritz Gschnitzer, as a legal state, while eliminating some older meanings such as 'common wealth' and 'common good' that had been tied to the use of the term *res publica*.²⁵⁸

The focus of contemporary ancient historical scholarship on the personal character of rulership as a yardstick for evidence of pre-statehood reflects the emergence of the state in modern times and projects this back onto antiquity. Contemporary debates on statehood are overly concerned with the distinction between personal/informal and impersonal/institutional forms of rule; they neglect the fact that ancient systems of rulership, not unlike those of the early modern age, may have been personal in character but highly varied in their institutions. This is as true of Imperial and Republican Rome as it is of classical Athens. The ability to establish personal networks was indeed an essential precondition for the achievement of leadership positions. Whereas in Rome one individual and one family eventually succeeded in monopolising such networks, Athens used ostracism and other institutional means as a way of preventing the centralization of allegiances around one individual. The existence of such processes must not, however, be taken to prove the existence of statehood, as Jochen Martin has rightly insisted.²⁵⁹ If we can speak of statehood at all in antiquity, then it must be in the sense of the old term *res publica*, with its orientation towards the common good. The history of the ancient polity is to a great degree a history of the opposition between the common good and self-interest.²⁶⁰ Self-interest in antiquity is not individual self-interest but the interest of the social grouping to which an individual belongs,

---

255. Holenstein 1991: 472–78.
256. Holenstein 1991: 486–503.
257. Plumpe 2007.
258. See Hölscher 1979: 60.
259. Martin 1990: 229. Recently Arjan Zuiderhoek (forthcoming) has stressed the stateless character of the Greek *polis* and even the Roman empire.
260. Cf. Schmitt-Pantel 1992: 108–13; Patzek 1992: 133. See now Fraß 2014: 6–28.

the *oikos, familia,* or *domus*—the household. Unlike modern households, ancient households had political functions. It therefore makes sense to differentiate, as historians of the Medieval period do now, between different community groups or, preferably, between different 'Zugehörigkeiten',[261] or 'Bindungsverhältnissen', that is, different allegiances and relationships. These groupings could form a hierarchical structure as they did in classical Athens, where the community of citizens was more powerful than the community of the *oikos*. In Rome, the system of patronage meant that the *domus* became the dominant grouping. The point is that there was no centralized state power in antiquity. As von Jhering has shown, political office was considered an honour bestowed by the people to an elite group. In return, office holders were required to provide political services and financial outlay. In his work on statehood in Rome, Jochen Martin defines the political order of ancient communities as a system of acceptance, which presented itself, even in late antiquity, through the traditional structures of gift-exchange.[262]

In view of the fact that the idea of statehood is so deeply marked by modern ideas and developments, I prefer to avoid the term 'state' altogether. I am also not interested in situating the gift in a pre-state era, as most recent scholarship has done. Given the problematic definition of the concept of gift-exchange, which I have demonstrated in my discussion of the history of Maussian gift theory, I do not advocate for the general presence of gift-exchange in the ancient world. It seems to me to make a lot more sense to consider the emergence of the *polis* from a spatial perspective. Even though immediate analogies between modern and ancient processes of state-building are not possible, the ancient process of structuring allegiances hierarchically does have a spatial component, which we can see from the location of tomb monuments by roadsides and temples on the periphery of *poleis*.[263] The concept of the territorial state, which implies spatial enclosure through the drawing up of boundaries, is not especially useful for understanding this process. It is more useful to think in terms of centre formation, a concept from settlement geography which has long been used by prehistorians and archaeologists and has gained prominence

---

261. Stein-Hölkeskamp 1989: 52 also uses the term 'belonging' ('Zugehörigkeit'). Looking back to Finley she also assumes that guest-gifts form bonds by creating obligations and founding loyalties between hosts and visitors, and that they enable a relatively durable relationship to be formed between two *oikoi*.
262. Martin 1994: 108. Cf. also Veyne [1976] 1990; Winterling 1999.
263. Cf. de Polignac [1984] 1995. For more detail see ch. 5.4.

in ancient history too. In settlement geography, centres are places that fulfil central economic, administrative, or religious functions within regions. According to Colin Renfrew, centres emerge from increasingly intensive interaction for which there can be a variety of explanations. He views reciprocal and redistributive forms of exchange as typical for the types of centres he calls 'early state modules.'[264] According to Michael Rowlands, who uses the term 'centre' for the ancient Near Eastern cultures of the second millennium, centres are where networks of alliances come together and allow optimal access to resources. In Rowlands's interpretation, the circulation of gifts, here understood as prestige goods, is less a matter of status than of control of resources.[265]

The spatial concept underlying this definition of centres focusses on communication and routes rather than boundaries. It allows us to conceive of Greek *poleis* as networks of open communication with one or more centres and subcentres,[266] emphasising exchange relations much more than in the debate on state-building. While scholars interested in statehood consider gifts primarily from a political perspective as either a pre-state means of forging alliances or as a means of displaying status or obligation in hierarchical relations, the concept of centres allows more emphasis on economic factors. Another advantage is that this approach does not conflict with a view of ancient rulership as personal and informal, while also allowing a broader consideration of the material aspects of rulership. Rulership can then be considered as not a matter of obedience and subjection[267] but more as a question of the disposal of labour and the control of resources.

The concentration on the institutional aspects of the formation of the *polis* has meant that the material and economic aspects of gift-exchange have receded somewhat into the background. When economics was brought into the picture, this was often limited to investigating whether guest-gifts were primarily intended as initial gifts to establish trading relations,[268] or whether they had other purposes such as the acquisition of prestige

---

264. Renfrew 1978: 12; 1986: 1–18.
265. Rowlands 1987: 5–6.
266. See Rihll and Wilson 1991: 59–95 for the geometric period. Cf. also Cavanagh 1991: 97–118; Osborne 1994: 143–60.
267. This is Max Weber's classical definition of power, although he also stressed another feature, that of the existence of a monopoly of power ('Gewaltmonopol'). Cf. Reinhard 1999: 9–11. For more detail see ch. 4.1.
268. Stanley 1986: 5–15. A similar view can be found in von Jhering 1887: 387 and Bolkestein 1939: 222–23. According to Morris 1986: 5, the exchange of gifts served to create personal relationships which preceded any trade exchanges.

or status and the forging of political alliances. The world of material production, that is, the realm of the actual production and materiality of the gifts and the procurement of the raw materials needed for them, has been largely ignored. This is, however, largely connected to the interpretation of Homeric society as a conglomerate of economically independent households, which goes back to Finley and is based on Bücher's model of a closed economy: 'With their flocks and their labour force, with plentiful stones for building and clay for pots, the great households could almost realize their ideal of absolute self-sufficiency'.[269] Felix Somló had rightly argued against Bücher's model of original self-sufficiency, when he assumed that the very first phases of development relied on economic collaboration.[270] Homeric households consisted of, as we will see, a multitude of relationships of obligation, both hierarchical and equal. It is precisely the size of their flocks and herds that forced early Greeks to establish wide networks of communication; the effects of this on the process of *polis* formation have not to date been adequately acknowledged.[271]

Against the background of this overview it makes sense to return once again to Homeric epic and the origins of the gift-exchange debate, to reconstruct anew the patterns of communication that underlie the distribution of gifts in the poems, and so to arrive at a new interpretation of the significance of gifts in the process of *polis* formation. This is also a question of the dating of the world of Homeric epic. Since Finley, there has been a tendency to assume that the world of the epics represented the social realities of the early Iron Age. Other researchers, investigating connections between hero-cults and the emergence of the *polis*, have suggested a dating of the Homeric world to between the eighth and sixth centuries instead.[272] Questions remain, however, as to whether hero-cult

---

269. Finley 1967: 57–58. According to Finley, only the trade with metals required external contacts. Donlan 1982: 151 stresses the mutual exchange of 'food, shelter, protection and favors'. For the economic aspects of gifts see Veyne 1976, who discusses the Roman evidence. On Bücher's concept see Wagner-Hasel 2011; 2014.
270. Somló 1909: 177.
271. For further detail see ch. 5.4.
272. See Antonaccio 1994: 79–104. Arguments for dating the epics into the seventh century BCE can be found in Andersen and Dickie 1995 and Crielaard 2002. For an overview see Ulf 2011: 294 with n. 12. The majority of scholars choose the eighth century. See Raaflaub 1991: 205–56; Latacz 1988: 153–83 and Latacz 2001: 56–69. Latacz dates the written text around 730 BCE, but he does not consider hexameter poetry as such as a new creation and does not exclude the possibility of elements of Mycenaean tradition being present. Cf. also Pöhlmann 1990: 11–17. For a later dating in the sixth century see Jensen 1980: 164–71; Burkert 1976; Boyd 1995.

GIFT-EXCHANGE IN THE GREEK WORLD 75

was a consequence of the spread of heroic epic,[273] or whether the spread of epic beyond Ionia went hand in hand with the emergence of hero-cults around Mycenaean tombs.[274] There are also significant local variations in the practices of heroic cult, as James Whitley's comparison between Argolis and Attica has demonstrated.[275] What we can be certain of is that epic provides a picture of the social practice of hero-cults and therefore provides an essential source of information about the process of spatial communication. Such imagined practice can only provide an idealised image of reality; but in order to be comprehensible it must have some roots in the lived experiences of its recipients, notwithstanding some conscious archaising tendencies.[276] This must be true, whether the poems represent a purely aristocratic imagination, as Ian Morris has argued,[277] or whether they are to be seen as a general repository of cultural knowledge.[278] Of course it must be assumed that representation will be influenced by the multiple poets' own points of view and by the expectations of audience and patrons.[279] This is not to suggest literary homogeneity or unbroken congruence between poetic tradition and society, but it does assume that the poems refer to lived experience. It is necessary, however, to explore the internal logic of the circulation of gifts before any attempt can be made at a concrete historical categorisation. As will become apparent in what follows, the hero's burial is the central, crystallizing event in the Homeric world. It is here that things come together in such a way as to allow us, through studying the circulation of gifts, to gain insight into the ideal or typical circle of reproduction of an ancient society.

---

273. See Coldstream 1979: 341–46.
274. See Snodgrass 1982: 107–19.
275. Whitley 1988: 173–82. Cf. also de Polignac 1994: 3–18.
276. Cf. Kullmann 1988: 184–96.
277. Morris 1986: 81–129; Latacz 1989: 26, 40–47, 63–68 = 2001: 32–35; 1984: 15–39.
278. See Havelock 1963; 1978: 10–14. Cf. also Thomas 1992: 116, who views the poet as the trustee of cultural heritage. For another view see Kullmann 1988: 187–90. The fact of literary borrowings from the ancient Near East is a key counter argument for Kullmann, although he does not consider that such borrowings must also be integrated into the poet's social world in order to gain acceptance. Within a culture of increased communication between the Greek and Near Eastern worlds, which reaches its apex during the seventh century, there is clearly room for such 'orientalising' elements. These borrowings do not undermine Havelock's thesis that the Homeric epic is an 'oral encyclopedia'. Cf. Burkert 1984; 1991: 155–81.
279. See Svenbro 1976: 16–34.

1.5. Methodological reflections: The sensory world of signs and the imagery of Homeric epic

Although the history of gift-exchange scholarship has ignored the sensory world since Mauss, we do find much more sensory reflections in older work. In his study *Ueber schenken und geben*, published in 1848 and examining the reciprocity of medieval and ancient gift-giving, Jacob Grimm sets his agenda as follows: 'Having made these preliminary remarks, I can now develop the customs of the past by speaking about individual objects as gifts: apart from land, by preference food and drink, livestock, clothing, rings, weaponry and other equipment'.[280] He then proceeds to examine individual objects, using ancient and medieval sources, in order to develop an etymology of the terms *schenken* ('to make a gift') and *geben* ('to give') that leads directly back to the objects discussed. Thus, he derives schenken from *einschenken* ('to pour'), the word used for serving food and drink, and *geben* from *binden*, *anheften* ('to bind', 'adhere'), used of clothing and jewellery.[281] I have no intention to pursue etymological research into the primary meanings of terms for gifts in Homeric epic, nor to order such terms into a historical sequence as Grimm does. We are, however, looking at a world in the poems in which concrete action and abstract meaning may come together in one term, that is, a world in which intellectual and sensory perception are on the whole not distinct from one another.[282] Indeed, it was only the philosophers of the late fifth century who separated the mind from the senses, as Eric A. Havelock has shown.[283] This is significant for understanding the message contained in the materiality of gifts.

In a series of studies Havelock pursued the connection between ways of speaking and ways of thinking in Greek poetry and philosophy. He argued that the connection between the senses and the mind is characteristic of the distinctive oral literacy of Homeric epic, which, although a result of early literate culture, maintains many features of oral poetry.[284] One

---

280. Grimm 1865: 175.
281. Grimm 1865: 210.
282. Onians ³1989; Dihle 1985.
283. Havelock 1986: 115–16.
284. Havelock 1986: 13 and 101. Here, he characterises Greek literature as 'written orality', although he had originally assumed entirely oral composition based on Milman Parry's research. German philologists increasingly emphasise the presence of elements of literary composition in Homeric epic. Cf. Latacz 1989: 83 = 2001: 66; Heubeck 1974: 146–52; Kullmann 1988: 193 with at times vehement rejection of Havelock's previous position. Cf. also West 1990: 33–50. On the transition from orality to literacy see Thomas 1992.

of these features is a poetics of visualization that is rooted in oral forms of transmitting knowledge. When knowledge is not transmitted through handbooks or other written means, there is a need for special memorizing techniques which are in keeping with oral ways of transmitting knowledge. This means that tradition is not illustrated through ideas and principles but through action.[285] Such action elucidates the rules of participation in civic life, both in the daily cohabitation of generations and in ritual actions. In poetic retellings of series of events this process of learning through participation is reenacted. Visuality and a focus on individual personalities are both key characteristics of early written as much as of oral poetry.

The German philologist Horst Wenzel applied Havelock's ideas to his analysis of medieval poetry, and in doing so he paid special attention to strategies of visualization. Wherever writing plays a secondary role in the transmission of knowledge, so Wenzel argues, there is a dominant focus on eyes, ears, gestures, facial expression, dress and bodily presentation, and the placement of people in space. According to Wenzel, the collective traditions of preliterary communities, and their entire social order, are visible 'in the organisation of settlements, houses, paths, and clothing, and especially in the configurations formed by people'.[286] Wherever poetry has to fulfil its function as the repository of memory, Wenzel suggests, poets need to create mental images that reproduce the bodily perceptions in the world of literature. Narrated events and phenomena need to take concrete form in order to make a strong visual impression and thus be memorable.[287] According to Wenzel, poets achieve vividness and visuality through a range of aesthetic means: a language rich in metaphor and allegory, vivid images, emphasis laid on gesture, bearing, and the dress of characters.[288]

For the present question, such a poetics of visualization is not without importance. In order to fulfil their memorializing function, poetically produced worlds of imagery must be distinguished by a clear reference to lived experience. Although Albin Lesky claimed that Homeric similes open a window onto the world outside the epic,[289] it seems, in fact, that connection

---

285. Havelock 1986: 15.
286. Wenzel 1994: 421.
287. Wenzel 1994: 422.
288. Wenzel 1994: 10 and 340.
289. Lesky 1971: 85: 'Hier öffnet der Dichter die Grenzen der Heroenwelt und läßt die Fülle des Daseins ein, in dem er selber lebt.' Lonsdale 1990: 125 discusses how animal similes serve to visualize the emotions of the warrior: 'The vivid depiction of the boar's furor in the simile is then metaphorically transferred back to the

to the real world is a characteristic of epic poetry itself. The representation of a heightened, heroic reality must be recognisable in such a way as to enable participation through the interpretation of the poetic images, and to allow an audience to acquire knowledge from these images. When the scholiasts began their work on the exegesis and interpretation of the epics, they needed to renew and reestablish those references to the lived world that had been guaranteed by the participation of the original audiences.[290]

If the epics belong to a world in which social order is visualized, then it makes sense that this order should be recognisable in the material world represented in the poems. This has long been proven for individual objects, such as the shield of Achilles, which contains a pictorial representation of the entire cosmos.[291] The same could be done for other objects that as gifts in social communication have significant memorial functions. Amongst them are textile gifts whose symbolic value is known to us from other societies.[292] Ioanna Papadopoulou-Belmedhi has shown the central role played by Penelope's shroud in the poetics of the *Odyssey* by drawing out the symmetries between the trick of the weaving and the poet's own ambiguities.[293] Material signs and poetic images may not be repositories of memory like the epic itself, but they do serve as thinking aids to memorise specific circumstances.[294] For this reason it is such images that provide a key to the world of the epic and its values. As we will see, there are certain terms used for gifts in which it is possible to find concrete manifestations of that world and its materiality. This is

---

   human counterpart in the narrative in such a way as to exhort him to unleash his anger against his opponent' (125). On similes in the *Iliad* see now Ready 2011. On similes of weaving see Bergren 1980; 2008; Clayton 2004.
290. Theagenes is said to have been the founder of the tradition of Homeric commentary. The development is discussed by Svenbro 1976: 108–20. See also Rösler 1980: 283–319; Pöhlmann 1990: 11–17; Feeney 1991: 5–56. For further arguments that an epic poet has to take 'his inspiration from the contemporary world' see Crielaard 2002: 242.
291. Cf. e.g. Stanley 1993 who analyses correspondences between narrative structure in the epic poems and the pictorial representations of the cosmos. Cf. also Becker 1995.
292. See Weiner 1976; 1989 (cf. ch. 1.3); Wunder 1994; Kahn-Majlis 1991; Slanicka 2002.
293. Papadopoulou-Belmehdi 1994. Cf. also Winkler 1990: 129–61. See now Canevaro 2018.
294. Wenzel 1994: 65–66 with respect to medieval memory signs. I will return to this in ch. 4.1.

especially true of the term *charis* because it denotes a gift of thanks but also in its more abstract meaning suggests the grace or radiance that emanates from a person. Since this abstract meaning draws on the effect created by crafted images, it also becomes a metaphor of the power of visualization that is connected to poetry itself.[295]

My primary method is entirely text-based and focussed on determining the material significance of terms for gifts as they occur in the epics. The selection of terms is determined by the research questions set out above. The starting point is an examination of the term *xeinion*, used for guest-gifts thought to support the forging of political alliances. Along with this, we will consider other terms sometimes used as synonyms, such as the general term for a gift, *dōron*, as well as the terms *dosis* and *dotinē*. The analysis of the concept of *charis*, which occurs in the context of every type of relationship, allows us an insight into Homeric society's internal structures of exchange. The problem of the nature of Homeric rulership, outlined above, is illuminated through examination of the terms used for gifts of honour, *geras* and *timē*. These play an important role in the relationships between Homeric leaders and collectives such as the army or the entire *demos*. In addition, in discussing the trading terms *prēxis*, *chreios*, *amoibē*, *kerdos*, and *ōnos*, we will consider the economic aspects of rulership, not at least those that are concerned with access to external resources. The growth of communication that can be viewed as a consequence of interest in these external resources forms the subject of the final part of this investigation through an examination of the symbolic function of the tripod and the emergence of a central location at which the exchange of resources takes place. Thus, we return to the initial question around which the debate about gift-exchange grew: the problem of the emergence of the state and the formation of the *polis*.

---

295. For further detail see ch. 3.

CHAPTER 2

Guest-Gifts and Relationships in Homer: *Xeinia* and *Phila Dōra*

In his study on guest-friendship in antiquity, published in 1887, the Romanist Rudolf von Jhering proposed a utilitarian interpretation of the institution. He illustrated this with a striking contemporary example: 'The anxious care with which he [the guest] was looked after finds its exact ethical parallel in the care with which bathers are looked after in spa-towns, or students at universities. There is the utmost concern for their safety and comfort, they are the darlings of public interest, but the motivation for this is not disinterested benevolence, or sheer love of mankind, but naked egoism. They are looked after because they must be kept satisfied: everyone is aware that if the reputation of the place were to suffer, so would the visitor numbers, and thus everything possible is done to maintain them'.[1] In von Jhering's view, which was developed in opposition to the ethical idealism that prevailed amongst his philosophical colleagues, it was public interest, and specifically interest in trade, that was responsible for alleviating the stranger's rightlessness through religion and custom. The development of guest-friendship was for von Jhering the beginning of 'international rights in antiquity' and, indeed, of 'civilisation' as a whole, since he takes the concept of guest-friendship to be the origin of sociability.[2]

Almost a century later, in his 1978 essay 'From Xenophobia to Altruism: Homeric and Roman Hospitality', Ladislaus J. Bolchazy takes the opposite perspective to von Jhering. For Bolchazy, progress is not to be found in the stranger's change of status from rightlessness to right, or in the pursuit of the selfish interest of the community (rather than the individual). According to Bolchazy, progress is made when magico-religious xenophobia is overcome and its place is taken by forms of guest-friendship which are at first self-interested and contractual and later become altruistic. In the

---

1. Von Jhering 1887: 380. Cf. also Finley 1967: 103–5, where fear of the stranger goes hand in hand with his rightlessness.
2. Von Jhering 1887: 357–58, 374, 381.

world of Odysseus, he sees just this stage of altruistically motivated hospitality: 'In the *Odyssey*, to conclude, we find that hospitable treatment of strangers is a distinguishing mark of civilization. To offer hospitality in all its refined aspects is the right and the wise thing to do. A stranger is to be treated like a brother. In Homeric culture we see, in other words, the conceptualization and the practice of altruistic hospitality'.[3] In this case it is not the stranger who initially needs to be fearful because of his powerlessness, as is the case in von Jhering's concept. It is society itself which confronts the stranger with irrational fear and rejection.[4] Progress is not found in the rule of law or in the realisation of economic interest but in ethics.

With these two positions the entire spectrum of the debate on Homeric guest-friendship is sketched out: self-interest against altruism, economics against ethics. Although von Jhering's position is focussed on the law, he did not, unlike his colleague and contemporary Theodor Mommsen,[5] consider guest-friendship to be purely a judicial matter but thought of it instead as a social institution. We can thus see in von Jhering the beginning of the interpretation of guest-friendship as a mechanism for social integration.[6] While von Jhering's legal argument is linked with one of economic purpose, his followers see social alliance itself as the main objective and do not pursue the issue of economic advantage. So Évelyne Scheid-Tissinier is able to conclude in her study on the use of the gift in Homer that the gift of guest-friendship 'normally sanctions the establishment of a bond of alliance or friendship'.[7] Emphasizing the contractual aspect of guest-friendship, Scheid-Tissinier, like von Jhering and Mommsen, the nineteenth-century law historians, stresses the necessity of reciprocity while keeping ethics and altruism at arm's length.[8] Bolchazy, on the other hand, looks back to the ethical position and places altruism above reciprocity.

In more recent conceptualisations, the stranger is no longer viewed, as in the nineteenth century, as the weaker party to whom security and rights

---

3. Bolchazy 1978: 63. Donlan 1982 combines the idea of altruism with the concept of 'balanced reciprocity'.
4. See also Pitt-Rivers 1977: 95-112. Here too emphasis is put on the perceived menace of the stranger in archaic societies, often ascribed to the stranger's possession of occult powers.
5. Mommsen 1859: 334.
6. See ch. 1.2, p. 31-34.
7. Scheid-Tissinier 1994: 158 (sanctionne normalement l'instauration d'un lien d'alliance ou d'amitié).
8. Mommsen 1859: 330; von Jhering 1887: 370.

are granted because he proves useful. Instead, he is viewed as one who represents a fundamental threat. To overcome this threat through altruistic behaviour is a mark of progress. In this view, von Jhering's contemporary example of purpose-driven motivation is no longer applicable, not because there is no experience of strangeness but because strangeness is everywhere. What remains is the appeal to individual conscience, while the nineteenth-century legal scholar's view still testifies to the self-awareness of a society that grants rights.

This is not the place for pursuing further the tendencies towards presentism that are part of such changes in perspective; instead we want to map the coordinates for an examination of ancient hospitality. Did Homeric guest-friendship possess the economic purpose suggested by the nineteenth-century legal scholar?[9] Or was political alliance the driving factor in guest-friendship, as is now argued with more frequency? And is guest-friendship an expression of progress as the rightlessness of the stranger is gradually eliminated, while irrational xenophobia changes into welcoming hospitality and into a more generally philanthropic attitude?

Viewed from the perspective of the material content of gifts, it becomes quite clear that Homeric guest-friendship must be multifunctional. Gifts in epic poetry can be natural produce or manufactured goods such as foodstuffs, weapons, metal vessels, and textiles. The technical term for them is ξεινήιον/ξείνιον (*xeinēion/xeinion*), which can be replaced with the more general term for a gift δῶρον (*dōron*) when the gifts are household treasures.[10] The word is an adjectival noun, derived from ξεῖνος/ξένος (*xeinos/xenos*), and it is mostly used in the plural. The term *xeinos* is ambiguous and can describe a stranger, a guest, or a host.[11] The host can be described as ξεινοδόκος (*xeinodokos*), one who receives a guest (*Il.* 3.354; *Od.* 7.210 and 543; 15.55 and 70; 18.64), and as φιλόξεινος (*philoxeinos*), one who observes the divine rule of hospitality in caring for strangers (*Od.* 6.121 and 144; 8.576; 9.176; 13.202). The adjective ξείνιος/ξένιος (*xeinios/xenios*) is a

---

9. Von Jhering (1887: 387) did, however, contradict his main position by ascribing to Greek hospitality a more convivial and friendly character, distinguishing it from the more commercial guest-friendships of the Phoenicians.
10. On the terminology of guest-friendship see Stählin 1954: 1–36; Hiltbrunner et al. 1972; Scheid-Tissinier 1994: 115–76.
11. See Scheid-Tissinier 1994: 115–29. On the ambiguity of *xeinos* cf. Gauthier 1972 and van Wees 1992: 228–37, who speaks of the hospitality-racket. See now Tracy 2014. She operates with the game theory, which is based on the idea of egoistic exchange, and argues that self-interest of strangers does not contradict cooperative behaviour.

frequent epithet for Zeus, underlining his role as the protector of strangers (*Il.* 13.625; *Od.* 9.271; 14.284 and 389).[12] Several times a table prepared for a stranger is described as *xeinios* (*Od.* 14.148; 17.155; 20.230).[13] The verbs ξεινίζειν (*xeinizein*), κομίζειν (*komizein*), τρέφειν (*trephein*), φιλεῖν (*philein*), and τίειν (*tiein*) are used to describe the range of activities involved in the process of receiving a guest: the serving of food, the provision of clothing, bath and bed, the reception into the domestic community, the giving of gifts.[14] The handing over of *xeinia* is expressed with the verbs τίθημι/παρατίθημι (*tithēmi/paratithēmi*), δίδωμι (*didōmi*), and πορεῖν (*porein*). As an institution guest-friendship can be discerned in the words ξένια (*xenia*) and ξεινοσύνη (*xeinosynē*), although these appear only in the final books of the *Odyssey* (*Od.* 21.35; 24.286 and 314). The usual term for this relationship in epic poetry is φιλότης (*philotēs*), which expresses a sense of belonging to a community based on ritualised guest-friendship, and also on the giving of gifts that serve to strengthen the bond between guest and host (*Il.* 3.354; *Od.* 15.55).[15]

The structure of the present examination of Homeric guest-friendship is based on the range of material contents of *xeinia* (natural goods, weaponry, and metal or textile goods), which represents the types of relationships characterised by exchange and alliance. We begin with the natural *xeinia* and in this context discuss the exchange-relationship between the herdsmen's community and the household of a *basileus*, and the question of the stranger's rightlessness. Next we find that when *xeinion* takes the form of a weapon, military alliance and the question of gift-giving as a form of political treaty are addressed. Finally, when *xeinia* are treasures of metal and cloth, the issues at hand are bonds between individual households and internal domestic structures.

2.1. *Xeinion* and *dōtinē*: The hospitality of the herdsmen Eumaeus and Polyphemus

Xeinion is that which is due to the stranger, and in most cases in epic poetry it takes the form of food and drink. The word is used with this meaning in classical literature too, although here *xeinia* may also be

---

12. For further examples see Scheid-Tissinier 1994: 136–43.
13. Ibid.
14. On *xeinizein* and *philein* cf. Scheid-Tissinier 1994: 129–35.
15. Cf. Konstan 1997: 33–37.

tribute or levies in the form of natural produce.[16] There is a hint of this double meaning in the epic, albeit in a different context, where *xeinion* does not only occur when meeting with strangers but also as part of the formalised exchange of goods between the world of the herdsmen and the household of a *basileus*.

In both the *Iliad* and *Odyssey*, *xeinia* can describe a meal given to gods or humans. In the divine sphere, this meal will be nectar and ambrosia, while for humans it will be a sacrificial or otherwise carnivorous feast to which strangers are invited. The hosts therefore tend to be those persons who have access to livestock, both owners and herdsmen. The guests include envoys seeking military assistance, friends and relatives of guest-friends looking for support, and also the (high-ranking) visitors of herdsmen, most importantly Odysseus in disguise.

In the *Iliad* we have two instances of *xeinion* as a feast granted to strangers. The first, remembered by Nestor in conversation with Patroclus, is Nestor's visit to Peleus in search of support and troops for the campaign against Troy—the occasion of his, Nestor's, first meeting with Achilles. He remembers that Achilles led him straight into the courtyard (*aulē*) and placed before him the *xeinia* due to the stranger according to divine right (ξείνιά τ' εὖ παρέθηκεν, ἅ τε ξείνοις θέμις ἐστίν, *Il.* 11.778). In detail these *xeinia* are itemised as food and drink (ἐδητύος ἠδὲ ποτῆτος, *Il.* 11.780), and specifically as wine and a portion of sacrificial beef (*Il.* 11.773–75).

While this example shows a guest participating at a sacrificial feast that would have taken place in any case, the other instance is one where the guest is treated to exclusive hospitality. When Thetis arrives to visit Hephaestus to place her order for new weapons for her son Achilles, Charis asks her divine visitor to follow her so that she may place the *xeinia* before her (ἵνα τοι πὰρ ξείνια θείω, *Il.* 18.387). A few lines later, the poet has Hephaestus repeat this invitation and request that Charis prepare the *xeinia* for the visitor (ἀλλὰ σὺ μὲν νῦν οἱ παράθες ξεινήϊα καλά, *Il.* 18.408). The verb used is *tithēmi* (to place) and then *paratithēmi* (to place beside), both used multiple times in the *Odyssey* for the serving of dishes by

---

16. Plato describes fruit picked at the roadside by travelling strangers as *xeinia* (*Laws* 845a). Herodotus (7.29) and Xenophon (*Hell.* 1.1.9) use the term to describe natural produce provided for travelling armies. Rich Athenians such as Miltiades are said by Herodotus (6.35) to keep an open house, offering shelter (*katagōgē*) and hospitality (*xeinia*) to strangers. The construction of lodges for strangers seems to be a development of Late Antiquity. See Hiltbrunner 2005; Constable 2003.

the female housekeeper (*tamiē*).[17] There can be no doubt then that *xeinia tithēmi/paratithēmi* must be taken as the providing of a meal, even in instances where the precise content of *xeinia* is not made explicit.[18]

In the *Odyssey* too, the presentation of *xeinia* as food and drink takes place both in the human and in the divine sphere. In Book 4, when Telemachus arrives with Peisistratus, the son of Nestor, to visit Helen and Menelaus in Sparta, Eteoneus, a retainer (θεράπων) of Menelaus is doubtful about whether to admit the recent arrivals. Menelaus reminds him of the times that they themselves consumed many *xeinia* (ξεινήια πολλὰ φαγόντες, *Od.* 4.33) and asks the servant to lead the two strangers to feast (θοινηθῆναι, *Od.* 4.36). The use of the verb *phagein* (to eat), together with the invitation to the *thoinē* (feast), leave no doubt that *xeinia* in this case is the meal offered to the strangers.

Such a meaning of *xeinia* can also be inferred from the nymph Calypso's invitation to the divine messenger Hermes to follow her so that she may place *xeinia* before him (ἀλλ' ἕπεο προτέρω, ἵνα τοι πὰρ ξείνια θείω, *Od.* 5.91). Indeed, the goddess fetches a table and serves the food of the immortals, nectar and ambrosia (*Od.* 5.92–93). A similar turn of phrase is used to describe Telemachus's and Peisistratus's stay at the home of Diocles on the way from Pylos to Sparta and on the return journey. Here, shelter for the night is granted as well as *xeinia*: 'There they spent the night, and he [Diocles] placed the *xeinia* before them' (ἔνθα δὲ νύκτ' ἄεσαν ὁ δὲ τοῖς πὰρ ξείνια θῆκεν, *Od.* 15.188).[19]

We can also conclude indirectly that *xeinia* involved a meal from the remark made by the swineherd Eumaeus to his master Odysseus, who is disguised as a beggar. When Odysseus asks to be thrown off a cliff should his prediction of the return of the missing master (*anax*) not come true, Eumaeus answers:

ξεῖν', οὕτω γάρ κέν μοι ἐϋκλείη τ' ἀρετή τε
εἴη ἐπ' ἀνθρώπους, ἅμα τ' αὐτίκα καὶ μετέπειτα,
ὅς σ' ἐπεὶ ἐς κλισίην ἄγαγον καὶ ξείνια δῶκα,
αὖτις δὲ κτείναιμι φίλον τ' ἀπὸ θυμὸν ἑλοίμην
πρόφρων κεν δὴ ἔπειτα Δία Κρονίωνα λιτοίμην.

---

17. Compare, e.g.: *Od.* 10.371–72; 4.57–58; 4.65–66; 3.40 = 20.260; 14.76; 17.258; 20.28–29. Herodotus uses a similar expression for the hospitality offered to Spartan ambassadors by the Persians (Hdt. 7.135.5: ὅς σφεας ξείνια προθέμενος ἱστία).
18. See Scheid-Tissinier 1994: 139. On *xeinia* as meaning food and drink see also Bolkestein 1939: 219 and 231.
19. Compare *Od.* 3.490 with *tithēmi* replaced by *didōmi*: ὁ δ'ἄρα ξείνια δῶκεν.

νῦν δ' ὥρη δόρποιο· τάχιστά μοι ἔνδον ἑταῖροι
εἶεν, ἵν' ἐν κλισίῃ λαρὸν τετυκοίμεθα δόρπον.

> Stranger (*xeinos*), that would earn me a fine reputation for virtue amongst men, both right now and hereafter, if I brought you into my hut (*klisia*), and provided hospitality (*xeinia dōka*), and then I killed you and seized your dear life from you. And then I would be happy to go and pray to Zeus, the son of Cronos. But it is supper-time now, and my companions should be here any moment so that we may get a tasty meal ready in the hut (*Od.* 14.404–8).

The swineherd then gives his disguised master the prime cut of a haunch of the slaughtered boar to honour him (γέραιρεν, *Od.* 14.437–38) and serves him bread and wine (*Od.* 14.447–49). The context in which the phrase *xeinia didōmi* is placed leaves little doubt as to the interpretation of *xeinia* as a meal served to the guest. Eumaeus's response to Odysseus's suggestion also makes it clear that the sharing of a meal implies a bond of protection which is subject to public scrutiny, and that Eumaeus would be putting his reputation at risk were he to do any harm to the stranger.[20] The underlying relationship between Eumaeus and Odysseus as master and servant adds a further dimension to this guest-friendship, which is alluded to with the characterisation of Odysseus as master, *anax*, and the designation of his portion of meat as that given to a guest of honour. In this scene a hierarchically structured bond such as the one between a warlord and his warriors, or a landowner and his herdsmen, is alluded to, which indirectly also applies to Odysseus's visit to the Cyclops Polyphemus.[21]

In the Polyphemus episode we find the notion of *xeinia* as a meal offered to strangers turned on its head. Upon arrival at Polyphemus's cave, Odysseus's companions suggest that they should take away the cheese that is stored there along with the lambs and kids. Odysseus rejects this proposal because he is curious to know whether the Cyclops would offer *xeinia* (ὄφρ' αὐτόν τε ἴδοιμι, καὶ εἴ μοι ξείνια δοίη, *Od.* 9.229). But upon his return to the cave, Polyphemus refuses Odysseus's request for *xeinion*, or any kind of *dōtinē* (ἱκόμεθ', εἴ τι πόροις ξεινήϊον ἠὲ καὶ ἄλλως | δοίης δωτίνην, ἥ

---

20. On guest-friendship as divine law see Flückinger-Guggenheim 1984; Scheid-Tissinier 1994: 143–48. Therefore, Eumaeus is considered the ideal host. See Newton 2015: 257 with further references.
21. See ch. 4.1.

Polyphemus even lives without a wife and children (resembling Eumaeus in this aspect). This has been taken as a sign of his uncivilised character,[36] but it is well suited to the narrative context. When Odysseus brings the dark sweet wine into Polyphemus's cave, he is inverting the logic of guest-friendship, but his action is in keeping with the logic of exchange between the herdsmen's station and the farmer's household in bringing goods produced in the home to the herdsman's shelter. Odysseus had received the wine from Maron (*Od.* 9.196–215),[37] a priest of Apollo, along with other goods as a form of ransom for protecting the priest (*Od.* 9.197–200).[38] Polyphemus consumes the drink which is unknown to him (but significantly not unknown to the other Cyclopes[39]), but he offers none of his own goods (milk, cheese, and meat) in return.

There are significant points of contact between the depiction of Polyphemus and Odysseus's stay with Calypso. As a nymph she belongs, just like the Cyclops, to the pastoral world. Nymphs are guarding the cattle of Helios when Odysseus's companions commit their fatal mistake by slaughtering the holy animals (*Od.* 12.134–36). There is also an uninhabited island near the dwellings of the Cyclopes, where nymphs are hunting goats (*Od.* 9.154–56). At the same time, however, Calypso also represents that part of the exchange-relationship between farmer's household and herdsmen's station occupied by Penelope, the *despoina*, in the Eumaeus episode (*Od.* 14.127 and 377).[40] This becomes clear when Hermes arrives and finds her singing and working at the loom (*Od.* 5.61–62). As she does so, she produces just those goods which Eumaeus had received from Odysseus's mother, and which presumably are those goods that warm the hearts of the servants (*dmōes*), namely woven cloths and garments. She compares herself with Penelope, telling Odysseus, whom she wishes to keep as her own bed-fellow

---

36. O'Sullivan 1990: 9.
37. This state of affairs irritates those who view the Polyphemus episode as conforming to a universal narrative pattern of the hero's return, from which, however, the giving of wine is omitted. Compare, e.g., Page 1955: 7–8; Schein 1970: 78. According to Calame 1976: 328, from a structuralist point of view, the wine episode radicalises the confrontation between 'sauvagerie et civilisation'.
38. Odysseus is represented as more generous than Agamemnon, who denies Chryses, another priest of Apollo, the return of his daughter in return for *apoina*. See Nestle 1942: 60.
39. *Od.* 9.109–10. According to Kirk 1970: 169, this indicates that the other Cyclopes possess a modicum of civilisation.
40. On the parallels between Calypso and Penelope, see Papadopoulou-Belmehdi 1994: 105–8. Belmehdi sees the similarity between Penelope and Calypso in the status of the nymph as a much-desired bride.

(*Od.* 5.120), that 'surely not inferior to her do I declare myself to be either in form or stature' (*Od.* 5.211-12). Here, too, the flow of goods is one-sided. Calypso provides food and drink for Odysseus (*Od.* 5.68-69; 196-97; 265), gives him clothing and wine for the journey, and makes a sail for the raft he builds for himself (*Od.* 5.165-67; 258-59; 264-67). Odysseus himself is damned to inaction during his stay with Calypso, spending his days sitting by the shore and grieving.[41] In the meantime, Penelope, by contrast, is not keeping up with her obligation of weaving and does not complete the cloth on her loom.[42]

The disturbed flow of goods between the world of the herdsmen and the farming household corresponds to a double break of the rules of guest-friendship caused by the shepherd Polyphemus and, in the house of Odysseus, by the suitors. They not only refuse *xeinion*, in this case participation in their meals, to the disguised Odysseus, but they also plunder their host's house. The suitors' consumption of Odysseus's livelihood (*biotos*) and goods (*ktēmata*) without reimbursement or compensation is a cause of constant complaint for the loyal Eumaeus as well as for Telemachus and Penelope.[43]

The comparison will allow us to understand the meaning of another term: *dōtinē*. The suitors' excessive consumption and Polyphemus's inhospitable behaviour stand in direct opposition to the hospitable Eumaeus and the welcoming Phaeacians. Like the Cyclops's inhospitality, their hospitality is played out in a mythic landscape so that it, like Polyphemus's behaviour, functions as an inverted image. While Eumaeus offers natural *xeinia* to the disguised Odysseus, the Phaeacians give him *xeinia* in the form of textile and metal treasures; they also grant him the *dōtinē* which Odysseus had vainly asked the Cyclops for (*Od.* 9.268). The Phaeacians thus afford Odysseus with the honours promised in Agamemnon's conciliatory offer to Achilles. 'Men [...] rich in flocks and herds (ἄνδρες [...] πολύρρηνες πολυβοῦται)' will 'honour [him] with gifts (*dōtinai*) like a god (οἵ κέ σε δωτίνῃσι θεὸν ὣς τιμήσουσι)', if he should agree to marry one of Agamemnon's daughters (*Il.* 9.296-97). Interpreted as extraordinary devotion by

---

41. On the grief of Odysseus, which is equated to death, see Vernant 1982: 15. Crane 1988: 20 draws a parallel between Odysseus's stay with Calypso and Persephone's stay in Hades. See also ch. 3.3.
42. See in more detail ch. 4.2.
43. See for instance: *Od.* 1.160; 14.417; 18.279: βίοτον νήποινον ἔδουσιν. At 16.431 Penelope accuses Antinoos: τοῦ νῦν οἶκον ἄτιμον ἔδεις. Telemachus complains before the disguised Odysseus at 16.127-28: ἔδοντες | οἶκον ἐμόν.

the community to kingly households,[44] or as special gifts associated with obligation or contract,[45] it appears that these honours are, in the epics, specific benefits or services afforded by people who are in a position to grant safe passage to strangers. When the blinded Polyphemus promises to provide the benefits he had previously refused, he does not offer *dōtinē* alongside *xeinion* but safe passage or conduct (*pompē*). This is also granted to Odysseus by Alcinous when he declares: 'I shall complete our *dōtinē*' (δωτίνην τελέσω, *Od.* 11.352). His *pompē* concerns all the men. While the Phaeacians accomplish the task of *pompē* with their ships, it can be assumed that the herdsmen like Polyphemus will make use of their animals for the purpose. More concretely this will mean, in the case of Odysseus, the transport of the *xeinia* given to him by the Phaeacians; in Achilles's case it means the *themistes* who are proposed to him so that he may carry out his judiciary tasks.[46]

The episodes concerned with hospitality granted to Odysseus are not solely interested in the treatment of the stranger but also, and indeed more so, with the cessation of the orderly exchange between domestic production and the world of the herdsmen, that is between, on the one hand, grain and bread, wine, and cloth, and on the other hand the sheep and goats and their products such as milk, cheese, and wool. Since Odysseus is a stranger, *xeinos*, and master of his herdsmen, *anax*, at the same time, the question arises whether the natural *xeinia* he is given should really be seen as gifts for a guest. They might equally be the goods given by economically independent herdsmen to strangers in exchange for other goods. This might also explain why Polyphemus is asked for both *xeinia* and *dōtinē*, even though *dōtinē* is usually only afforded by owners of livestock or ships in epic and has therefore been interpreted above as safe passage. Unfortunately, the epic is extremely unclear in this respect.

Homeric epic knows of three different types of herdsmen. First there are sons, such as the sons of Priam, who take herds out to pasture in the valleys of Ida (*Il.* 11.104-6). Second there is the hired herdsman, who gives his services for a certain amount of time and in exchange for a

---

44. See the argumentation of Andreades 1931: 19; Bolkestein 1939: 221.
45. So Benveniste 1969: I, 69: 'C'est pas seulement un présent, un don désinteressé; c'est un don en tant que prestation contractuelle, imposée par les obligations d'un pacte, d'une alliance, d'une amitié, d'une hospitalité: obligation du *xeinos* (de l'hôte), des sujets envers le roi ou le dieu, ou encore prestation impliquée par une alliance'. Scheid-Tissinier 1994: 225-26 also stresses the obligatory character.
46. Posthomeric usage also fits with this interpretation. So, in Herodotus (6.89) *dotinē* means the fee charged for ships loaned to strangers. See in more detail ch. 4.1.

wage (μισθός).⁴⁷ The wage takes the form of goods from the household of the herd-owner; in one case these are specified as the sorts of goods Eumaeus may expect to receive from Odysseus's household in exchange for his services. The suitor Eurymachus promises clothing (εἵματα) and bread or grain (σῖτον) for the work on the *agros* in the *eschatia*, to the disguised Odysseus (*Od.* 18.360-61).⁴⁸ Although ἐσχατιᾷ would indicate that the work should be pastoral, since this is normally the location for taking animals out to graze, the work is actually to gather stones and plant trees (*Od.* 18.357-59).⁴⁹ A third type of herdsman has a permanent and open-ended exchange-relationship with the herd-owner, as is the case for Eumaeus and Odysseus's other herdsmen. This type of herdsman is socially dependent but economically autonomous and is tied into a reciprocal exchange-relationship between the herding station and the herd-owner's household, where goods of agriculture and craftsmanship are produced. These herdsmen may have permanent dwellings on the borders of a region or they may, like Philoetius, Odysseus's cattle-herdsman, travel through strange lands (*Od.* 14.96-104; 20.209-20). The reward for their labour is described in one instance with the same word as that for the reward given for a warrior's labour, namely κάματος (*kamatos*),⁵⁰ while the profit earned by herd-owners who leave their herds to independent herdsmen for pasturing is evidenced as κέρδος (*kerdos*) in the Homeric hymns.⁵¹ Given his location some way removed from the dwellings of the other Cyclopes, Polyphemus is closest to this third type of herdsman, who is represented by Eumaeus. Polyphemus's situation also approximates that at Ithaca, where animals are kept for both the

---

47. The relationship between employer and hired help is called θητεύειν (*thēteuein*). See Poseidon, reminding Apollo of their time serving the Trojan leader Laomedon, Apollo as shepherd and Poseidon building the wall: 'we served the lordly Laomedon for a year's space at a fixed wage' (θητεύσαμεν εἰς ἐνιαυτὸν | μισθῷ ἔπι ῥητῷ', *Il.* 21.444-45). See also the double *misthos* that a sleepless man is able to earn in the land of the Laestrygonians, 'one by herding cattle, and one by pasturing white sheep; for the paths of the night and of the day are close together' (*Od.* 10.84-86). On the seasonal aspects of such work see Walcot 1970: 37-44.
48. A *misthos* is also given to warriors, such as Dolon who keeps look-out for Hector (*Il.* 10.304), and to a female spinner whose wage is described as meagre (ἀεικέα μισθόν, *Il.* 12.438). By contrast, Hector promises Dolon a chariot and two horses as his wage. The watchman hired by Aegisthus to look out for Agamemnon's arrival receives an especially generous *misthos* of two talents of gold (*Od.* 4.525-26).
49. On *eschatia* as pastureland see Audring 1989.
50. *Od.* 14.417. In more detail ch. 3.2.
51. For evidence see ch. 5.2.

consumption of meat[52] and the production of wool.[53] Thus Polyphemus with his animals represents a multiplicity of possible preferences for breeding livestock, which a single herdsman would not in fact be able to realise. The designation of his animals as 'fat' (πίονα) points to meat-production (*Od.* 9.217 and 315). On the other hand, the animals are also said to have luxuriant fur (καλλίτριχα, *Od.* 9.336 and 469) and to be thick-fleeced (δασύμαλλοι, *Od.* 9.426), which would indicate an interest in the production of wool. The male gender of the sheep would also point to this, as we are told that Polyphemus leads *arsena mēla* (ἄρσενα μῆλα) to pasture in the morning (*Od.* 9.438). Male, especially castrated, sheep are thought to have thicker fur than ewes.[54] But Polyphemus's animals are milked in the evening (*Od.* 9.244 and 219), which would indicate a different composition of the herd and would lead us to expect the mention of ewes rather than rams.[55] With this lack of clarity the circumstances in the world of the Cyclopes are almost identical to those in Odysseus's world. While at Ithaca the multitude of herdsmen associated with the household makes the existence of a variety of herds and flocks feasible and realistic; the depiction of Polyphemus's circumstances with its contradictions evokes a utopian and hostile imaginary.

Were we to view the behaviours of Polyphemus and Eumaeus as expressing a fundamental opposition between xenophobia and hospitality, between savagery and civilisation, this would mean falling into the trap of the inversions created by the poet to indicate the cessation of orderly exchange between the pastoral world and agricultural production. It would also mean that this cessation is reproduced through the use of universal categories in which any concrete reality is destroyed beyond

---

52. Philoetius brings lambs for the consumption of meat from the mainland (*Od.* 20.209-10). Brendel 1931: 6-8 assumes an interest in wool as well as milk and meat.
53. On the other hand, the metaphorical use of the 'shearing' of the goods of Odysseus through the suitors' constant feasting alludes to the breeding of sheep for wool, especially as the mistress and maids are busy with spinning and weaving. See *Od.* 2.312-13 (ἐκείρετε [...] κτήματ') and 2.142-43 (βίοτον [...] κείρετ'). At one point, Telemachus specifies the livelihood which is 'shorn off' by the suitors as sheep, wine, and bread (*Od.* 20.312-13).
54. The explicit reference to uncastrated rams in the *Iliad* (23.147) is also an argument for the existence of castrated animals. On the quality of the wool of castrated sheep see Halstead 1987: 77.
55. Halstead 1987: 77-83.

recognition. This is not to deny that factual experience with strangers influenced the tales.[56]

Such experience, however, does not rule the logic of the depiction nor the image of the person of Polyphemus. The Cyclops's main distinguishing feature, his single eye, characterises him as one who can only half see. Norms and values, such as the law of hospitality guarded by Zeus, are thought of as clearly understandable in the epic.[57] Yet Polyphemus does not know what the 'stranger's right' is (ξείνων θέμις, *Od.* 9.267). Were we to take him as a prototype, the Cyclops, because of his lack of insight, would embody the not-seeing of the very values the poem defends through the design and structure of the episode.

2.2. Exchanging arms: Glaucus and Diomedes

The exchange of armour between the Argive Diomedes and the Lycian Glaucus in *Iliad* 6 is often referred to when scholarship ascribes a peacemaking or bond-forming function to guest-gifts. In Bolchazy's scheme, this exchange conforms to the contractual rather than altruistic forms of guest-friendship;[58] Walter Donlan places it into the category of balanced reciprocity and views it as possessing the character of a peace-treaty.[59] For Finley, the exchange of arms between Glaucus and Diomedes gives rise to fundamental thoughts on guest-friendship and the forging of bonds and alliances in the early Greek world. Finley views this critical moment as the most dramatic possible test of the cohesion of the network of personal alliances established through guest-friendships.[60] Significantly, the arms-exchange occurs in the midst of battle, just as the opponents trade insults intended to lead up to a duel. When Diomedes, fighting with the Achaeans against the Trojans, recognises his opponent Glaucus as a guest-friend, a *xeinos* going back to their grandfathers' generation, he suggests the exchange of arms:

56. The word ἄγριοι, used for the Cyclopes and the Laestrygonians (*Od.* 10.100–32; 11.175), does not describe savages as Gauthier 1972: 5 claims but the inhabitants of the *agros*, i.e. pastureland. See also Audring 1989. The classical term *barbaros* to identify a stranger who does not speak Greek does not occur in Homeric epic, although we do find the epithet βαρβαρόφωνοι (*Il.* 2.867). The epic term for this kind of stranger is *allothroos*. Compare Vasilescu 1989: 70–77.
57. Compare ch. 3.
58. Bolchazy 1978: 57. See also Gauthier 1972: 10.
59. Donlan 1982: 145.
60. Finley 1967: 104–8. See also Hands 1968: 28. Similar Herman 1987: 2: '[…] the guest-friendship he [the heros] contracted were his own private affair'.

τε ξείνων θέμις ἐστίν, *Od.* 9.267-68). The only *xeinion* he is willing to give is to grant Odysseus the favour of eating him last (*Od.* 9.376). Only after he has been blinded by Odysseus does Polyphemus promise *xeinia*: 'Come here', he invites Odysseus, 'so that I may place the *xeinia* before you' (ἀλλ' ἄγε δεῦρ', Ὀδυσεῦ, ἵνα τοι πὰρ ξείνια θείω, *Od.* 9.516), and he promises safe passage too (*Od.* 9.517). The formulaic turn of phrase is identical to that used when Calypso receives her visit from Hermes cited above (*Od.* 5.92). Polyphemus's refusal of a meal to Odysseus contravenes the laws of hospitality, and this contravention marks the Cyclops out as the incarnation of the wild and uncivilised.[22] Nonetheless his behaviour as represented in the poem moves within the framework of the logic of hospitality, albeit in an inverted form: he refuses a meal to the stranger, but he makes a meal of the stranger.[23]

This logic of inversion also applies to the case of the Laestrygonians, who live off fishing rather than livestock. They prepare their meal (δεῖπνον, *Od.* 10.116) from the companions of Odysseus, as the Cyclops does, and they are described as spearing Odysseus's men like fish (ἰχθῦς δ' ὣς πείροντες, *Od.* 10.124).

A similarly upside-down sense of *xeinion* is at play in Ithaca, where the positions of host and guest have become reversed: here the suitors act as hosts to the real master of the house, Odysseus, in his disguise as a beggar.[24] Just like the Cyclops, they also refuse Odysseus the *xeinion* that is due to him. When the suitor Ctesippus finally offers a *xeinion* (ἐγὼ δῶ ξείνιον, *Od.* 20.296), this generous offer turns out to be the cow's foot (βοὸς πόδα) he throws at Odysseus's head (*Od.* 20.299). This guest receives payment in kind for his presumption: the *xeinion* of the cow's foot is repaid when Odysseus's cowherd pierces Ctesippus's breast with an arrow (τοῦτό τοι ἀντὶ ποδὸς ξεινήιον, ὅν ποτ' ἔδωκας | ἀντιθέῳ Ὀδυσῆϊ δόμον κάτ' ἀλητεύοντι,

---

22. See for example: Hiltbrunner 1972: 1078; Scott 1982: 12; Gauthier 1972: 5; Bolkestein 1939: 216; Scheid-Tissinier 1994: 141-42.
23. Compare the argument in Reece 1993: 142 according to whom Polyphemus 'has perverted the normal diction of the hospitality-scene and generally turned the type-scene on its head.' Vidal-Naquet 1983: 53-56 similarly categorises the Cyclops and the Laestrygonian episodes as being in line with a model of 'le thème du renversement' (54). Podlecki 1961: 125-33 sees the wordplay with the name *outis* as part of a logic of inversion. According to him, Odysseus responds to the nongiving of *xeinia* by being nobody. See also Lavelle 1980-81: 197-99 on ironic use of the word *xeinia* in the Cyclops episode.
24. See Pitt-Rivers 1977: 112, who draws attention to this role reversal.

Od. 22.290-91). Just as Polyphemus promises to eat Odysseus last, the cowherd will give death as *xeinion* to the presumptuous guest.[25]

The game of inversions does not only take place on a linguistic level; it is continued also in the various connections that are drawn between individual scenes. In studies of Homeric guest-friendship, the Polyphemus episode has held a prominent position. Negative characterisation of the Cyclops accounts for the concept of a primitive magico-religious xenophobia as well as for the assumption of an early stage during which strangers possessed no rights.[26] Equally, structuralist interpretations of mythology have shown how fruitful comparisons can be made regarding the treatment of strangers in the world of the Cyclops and the world of the heroes.[27] These comparisons are in no way limited to the general oppositions between nature and culture, or the wild and civilisation, as is often suggested.[28] The real common denominator in the various scenes of natural *xeinia* granted are not abstract values but rather concrete problems of exchange which exist between the pastoral world and the household of a *basileus*.

It is striking that natural *xeinia* are mostly granted in places associated with herdsmen. So, when Eumaeus, Odysseus's swineherd, lets his master participate in the herdsmen's supper and promises to provide *xeinia*, they are at a herdsman's station, *stathmos*, or hut, *klisia* (*Od.* 14.381 and 404). The upside-down game of *xeinia* between Polyphemus and Odysseus takes place in a grotto (*speos*) or cave (*atron*) used as shelter (*aulē*) for goats and sheep in the mountains (*Od.* 9.462 and 216-18). Calypso, too, places her *xeinia* for Hermes in a remote island grotto surrounded by flower-meadows (*Od.* 5.57 and 72). As a nymph she belongs, like Hermes the divine protector of herds, to the pastoral world; but unlike Eumaeus and Polyphemus she also has at her disposal the sorts of goods usually only available at the palaces of wealthy men: garments and textiles for bedding.[29] On the other hand, there are herd-owners, such as Peleus who looks after his guest in just such a courtyard (*aulē*) as is used at Eumaeus's farm as shelter for the

---

25. Polyphemus's 'raw eating' also belongs in this context. It is to be understood as a metaphor of revenge for death, and as anticipation of Odysseus's actions towards the suitors who consume his goods. In *Iliad* 24 Hecuba wishes to avenge her son by eating the liver of the man who killed him (*Il.* 24.212-14). See ch. 4.4.
26. Bolchazy 1978: 46-47; von Jhering 1887: 367; Bolkestein 1939: 216; Köstler 1950: 17-20.
27. Vidal-Naquet 1983: 39-68 (Valeurs religieuses et mythiques de la terre et du sacrifice dans l'*Odyssée*).
28. Calame 1976: 311-28; O'Sullivan 1990: 7-17.
29. Cf. ch. 2.3.

animals (*Il.* 11.774). The only time an actual house (*dōma*) is mentioned is in the case of Diocles of Pherai, who provides *xeinia* for Telemachus and Peisistratus (*Od.* 3.488).³⁰ It is therefore possible to conclude that where the offering of natural *xeinia* is described we are dealing with a specifically pastoral form of hospitality, especially as whenever *xeinia* take the form of manufactured goods such as textiles or metal objects in the epic poem, the hospitality in question is offered by high-ranking *basilēes*.³¹

Polyphemus's negative depiction notwithstanding, there is an ancient tradition of pastoral hospitality. Vidal-Naquet has drawn attention to the fact that Homer knows of a kindly species of Cyclops, 'the *abioi* (without food), who milk mares and live on milk and are "the most just of humans" (*Il.* 13.5–6)'.³² They also feature in a fragment from Aeschylus's drama *Prometheus Unbound*, where they are called the Gabioi (*Prometheus Unbound* fr. 196). Here they are referred to as hospitable as well as just and are granted nourishment from the earth without knowledge of agriculture.³³ Hellenistic poetry especially features hospitable herdsmen.³⁴

Eumaeus represents the hospitable herdsman who shares all his available resources with the stranger. The Cyclops, who disregards or inverts the norms of hospitality, is in a sense antithetical to Eumaeus while also resembling him. While Polyphemus is autonomous, Eumaeus's position is part of a herd-owner's household. Eumaeus had originally been procured by Laërtes for an *ōnos* (*Od.* 15.483; 15.452–53)³⁵ and was then sent by Laërtes and Odysseus's mother to the countryside, to the *agros* (ἀγρόνδε), as a youth. They provided him with a cloak, *chlaina*, and a tunic, *chitōn*, and further good garments and textiles, *heimata kala* (εἵματ' [...] καλὰ μάλ', *Od.* 15.370). Eumaeus complains, however, that this provision with textiles is no longer possible since Penelope's suitors at Odysseus's house are eating up all the cattle, pigs, goats, and lambs. His work (ἔργον) brings in enough to eat and drink, which he is able to share with strangers (*Od.* 15.372–73).

---

30. Compare the reference to the hospitality of Axylos whose house was by the roadside (πάντας γὰρ φιλέεσκεν ὁδῷ ἔπι οἰκία ναίων, *Il.* 6.12–15). In epic poetry *oikia* can refer to the herdsman's station, the animal shelter, or the house itself. See Knox 1970: 117–20.
31. See in more detail ch. 2.3.
32. Vidal-Naquet 1986: 22 (= 1983: 52): 'Homère [...] connaît en quelque sorte de bons Cyclopes, les *Abioi* (sans nourriture), trayeurs de juments galactophages, qui sont "les plus juste des hommes".' Cf. *Il.* 13.5: δικαιοτάτων ἀνθρώπων.
33. Vidal-Naquet 1983: 52.
34. See Hiltbrunner 1972: 1083.
35. Cf. ch. 5.2.

But from the mistress, *despoina*, nothing is forthcoming:

> οὔτ' ἔπος οὔτε τι ἔργον, ἐπεὶ κακὸν ἔμπεσεν οἴκῳ,
> ἄνδρες ὑπερφίαλοι μέγα δὲ δμῶες χατέουσιν
> ἀντία δεσποίνης φάσθαι καὶ ἕκαστα πυθέσθαι
> καὶ φαγέμεν πιέμεν τε, ἔπειτα δὲ καί τι φέρεσθαι
> ἀγρόνδ', οἷά τε θυμὸν ἀεὶ δμώεσσιν ἰαίνει.

> There is no getting a kind word or deed [...], for the house has fallen into the hands of wicked people. Servants want sometimes to see their mistress and have a talk with her; they like to have something to eat and drink at the house, and something too to take back with them into the country (*agros*). This is what will keep servants' hearts (*thumos*) warm (*Od.* 15.374-79, tr. Butler, modified).

This 'something' that keeps 'servants' *thumos* warm' could be agricultural goods such as grain or wine, or textile goods such as those the young Eumaeus received from Odysseus's mother when the mechanism of exchange between the herdsmen's station and the main household was still functional. Now the flow of goods between the herdsmen's station in the countryside (*agros*) and the herd-owner's household, represented by the *despoina*, has become one-sided. Eumaeus sends animals for slaughter but receives nothing himself by way of food and drink or those other items that warm the *thumos*.

While at Ithaca the breakdown of the exchange is caused by the *despoina*'s problems in the household; in the case of the Cyclopes, it is the herdsmen who are not fulfilling their side of the relationship. The Cyclopes live by themselves without exchange amongst one another and lacking rules that govern relationships beyond individual households. As Odysseus tells the Phaeacians:

> θεμιστεύει δὲ ἕκαστος | παίδων ἠδ' ἀλόχων, οὐδ' ἀλλήλων ἀλέγουσιν.

> Each makes the rules for his children and his wife, but they do not care for each other (*Od.* 9.114-15)

Figure 3.1. Alfred R. Waud, "Scenes in Memphis, Tennessee, During the Riot," *Harper's Weekly*, May 26, 1866, 321. Wood engraving, Prints and Photographs Division, Library of Congress, LC-USZ62-111152.

emotion-laden imagery, the report established violence in the South as an acute threat to freedpeople's emotional reformation. Stifling the hopes associated with the intimate relationship of teacher and pupil, such violence prompted a reinvigorated focus on the bureau as a military barrier between the classroom and the unruly ecology of feeling outside it.

When Eliot introduced a revised bureau bill, on May 23, 1866, the legislation more narrowly emphasized protection for freedpeople, with a specific emphasis on missionary-sponsored public schools. To assuage concerns about freedpeople's "idleness," the bill indicated that material aid could not be administered to anyone "able to find employment, and [who] could, by proper industry or exertion, avoid such destitution, suffering, or dependence."[64] In practice, this revision led bureau administrators to be more selective in providing food, medical supplies, and other material aid while dedicating greater resources to education.[65] Yet even as the bill positioned education as more central to the bureau's mission, it also more starkly separated the bureau's protective role from the labor of teachers. Accepting contentions that "the United States ought not to educate," Eliot clearly delineated where the bureau ended and philanthropy began: "The object ... is to provide school-houses and protect those school-houses, while the schools themselves are conducted by associations of benevolent individuals from the North and West." Alluding to the violence of the previous months, Eliot added, "It is perfectly plain that education cannot be secured to these freedmen unless the Government, for the present, shall protect the buildings in which the schools are conducted." Premised on the logic of patriarchal protection, Eliot's bill assuaged enough moderates to pass by veto-proof majorities in July.[66] The revised legislation thus placed the bureau atop a discursive fault line. If the government engaged in actual benevolent work—for instance, by directly paying for teachers' labor—it infringed on the voluntary realm of civil society. Likewise, missionary teachers could not move beyond their appropriate roles as pseudo-mothers to freedpeople lest they face accusations of engaging in political agitation. The bureau's future thus depended on how it negotiated the tensions between public and private, government and philanthropy, protection and education. With the enactment of Black suffrage in the South, maintaining the bureau's relationship to these binaries grew more fraught by the year.

"RADICAL EMISSARIES": BLACK IMPRESSIBILITY AND CORRUPTION ALLEGATIONS, 1867-1868

During the 1866 debate, many Republicans in Congress argued on behalf of educating freedpeople as preparation for their eventual political rights. Gesturing to some undefined moment in the future, these politicians defended Black suffrage in principle while deferring it until, as Representative James A. Garfield (R-OH) put it, "they are worthy [and] qualified, by intelligence, to exercise it."[67] Black men in the South gained the ballot far faster than most legislators anticipated. Passed in March 1867, the first Reconstruction Act established conditions for Southern states' readmission to the Union. Part of an effort to limit the political power of Southern whites responsible for the rebellion, the law empowered Black men in the South to participate in state constitutional conventions, vote, and hold office.[68] Following what Eric Foner describes as an "astonishingly rapid evolution of Congressional attitudes," the Reconstruction Act represented a major victory for Black activists and Radical Republicans and a leap of faith for moderate Republicans who doubted Black capacity for fellow feeling.[69] Complicating the political calculations of Northern moderates, the bill accelerated conversations about Black suffrage in the North and heightened Northern constituents' anxieties about Black political participation. Democrats eagerly stoked these anxieties, reading petitions from white Southerners attesting to the region's alleged subordination by "unlettered and capricious barbarians ... without control over their own caprices and strong passions."[70] For bureau supporters, the Reconstruction Act transformed the terms of debate about freedpeople's protection and schooling. Before 1867, education had provided Republicans a way to gesture toward a hopeful moment when Black men would be worthy of the ballot. After 1867, party members defended the position that freedmen were already worthy while continuing to promote bureau-backed education to assuage constituents' apprehensions.

As Republicans oscillated between defenses of enfranchisement and urgent appeals for education, their opponents accentuated the party's divides by positioning bureau advocates as caught in a double bind. As Senator Thomas A. Hendricks (D-IN) argued, claims that freedpeople still needed education revealed hypocrisy in Republican policy: "You say the wisdom of the negro race has been quite sufficient ... to decide the political fortunes of one third of this country, and to-day you propose to declare these same people not competent."[71] Tapping into the same assumptions of Black impressibility that warranted the bureau's renewal in 1866, opponents like Hendricks built a conspiratorial argument to exacerbate this alleged contradiction in Republican policy. Bureau critics alleged that the agency's officers—and by proxy, its affiliated teachers—had radicalized Black pupils against Southern whites to disrupt the formation of fellow feeling in the South. Undercutting imagery of bureau teachers as paragons of domesticity, this argument collapsed Republicans' already-tenuous distinction between federal authority and classroom teaching. Citing yet another surge of violence in the South, bureau supporters once again secured its renewal in 1868 by emphasizing its protective role. Yet critics' efforts to erode the bureau's perceived separation from the classroom set the stage for its demise in 1870.

Vacillating Accounts of Freedpeople's Civic Readiness, July-December 1867

As the bureau's 1868 expiration approached, white anxieties about Black feeling weighed on the agency's supporters. Throughout the summer of 1867, Northern newspapers raised alarms about Black labor protests, political conspiracies, and rejection of free labor ideals. As Heather Cox Richardson writes, these reports incited Northern fears of Black militancy by claiming that freedpeople had been swayed by passion-arousing demagogues in their midst.[72] By the fall, these concerns coalesced in the failure of a statewide universal male suffrage amendment in Ohio. Coupled with major losses for Republicans in local elections in crucial swing states, the outcome led moderates to fret about a white backlash against Radical Republican policy.[73]

Meanwhile, Freedmen's Bureau officials' reports to Congress seemed to confirm constituents' fears about Black feeling. Alvord's July 1867 report included his apprehensions about freedpeople's illiteracy: "At the place of voting they look at the ballot-box and then at the printed ticket in their hands, wishing they could read it. The party politician is at their side with professions and assertions, and they feel their ignorance. . . . 'I want to know what is on the ticket myself,' said one to me."[74] In December, Representative Eliot received letters from bureau agents reiterating the same theme. Samuel Chapman Armstrong, a Virginia agent whose industrial schooling model would soon play a central role in postbellum Black education, lamented that "the ignorance of the freedpeople" left them susceptible to passionate whims: "Freedmen need warning from unprincipled men of the North, as well of the South, who are now, with selfish ends, travelling up and down the country seeking with smooth and flattering words, the suffrages of an ignorant people." Teachers needed to counteract these influences lest "the evils of their ignorance are liable to produce general disaster."[75] Fears of freedpeople's emotional exploitation shaped the priorities in Eliot's 1868 renewal bill. The bill called to discontinue the bureau in all areas except its educational division, which would remain until states established their own school systems.[76]

In pursuing schooling as an adjunct to suffrage, bureau advocates found themselves caught between conceptions of civic worth predicated on loyalty and education. To warrant Black suffrage in the Reconstruction Acts, Republicans had invoked the wartime loyalty of formerly enslaved people as evincing a depth of feeling for the nation. Loyalty provided Congress a justification to enfranchise Black Southerners while limiting white rebels' political rights.[77] The case for loyalty insisted on Black civic worth in the present tense, proclaiming, in Sumner's words, that "the freedman already knows his friends by the unerring instinct of his heart."[78] Yet the loyalty argument began to lose its persuasive appeal in Congress early in Reconstruction.[79] By late 1867, the depth of Black feeling for the Union could even be contorted into further evidence of freedpeople's dangerous impressibility. As Armstrong wrote, "Simple loyalty is all the freedman has to qualify them for the franchise, and that, in its simplicity is liable to be, and is sometimes misled."[80] Logics of loyalty and education thus had competing implications for Black citizenship: the former conferred civic worth in the present; the latter pushed it into the future. As Eliot introduced the 1868 renewal bill, then, he wrestled with these conflicting logics. Most of his speech emphasized protecting loyal Black and white Southerners from violence. In a revealing passage, though, he stumbled into the tension between loyalty and the educational emphasis of the bill itself: "It is said that these men are unfit to vote. Well, sir, this bureau is doing all it can to qualify them in all respects. But how is it they are unfit? Rebels are qualified because they are white. No matter how disloyal or how ignorant or how vicious, they ought to vote!"[81] Eliot had begun to concede that freedpeople lacked preparedness to vote before shifting midargument to reject the premise that level of education was an arbiter of civic worth. In this moment of vacillation, he accentuated the conflicts animating Republican conceptions of Black preparedness. The basis of Eliot's hesitancy provided the fulcrum of opponents' attack on the bureau.

Conspiratorial Charges of Radicalizing Freedpeople, January–July 1868

As bureau supporters premised renewal on the need to protect freedpeople's education, opponents invoked Black impressibility to portray the agency as a vast Radical scheme. As a conservative opponent to Black suffrage on the verge of breaking from the Republican Party, Senator James R. Doolittle (R-WI) led in making conspiratorial charges. During a January 1868 debate, he quoted former Confederate vice president Alexander H. Stephens while outlining the arguments against Black suffrage and the bureau. According to Stephens, Radical policy had deepened "the estrangement between the races" through "the effects of such instruction as teaches [Black Southerners] to distrust and oppose the whites." Through the work of "Radical emissaries from the North," Congress had "sown the seeds of evil dissension with a terrible earnestness" that would induce "fearful collisions" between Black and white Southerners.[82] Rather than apolitical figures sacrificing themselves to promote fellow feeling, bureau-affiliated teachers were depicted as partisans inflaming racial animosities.

Elaborating on Stephens's claim, Doolittle presented bureau agents and teachers as part of a plot to retain Radical power in Congress. "The negroes," he claimed, "under the tutillage [sic] of the Freedmen's Bureau, led by Radical emissaries, or pushed by Federal bayonets, must take political control of these States in order to obtain their votes."[83] Underpinning Doolittle's account of Radical motives were his views of Black susceptibility to emotional appeals. Speaking to a Democratic meeting in March, he asserted that "there never was such a wide field for demagogues and aspirants for office as is now opened among these colored people." That field had been prepared by "emissaries from the North" who had "prejudiced [the newly emancipated] against the white race."[84] In Doolittle's view, Black prejudices could not derive from formerly enslaved persons' analysis and reflection on the conditions they had experienced. Rather, such prejudices had been inculcated in freedpeople by those who preyed on their unique emotional susceptibility. In this way, Doolittle reframed bureau-sponsored education as a mode of political indoctrination.

The reframing of missionary teachers as Radical emissaries fit into a larger Democratic narrative about bureau influence on Black Southerners. At the heart of that narrative were the Union Leagues (or Loyal Leagues), political groups established by Republicans that aimed to organize Black Southern voters.[85] As Mark Wahlgren Summers writes, throughout 1867 Democratic newspapers and politicians misrepresented the leagues as not merely "recruiting agencies for a biracial Republican Party" but also "paramilitary groups, out to prepare the blacks for warfare."[86] Between March and July 1868, Democrats seized on this conspiratorial image of the Union Leagues as bureau-fueled engines of Black radicalism and Republican partisanship. Senator Hendricks alleged that the bureau placed Republican political operatives in the South "for the purpose of managing, manipulating, and controlling the elections that are to take place" while "organizing [Black voters] through the loyal leagues." House Democrats agreed, calling the bureau "a political machine to control political sentiments" and "a contrivance of this Congress to manipulate, control, regulate, and dominate the southern States." Representative James Brooks (D-NY) declared that this assertion of political control relied on Black impressibility: "The negro is . . . being used, as his donkey or mule or his horse is used, by northern adventurers for the purpose of riding into the capital of the United States." Though most Democrats did not directly address the bureau's work in classrooms, the association of its officials with partisan motives undercut Republicans' insistence on a separation between military protection and missionary education. Illustrating the force of the conspiracy theory, Representative George W. Woodward (D-PA) explicitly blamed ongoing conflict between white and Black Southerners on "your agents of the Freedmen's Bureau, your teachers of negro children, the negroes themselves, . . . those organized in loyal leagues and other treasonable combinations."[87] In the ensuing years, House Democrats developed a narrative to connect the various actors in Woodward's account.

Amid intensifying scrutiny of bureau political activity, the agency's proponents doubled down on the need to protect teachers from violence. Near the close of the debate in mid-July, Representative Samuel Arnell (R-TN) painted a dire portrait of the insurgent Ku Klux Klan's attacks on schoolteachers, depicting a "Mr. Dunlap" in terms that reflected the domestic expectations of the classroom: he was "quiet, unobtrusive [and] attended to his own business," willfully "disbursing his charities and benevolence." On the July 4, 1868, after leading his Black pupils in a day of patriotic celebrations, Dunlap was visited by "about fifty" Klan members in the dead of night. They "fired a shot into the house; forced the doors," dragged Dunlap to the town square, and whipped him "unmercifully, cruelly, and shamefully, with orders . . . to leave immediately, or his life would be taken."[88] Building on Arnell's brutal account, Eliot bluntly stated that without the bureau, "there is no doubt at all that schools would be abolished and a war upon the freedmen be begun."[89]

As supporters reinforced the necessity of protection, they also again asserted teachers' independence from the bureau's military work. Eliot repeatedly reminded his colleagues that "teachers are chiefly supplied and paid by northern and western benevolent associations" and operated in buildings "mainly built from private funds of freedmen and contributions from loyal men," and these arguments again helped propel the agency's renewal over Johnson's veto.[90] Yet congressional support only continued through January 1869. The agency's funding and field operations subsequently declined rapidly, prompting one last-ditch effort to preserve its educational work as a civilian agency.

"TAUGHT A HATRED OF HIS BEST FRIENDS": THE TRANSFER DEBATE AND THE HOWARD INVESTIGATION, 1870

By the beginning of 1870, the bureau's financial situation was dire as a consequence of diminished federal support. At the same time, its missionary partners faced a rapid decline in donations. Lamented Alvord, "The open hand [of northern benefactors], which at the close of the war poured forth its treasures without stint, has been somewhat withdrawn."[91] Meanwhile, the language of the soon-to-be-ratified Fifteenth Amendment created new concerns for Republicans in Congress. During debates over the amendment, Radical Republicans led by Wilson sought revisions to prevent educational restrictions on voting rights.[92] Wilson's language was rejected, leaving a loophole that could—and soon would—be used to suppress Black suffrage.[93] The Republican Party's foothold in the South thus depended on ensuring that Black voters could withstand state legislatures' attempts at educational exclusion.

White anxieties about Black feeling also still threatened the Republican coalition across the North, West, and border states, leading voters in Ohio, California, and Tennessee initially to reject the Fifteenth Amendment.[94] Animated by these concerns, Howard advocated that Congress continue the bureau until Southern states developed stable programs for Black education. Keenly aware of congressional resistance to the ongoing use of wartime military power, Howard knew that his agency had no future in the military.

Instead, he argued that the bureau's operations should be transferred to the recently founded civilian Bureau of Education.[95] Setting the stage for a final collision over the agency, Republicans in Congress took up Howard's proposal but quickly found that without the appeal to military protection so crucial to the bureau's renewal in 1866 and 1868, a more direct appeal for federal involvement in schools was required. The bureau's opponents, in turn, honed their loose claims of corruption into a set of formal charges. The result was a debate that halted the bureau's transfer, diminished its legacy, and limited the scope of federal influence in the classroom.

Advocating for a Civilian Freedmen's Bureau, March 1870

From the start of the 1870 debate, Republicans framed the bureau's continuation as a response to concerns about the preparedness of newly enfranchised Black voters. With the ratification of the Fifteenth Amendment on March 30, 1870, President Ulysses S. Grant took the unusual step of appending a special message to the secretary of state's ratification proclamation. Firmly linking enfranchisement to education, Grant insisted on "the newly enfranchised race ... striving in every honorable manner to make themselves worthy of their new privilege." With these words, Grant departed from the justifications bureau proponents had used two years earlier. Whereas Eliot vacillated between loyalty and education as prerequisites for the ballot, Grant's message was unequivocal: freedpeople were not "worthy of their new privilege" unless they pursued education. To ensure that Black voting rights would be "a blessing and not a danger" to national sentiment, he thus implored members of Congress to "take all the means within their constitutional powers to promote and encourage popular education throughout the country."[96]

Arnell immediately responded to Grant's call by introducing a bill to continue the Freedmen's Bureau's educational operations. Adopting Howard's suggestion to transfer the agency's work to the Bureau of Education, Arnell amplified Grant's statement. To date, Arnell argued, the bureau had reached only "a small portion of the four million colored people, all ignorant." The bureau was thus needed as a federal bridge until states created taxpayer-funded systems.[97] Arnell's bill represented a departure from the previous legislation. Whereas the bureau had previously constituted a military agency responding to a humanitarian exigency of displaced enslaved people, it would now become a civilian agency working to redress a civic exigency created by the Fifteenth Amendment. Bureau supporters who in 1866 and 1868 had downplayed the agency's direct educational work and emphasized military protection could no longer use that argument.

Unable to cite military protection as the bureau's purpose, proponents instead defended its educational work on its own terms. Their words contrasted strongly with Eliot's almost exclusive focus on protection. Representative Oliver Dockery (R-NC) used the bill as an opportunity to extol education as what "underlies the entire fabric" of American government. Noting that freedpeople were "unaccustomed to the exercise of thought and care 'for the morrow,'" Dockery insisted that the bureau was vital to freedpeople's exercise of citizenship and assimilation into fellow feeling: "The tranquility and order of our common country demand it." Building on these appeals, Representative George Frisbie Hoar (R-MA) advocated the Freedmen's Bureau's continuation as part of his ongoing advocacy for a national system of education. Depicting schooling as a vital adjunct to civic participation, Hoar argued that converting the bureau into a longer-term civilian agency would "signalize the formal proclamation of the completion of [freedpeople's] enfranchisement," whereas allowing it to perish would provide "a declaration of the national Congress in favor of ignorance."[98]

With the proposed bureau severed from the military, appeals from Arnell, Dockery, and Hoar dispensed with discussions of protection. They likewise recognized that with public donations for missionary work declining, the bureau would need to directly engage in educational work without intermediaries. Noticing this change in emphasis, moderate representative William Lawrence (R-OH) fretted that the bill "presents the question whether we shall embark in the general business of taking charge of the educational interests of the States."[99] In defending federal involvement in schooling on its own terms, bureau advocates set aside the distinction between protection and education so essential to the agency's previous survival in Congress, a change that facilitated opponents' accusations that the bureau was exerting undue influence on the fragile maternal sphere of the classroom.

Accusations of Corrupting Feeling, March–July 1870

As supporters called for the bureau to directly intervene in schools, critics argued that the agency was already too closely involved in education and that this involvement was having nefarious results. By the 1870s, the topic of corruption had emerged as a driving force in Reconstruction politics. More than a concern for partisan machines, patronage, and unscrupulous uses of taxpayer funds, the corruption issue itself often acted as a rhetorical strategy for delimiting and redefining the scope of government authority during a period of flux.[100] In the 1870 debates, Representative Thompson McNeely (D-IL) positioned the bureau at the center of that negotiation. Echoing the words of his fellow Democrats two years earlier, he insinuated that the bureau existed to consolidate Republican political power. By shielding "agents, teachers, officers, and other emissaries of the bureau" from civilian oversight, he charged, the agency's "educational division... became a very consistent and appropriate part of that military despotism which then exercised its cruel sway over the southern people." McNeely was incredulous at Republican claims that the bureau would still rely on outside cooperation for its educational work. In his view, Congress had failed to define "what this new bureau may do under the head of 'coöperation,'" leaving room for corrupt schemes at public expense. He claimed that the creation of Howard University—a college for Black teachers named after the bureau's commissioner—had been such a scheme: "The coöperation in that job consisted in the joint action of a few gentlemen engaged in getting over half a million dollars out of the public Treasury" for their own profit and minimal public benefit.[101]

McNeely also implicated the bureau in corrupting the classroom itself. Developing an argument he later used against the Hoar Bill, McNeely indicated that the mere presence of federal power near the classroom intruded on the "delicate trust" granted to teachers. He insisted that schools could fulfill their purpose only when "free from any interference on the part of Federal officers acting under the pretense of 'coöperating' with them."[102] In McNeely's view, the bureau had violated a crucial political boundary line vital to education's claim of domesticity—the line between protecting the classroom and interfering with it. It thus had hurt rather than helped the efforts of missionary teachers.

The bill to transfer the bureau passed the House of Representatives, but its Democratic critics continued to try to thwart it. On April 6, the day the bill was introduced in the Senate, Representative Fernando Wood (D-NY) requested ten minutes to issue a "Personal Explanation" on the floor of the House. A notorious provocateur, Wood was reviled by Republicans for his wartime Confederate sympathies, opposition to the Thirteenth Amendment, and formal censure by the House for uncouth language.[103] True to his reputation, he used his speaking time to issue a tirade of insinuations. Citing a "common report and common rumor," he alleged that Howard had accrued a fortune through nepotistic impropriety in managing funds for Howard University.[104]

Wood went well beyond accusing Howard of personal enrichment, labeling him "one of a ring known as the 'Freedmen's Bureau ring,' whose connections and influences with the freedmen's savings-banks, the freedmen's schools of the south, the political machinery of a party in the southern States; and whose position has been to devote the official authority and power of the bureau to personal and political profit."¹⁰⁵ Threading together Democrats' conspiratorial arguments against the bureau, Woods's far-reaching claims prompted House Republicans to initiate a formal investigation in hopes of defending Howard's reputation. Over the next three months, members of the Committee on Education and Labor were joined by Wood and bureau critics McNeely and Anthony Rogers (D-AR) to question federal agents and missionary leaders about bureau operations. As they examined Howard's finances, Democrats on the committee also interrogated teachers and AMA officials about their political activities, religious instruction, and sources of revenue.¹⁰⁶ Through these questions, McNeely and Rogers claimed to expose a blurred line between the bureau and its partners, portraying the agency as involved in schools' day-to-day activities to partisan ends.

Vastly outnumbered by Republicans on the committee, McNeely and Rogers could not prevent Howard's formal exoneration but nonetheless used their minority report as a platform to synthesize claims about Black impressibility, Republican partisanship, and the exploitation of classroom space by federal influence. They insisted that a corrupt "ring" was indeed seeking political and financial gain "through the instrumentality of the officers and willing agents of the bureau, the freedmen schools and teachers, [and] the missionaries sent out by the" AMA. Together, these "emissaries ... with the Bible in one hand and the purse in the other" used federal money to plant partisan, anti-Catholic, and antiwhite ideas among freedpeople. Coached by AMA publications like the *American Missionary*, teachers were thus dispatched to classrooms "to create animosities and hatreds in the heart of the poor colored man against white men amongst whom he lives." Offering their account of the bureau's partisan influence, they summarized,

> Successful applications were made to the necessities and ignorance of a people who had not learned the arts of the demagogue, nor the wiles of politicians. Under the pretense of giving him protection, the negro was plundered of his just dues; under the pretense of teaching him religion and morality, he was taught a hatred of his best friends; under an avowed object of teaching him his political rights and duties, he was drilled into a voting machine, and made tributary to the aspirations of those who said they came to enlighten him.¹⁰⁷

Rendering Black voters of the South as passive containers for white influence, McNeely and Rogers's account foregrounded the ease with which freedpeople could be manipulated into feelings of hatred or loyalty toward scrupulous actors.

In 1866, Republicans had cited the unique impressibility of freedpeople as a justification for renewing the bureau. Four years later, McNeely and Rogers inverted the Republicans' appeal, arguing that Black voters' naive emotional receptivity made them easily exploitable by white Northerners, including through the classroom. In this way, McNeely and Rogers reframed the bureau as a force for destroying rather than generating fellow feeling. Rather than preserve a tranquil space of domesticity, the bureau exploited the intimacy of the classroom for political ends. Rather than protecting freedpeople from outside hostility, the agency turned them hostile. Rather than working against demagogues, the bureau empowered them.

Republicans' Retreat from the Bureau's Educational Achievements, July 1870

Amid an all-out attack on the bureau's imbrications with philanthropy, committee Republicans backed away from a direct defense of its work in public education. Attempting to secure the bureau's legacy, the majority report issued by Arnell instead reinscribed the distinctions between government and philanthropy that allowed the bureau to survive Johnson's repeated vetoes. From the start, Arnell argued, the bureau had an apolitical mission "too important to be associated in the public mind with anything of a partisan nature." Knowing that the bureau needed to remain apolitical, President Abraham Lincoln had selected Howard as its leader because of his benevolent reputation "as a Christian gentleman [with] the esteem of the humane and benevolent portion of the public."[108] Rather than engaging in illicit activities, Howard had cultivated partnerships outside the government that reflected his own character. Arnell contended that "the 'ring,' sneeringly so called, . . . was a noble band of patriots and philanthropists, of missionary associations, of educational institutions, of learned and eminent divines, of devoted and benevolent men and women."[109] Rather than aiming for partisan benefit, these Northerners had been "willing to leave the comforts of home, and the society of relatives and friends, for the purpose of carrying the lights of education and religious instruction among the newly enfranchised people of the South." By characterizing the work of education as undertaken through self-sacrifice, Arnell's report reinscribed the classroom as a space of fragile domesticity. Restoring a gendered conception of teachers, he included a lengthy report from a French observer: "It would be impossible to convey an idea of the energy and friendly rivalry displayed by the women of America in this truly Christian work."[110] Rather than a defense of federal involvement in education, then, Arnell's report returned to themes Eliot stressed in the 1866 debate, portraying schooling as the labor of altruistic outsiders, especially white women, untouched by federal power.

Dragging on from early April through mid-July, the Howard hearings helped to dampen enthusiasm for the bureau transfer bill in the Senate. Against that backdrop, Arnell's report seemed more concerned with controlling the narrative of the bureau's legacy than providing a basis for its continuation. Despite a wider push from Republicans to expand federal involvement in schools, the majority report downplayed the bureau's important role in providing financial support to public schools and shied away from arguing that more work remained in the arena of freedpeople's education; instead, the report proclaimed, "With God on its side, the Freedmen's Bureau has triumphed." To that end, the majority painted a far more positive portrait of the bureau's influence on public feeling than did their colleagues in the minority. Quoting at length from an editorial by author Sidney Andrews, the majority report claimed that the bureau had "rooted out old prejudices, . . . led bitter hearts into brighter ways, shamed strong hearts into charity and forgiveness, promulgated the new doctrine of equal rights, destroyed the seeds of mistrust and antagonism, cheered the despondent . . . inculcated kindly feeling, checked the passion of whites and blacks, . . . encouraged human sympathy, . . . upheld loyalty, [and] assisted in creating a sentiment of nationality."[111] The committee's majority framed the bureau's work as an extension of the atmosphere of altruism, a swelling of hopeful optimism that turned to a government agency for protection and support. Depicting the bureau this way helped to exonerate Howard and stave off political attacks on its recent work. Yet that portrayal also elided the bureau's direct role in promoting freedpeople's education, acquiescing to a view of the schoolroom as outside the sphere of appropriate federal support.

THE FREEDMEN'S BUREAU, EDUCATION, AND FELLOW FEELING

Congress embraced the Freedmen's Bureau's educational turn as part of a wider attempt to intervene in public feeling after the Civil War. The bureau allowed federal officials to channel the positive feelings associated with white women's domestic labor to teach emotional control to supposedly impressible Black Southerners. By pursuing that course while defending the bureau as a patriarchal protector of voluntary teachers, Congress sidestepped a debate over direct involvement in schools—but only at first. In marshaling a postwar zeal for benevolence, Congress built its policy for emancipated slaves atop a what Butchart describes as a "spasm of patriotism and emotional release at war's end . . . a wave of emotion that crested on the southern shore, then ebbed as quickly as it had come."[112] As these fleeting feelings subsided and public support for military intervention receded, the bureau's proponents tried and failed to continue federal sponsorship for freedpeople's education on its own terms. By 1870, bureau opponents accepted the core premises regarding Black impressibility and classroom domesticity, folding those ideas into conspiracy theories about Republican efforts to maintain power in the South. In this alternative rendering, the bureau's proximity to the classroom was reinterpreted as a harmful force responsible for interracial hostility. To counteract these allegations, supporters ultimately disclaimed the agency's considerable role in supporting freedpeople's education. Reinscribing a firm line between the bureau and missionary organizations, both supporters and opponents accepted the classroom's inherent domesticity, fragility, and susceptibility to partisan influence.

The outcome of the Freedmen's Bureau debate foreclosed a significant role for the federal government in shaping Black education in the South. Prior to the Civil War, combinations of federal authority and civil society were not unusual. However, as Brian Balogh writes, the Reconstruction era prompted a renegotiation of the relationship between federal government and civil society. By the period's end, federal policymakers generally accepted a "hard boundary" between interventions deemed acceptable for federal power and forms of "social or humanitarian reform" best left to philanthropic organizations.[113] The Freedmen's Bureau was at the center of that debate, representing the federal government's first systematic social welfare program and its most serious foray into public education during the nineteenth century. Even as the bureau's leaders and congressional officials downplayed its direct involvement in schools, the agency dedicated close to five million dollars to sustain—not merely to protect—more than four thousand schools.[114] As W. E. B. Du Bois argued, the bureau left behind a legacy of schools and teacher training colleges that were among the few educational footholds for Black people in the postbellum South.[115] In ascribing these accomplishments solely to independent missionaries, the bureau's supporters in Congress bypassed a chance to defend federal work in schools or advocate for that work's continuation.

The subsequent federal absence had serious consequences for the development of Black education in the South. As missionaries and bureau officials departed, Black communities were left to continue their fight for their public schools without a significant ally and amid growing hostility from white state officials.[116] The federal departure also created space for modern foundations like Baltimore industrialist George Peabody's Fund for Southern Education to assume a significant role in shaping national policy.[117] As a result, large-scale choices about education reform would be shaped by the whims of wealthy philanthropists. As with the debates over the Bureau of Education, the Hoar

Bill, and the Perce Bill, efforts to renew the Freedmen's Bureau thus limited the federal government to only indirect forms of involvement in schools.

The outcome of the bureau debate undermined a key support for freedpeople's education at the same time it reinscribed white fears about Black people's emotional capacities for civic participation. The argument that formerly enslaved persons could be uniquely susceptible to white teachers' impressions helped keep the bureau alive but proved to be a double-edged sword when Black political participation became a reality. Hope was rapidly converted into fear. With each expansion of Black political rights—first in the South in 1868, then nationally in 1870—white political anxieties intensified. It is not a coincidence that the day the Fifteenth Amendment was ratified, President Grant and bureau advocates in Congress doubled down on appeals that Black people needed more education to exercise the rights they had just received. These appeals sought to head off a perception among Northern whites that Black voters, with their unique susceptibility to emotional appeals, could be swept up by demagogues into causes deemed divisive. Democrats exploited these racial fears, propagating ideas about bureau-affiliated agents brainwashing their impressible charges into radical resentments and hostility toward white Southern elites. Whether invoked to save the bureau or to destroy it, assumptions about Black emotional impressibility suffused these debates. Those assumptions underwrote the backlash against Black political leadership, feeding stereotypes that underpinned the white counterattack on Reconstruction during the 1870s.

The bureau's fate underscores the inherent limitations Congress faced in tethering arguments for education to the promotion of good feelings. Part of the appeal of schooling was its possibility to bypass the seemingly intractable passions of present generations and inculcate different emotional investments in the young. At its heart, this understanding of schooling relied on an image of classrooms as apolitical spaces shielded from the angry, hateful, jealous, resentful, bitter, and otherwise divisive feelings on the outside. In the eye of the hurricane of feeling stood idealized women teachers, training pupils to control their feelings, share in sympathy with others, and orient themselves toward the appropriate objects of happiness. During the Freedmen's Bureau debate, the aim of preserving this mythic vision of schooling took precedence over the flesh-and-blood experience of learning in the South. Any effort to teach freedpeople, even efforts relying on the most sanitized AMA curriculum, still threatened to destabilize the emotional investments that sustained white supremacy. Rather than accept the stirring of "bad" feelings as an inevitable part of the process of undoing the South's hierarchies, policymakers recoiled at any sign that schooling had empowered Black people to express their politicized feelings in public. Believing that only the present-tense performance of good feelings could produce a sense of fellow feeling in the longer term, Republicans abandoned not only the bureau but also other educational causes.

The inherent volatility of the classroom as an instrument of reform continued to vex policymakers during the waning years of Reconstruction. Between 1872 and 1875, Congress reckoned with this volatility as it debated perhaps the most controversial education issue to arise during that decade: the desegregation of public schools as part of the broader Civil Rights Bill. In the view of Sumner and other proponents of "mingling" in the classroom, bringing together people from disparate backgrounds was a vital element of common schools' capacity to instill the dispositions needed for republican citizenship. Raising the question of whether mingling should encompass race, the debate over the Civil Rights Bill's educational provisions prompted sustained reflection on questions about the composition of classrooms and schools' role in forging a multiracial democracy. As Southern Democrats sought to galvanize resistance to the legislation, they invoked visceral rhetorics of racial hatred and disgust, claiming that their white constituents would sooner dismantle public schools than allow their children to attend with Black children. Republicans, fearful about the fragility of the South's nascent school systems and the political future, chose to remove education from the bill. Ultimately, the Civil Rights Bill debates cemented a reconciliationist vision of schools as managing and suppressing emotional tensions rather than intervening in their causes.

Chapter Four

THE METHOD OF MINGLING
The Civil Rights Act and Educational Reunion, 1872-1876

In November 1865, members of the Colored People's Convention of South Carolina passed a resolution insisting on their full inclusion in public life: "We are Americans in feeling, who desire to dwell among you in peace, and whose destinies are interwoven."[1] Francis L. Cardozo, an honorary member of the convention, shared its vision of Black and white citizens both dwelling and feeling together. The child of a free Black mother and Jewish father, Cardozo had attended a private school and later the University of Glasgow with white peers. After the Civil War, he founded a freedpeople's school and insisted on a multiracial teaching staff to serve its nearly one thousand pupils.[2] Over time, Cardozo came to understand interracial sympathy as a product of embodied interactions, especially in the classroom. As the chair of the Education Committee at the 1868 South Carolina Constitutional Convention, Cardozo expressed these views as delegates debated integrating the state's new common school system. Accepting separate schools as a compromise in the short term, he refused to see segregation enshrined in the state constitution as a permanent policy.[3] He insisted that when schools "allow children, when five or six years of age, to mingle in schools together, and associate generally ... prejudice must eventually die out." Such classroom proximity was vital to the delegates' alleged aim of preparing children for life in a multiracial democracy. Cardozo warned that if contact were postponed until children "become men and women, prejudice will be so established that no mortal can obliterate it."[4] For Cardozo, schools' capacity to promote fellow feeling would ultimately fail if Black and white Southerners never dwelled or felt together in the same physical space.

Cardozo's advocacy for racially integrated education extended a central idea of the antebellum common school movement: the idea of pedagogical mingling. Since the turn of the 1800s, reformers had touted schools' capacity to inculcate fellow feeling by placing children in contact with one another. Through shared experience on equal terms, children could internalize affinities toward people unlike themselves and in time form a love for a nation populated by diverse others. Pedagogical proximity was thus thought essential to schools' capacity to alleviate hostile sentiments based on religion, place of origin, or class.[5] In the view of Massachusetts secretary of education Horace Mann, a school could be considered republican only if pupils met "together, under the same roof, on the same seats, with the same encouragements, rewards, punishments, and to the exclusion of adventitious and artificial distinctions."[6] Mann and other reformers routinely invoked this idea to justify their vision of common education over extant private, parochial, and charity schools.

Despite Mann and other reformers' convictions about contact, they refused to support Black parents who cited the pedagogy of proximity to contest the segregation of their children.[7] Most white reformers viewed race as beyond the common school movement's sentimental powers, believing schools could not remedy the visceral prejudices of white people or ingrained abjection of Black people.[8] As public schooling became mainstream in New England and in states further west, Black activists and their allies challenged the exclusion of Black pupils from "common" schools. Citing the same appeals white reformers applied to promote the mingling of Catholics and those born into poverty with other children of the same age, Black activists insisted that schoolhouse walls include their children as well. After the Civil War, Cardozo and others carried these appeals into national debates over the role of educational proximity in forging racial, sectional, and religious fellow feeling. Debating questions of civil rights during the 1870s, Congress took up the same questions.

As initially proposed, the Civil Rights Act of 1875 called for racial integration of transportation, entertainment venues, juries, cemeteries, and schools, prompting a sustained reflection on the possibility of interracial democracy in the United States.[9] In the midst of debates over amnesty for former Confederates, Senator Charles Sumner (R-MA) introduced the legislation to ensure that white rebels' resumed political participation would be conditioned on the protection of Black Southerners' rights. The bill represented the pinnacle of Radical Republican efforts to reconfigure the emotional assumptions of Southern political culture. As Kirt Wilson argues, Radical Republicans sought to dismantle a politics of place that constrained Black political participation, substituting a rhetoric of equality that extended civic republican ideals to race.[10] While the bill sought to intervene in many realms of public life, school integration played an outsized role in Radicals' vision. Only schools seemed to provide a direct intervention into the supposedly cut-off world of private prejudices.[11] Even in the face of concerted attacks on the school clause, most Radicals—including several of the nation's first Black legislators—held steadfast to the principle of mingling until the waning days of debate. Like Cardozo, they believed classroom mingling to be essential to aims of civil rights and common schooling alike. To allow separate schools would be to reproduce conditions of racial hatred and thwart dreams of a nation united in fellow feeling.

For Democrats and disaffected Republicans, the school clause of the civil rights bill became central to efforts to reframe the causes of lingering bitterness between North and South. Evoking white Northerners' fatigue with Reconstruction, these critics of the bill contended that ongoing federal involvement in the South had inflamed, rather than diminished, racial and regional resentments.[12] Radical advocacy for racially integrated schools was, in their view, the pinnacle of this agitation. As one Democrat put it, the school clause was a plot to "irritate the feelings" of white Southerners and cause "the destruction of the common schools of the South."[13] In invoking the specter of white backlash, Democrats enacted a paradoxical rhetoric of feeling. On one hand, their attacks on integrated schools portrayed racial prejudice as rooted in visceral feelings: emotions too deep, natural, and self-evident to transform.[14] On the other hand, they invoked white constituents' fears that schools would succeed in promoting interracial friendships, marriages, and sexual relationships—thus raising anxieties about white racial purity becoming corrupted.[15] Though this portrayal of schools as both impotent and all-powerful rested on a contradiction, it nonetheless posed a formidable challenge for supporters of school integration. Critics claimed that their white constituents would sooner abandon their schools than integrate them.

Through visceral rhetorics of race, Democrats repositioned their party's relationship to public schools. After decades of opposing the principle of taxpayer-funded public education for even most white children, Democrats now portrayed themselves as defending schooling against Republican villains who would destroy the nascent system by introducing racial strife. Dissociating mingling from the broader rhetoric of common schooling, Democrats—with help from moderate Republicans—posited an alternative vision for schools' role in sectional reunion. In this view, it would not matter whether schools fostered contact across difference or even whether they taught similar curricula. Rather, to praise education as a unifying panacea was an end in itself, a way to signal an investment in the cause of national reconciliation.

Between 1872 and 1875, Congress renegotiated the rhetoric of education, rejecting the idea of mingling while reinforcing faith in schooling as a cornerstone of reunion. Persuaded by claims that visceral feelings would prompt Southern whites to dismantle their school systems, legislators stripped the Civil Rights Act of educational language before passing it. In the pursuit of national fellow feeling, they decided, it mattered less for students to encounter difference and more for them to have a similar institutional experience. In the sections that follow, I first detail the antebellum development of "mingling" discourses, their adoption by Black reformers, and the visceral rhetorics white opponents deployed to reject them. In 1872, Sumner and other Radicals posited educational mingling as a centerpiece of how civil rights legislation would alter feelings of racial prejudice. But as policymakers developed their educational arguments between 1874 and 1875, Congress discarded this method of mingling while affirming the common school's centrality to sectional reunion.

In the end, the Civil Rights Act debate represented the climax of postwar efforts to shape national education policy. Its outcome further severed the idealistic rhetoric of schooling from thorny policy questions about how fellow feeling would be forged in the flesh-and-blood contexts of actual classrooms. Among late-nineteenth-century policymakers, paeans to schooling thus remained appealing as a panacea for alleviating social hostility even as those policymakers established schools that overtly reinforced racial hierarchies. Reconstruction-era advocates left behind a contradiction that would haunt school reformers for generations to follow. The same schools deemed incapable of changing feelings among Black and white children living mere miles apart were nonetheless imagined as a means of fostering fellow feeling among diverse populations scattered across a vast continent. Schools thought too fragile to overcome local racial hostility were deemed strong enough to unite a nation.

"*ALL* SHALL BE TAUGHT *TOGETHER*": DEVELOPING A METHOD OF MINGLING, 1834-1861

Reflecting on the success of the common school movement in Pennsylvania, reformer James Pyle Wickersham praised the benefits of pedagogical proximity. Prior to the 1830s, schooling in the state was provided through a patchwork of parochial, private, and neighborhood prerogatives. Locales clung to such schools, he said, because they were moored in prejudices of sect and culture inherited from Europe. State common school laws weakened those prejudices. After people "mingled more and more together" in common schools, they abandoned their "customs of exclusiveness," recognizing "that neither sect, nor class, nor race, need stand in the way of the cordial union of all in the education of their children . . . and the moulding of the population into a common nationality."[16] As Wickersham's account suggests, faith in the ameliorative force of mingling played a key role in advocacy for common school reforms. The idea provided an affirmative argument for why states' disjointed schools should be fused into a public, class-neutral, nondenominational system. Yet Wickersham overstated how readily and rapidly community members accepted contact between their children.

A preferred term among reformers, the verb *to mingle* carried ambiguous meanings that reflected the vexing politics of pedagogical contact. The word could mean, as Wickersham implied, "to associate or unite in society or by ties of relationship." But opponents tended to abjure *mingling* as tantamount to *mixing*, going beyond sympathy to dissolve group identities.[17] Especially when reformers sought to extend the method of mingling to race, they collided with the visceral rhetoric of disgust implied by another common definition of the term: "to deprive of purity by mixture; to render impure; to contaminate."[18] As post–Civil War Republicans embraced *mingling* as part of their educational advocacy, they inherited the ambiguities involved in the idea and set the stage for a clash over integrated schools.

By the 1840s, education reformers synthesized various appeals to mingling to defend the common school's role in crafting a harmonious national culture. School leaders often cited an array of social categories of class, birthplace, and religion side by side in a single argument, as in Mann's 1848 annual report: "No child is met on the threshold of the schoolhouse door, to be asked for money, or whether his parents are native or foreign, whether or not they pay a tax, or what is their faith."[19] These rhetorical series tended to include groups reformers perceived as divided through social arrangements that foreclosed contact, such as class, religion, national origin, partisanship, or ethnicity.[20] By producing proximity before these distinctions took full form, schools were thus viewed as capable of preventing (or, more cynically, assimilating away) the artificial distinctions among these categories. Speaking to a group of Wabash College teacher trainees in 1840, prominent school reformer Calvin E. Stowe explained that common schools "bring together children of all ranks in life, of all political parties, and of all religious creeds, give them a common education, make them acquainted with each other, and thereby break down prejudice and alienation, and fit them, when they come to adult years, to feel and act together as a harmonious people."[21]

Schools' intervention in public feeling stemmed from the force of acquaintance at a formative age in the emotional space of the classroom. There, through participation in common experiences under conditions of equality, children would develop a sense of filiation reaching beyond their immediate peers' group identities. As Stowe put it, the school's production of proximity "is of the utmost importance in our nation, which is made up of so many heterogenous elements that must be amalgamated before we can have peace or stability."[22] The school served as a social crucible, a site where sentiments responsible for hostility and division could be forged into a more encompassing national feeling.

For the free Black community nearest the center of New England common school reform, the rhetoric of mingling provided one tool in their efforts to gain fuller recognition as citizens. Between 1844 and 1849, Black citizens in Boston petitioned the city's School Committee for the dissolution of the Black-only Smith School and the admission of its pupils to the same public schools as white students.[23] Invoking proximity as a means to foster sympathy, the petitioners argued that separate schooling "strengthens a feeling of prejudice between white and colored children, while [the school's] abolition will foster a regard for each other."[24] Their effort reached the Massachusetts Supreme Court in *Roberts v. Boston* (1849), in which Black attorney Robert Morris and Sumner, at the time a rising civil rights advocate, collaborated to challenge racial segregation.[25] As a proponent of Mann's reforms, Sumner understood embodied interaction as key to common schools' intervention in civic life. As he insisted to the Massachusetts court, "It is a narrow perception of [the common schools'] high aim, which teaches that they are merely to furnish an equal amount of knowledge to all, and, therefore, provided all be taught, it is of little consequence where, and in what company. The law contemplates not only that all shall be taught, but that all shall be taught together. . . . Prejudice is the child of ignorance. It is sure to prevail where people do not know each other."[26]

Sumner's remarks did not focus exclusively on race. He feared that granting the School Committee the power to exclude students based on race could undermine the whole method of mingling. If the committee separated Black and white students, he argued, they could also build "a separate school for Irish or Germans" or divide Catholics from Protestants or Protestants from one another; they could divide rich from poor or children whose parents held different occupations. Allowing racial separation would, in short, threaten "the grand fabric of our Common Schools . . . where, at the feet of the teacher, innocent childhood should come, unconscious of all distinctions from birth."[27] For Sumner, the question of school integration in *Roberts v. Boston* went beyond promoting racial equality. It also implicated the potential of public schooling as a mode of social reform.

By counting race among those categories schools must bring together, Morris and Sumner developed an argument soon taken up by other Black communities fighting for educational opportunities. To be sure, Black leaders vigorously debated integration, recognizing disadvantages to sending children to schools where white teachers and pupils would likely treat them as inferiors. Nonetheless, the proceedings of Black conventions in the late 1840s and early 1850s also showcased considerable support for educational mingling as a principle.[28] For some conventiongoers, support for integration stemmed from a sober awareness that separate Black schools, no matter how effective, would be regarded as inferior by whites and thus provide whites a way to legitimize future civic exclusions.[29] Others advocated that Black people needed to either fight for integrated schools or assert full autonomy over their own institutions, rejecting any school "which the malignant and murderous prejudice of white people [have] gotten up exclusively for colored people" as a space that would instill feelings of inferiority and degradation.[30] A subset of convention participants agreed with Bostonians' more optimistic view that mingling could promote feelings of interracial sympathy and erode logics of caste.[31] Some even argued that integrated schools could eliminate the prejudices that arose from a lack of mutual contact between Black and white people—what social reformers of the era called "colorphobia."[32] Leaders of the 1849 Colored Convention in Ohio, for example, marshaled the language of feeling to explain their opposition to separate schools: "In children thus divided by law, the most Satanic hate is likely to be engendered. . . . What feeling the school-room fosters appears in after life in the shape of a monster called law."[33] For these Black leaders, schools represented a key node in a cycle of emotional reproduction: hateful laws sanctioned separate schools, which led to prejudiced adults, who enacted hateful laws. Integrating schools could bring an end to that cycle.

The visceral rhetorics of white racism rapidly emerged as an obstacle to activists' efforts to include race in the rhetoric of educational mingling. As Jenell Johnson explains, visceral rhetorics argue for the protection of physical and social bodies by "gestur[ing] toward an *intensity* of feeling." Such rhetorics establish limits to what emotional communities accept, purporting to "reveal a primal truth outside of language, culture, or history" and thus beyond the scope of reason.[34] Nineteenth-century white Americans commonly spoke of racial prejudice as residing deep beneath the skin. Even abolitionists such as preacher Benjamin Parham Aydelott used such language, characterizing racial prejudice as a "deeply-seated dislike" welling from a "fountain of bitterness within us."[35] Framing prejudice in similarly visceral ways, opponents of racial mingling cited raw perceptions of smell, taste, and touch as proof of innate and unalterable feelings immune to persuasion or institutional reform.[36] In this way, Johnson observes, visceral rhetorics often allow communities to exert their "collective visceral feelings of vulnerability and fear" as "self-evident rationales for policy."[37] When Massachusetts Supreme Court chief justice Lemuel Shaw upheld segregation in the *Roberts v. Boston* decision, he reasoned that the "deep-rooted prejudice" of race decried by Sumner "is not created by law, and probably cannot be changed by law."[38]

Yet even as critics portrayed white prejudices as too visceral to change, they also paradoxically treated classroom contact as a unique threat to those prejudices. Critics of racial mingling frequently charged that school integration would lead to what one Boston editorialist termed "the matrimonial amalgamation of the Saxon and Negro races."[39] This appeal evoked white readers' fear and disgust regarding interracial sex, thus reinforcing a visceral sense of racial separation as self-evident and natural.[40] At the same time, the argument tacitly accepted that schools could indeed erode children's supposedly innate racial prejudices, leading not only to feelings of sympathy but even romantic and sexual relationships. Ironically, fear that schools might erode prejudice reinforced segregationists' conviction regarding that prejudice's untouchable depth.

"A SENTIMENT OF FRATERNITY": RECONSTRUCTION AND RACIAL MINGLING, 1867-1872

During and after the Civil War, rhetorics evoking the depth of white emotional resistance continued to pose an obstacle to integration.[41] Despite the escalation of visceral racist rhetorics, a small but vocal subset of Black leaders extended prewar advocacy for racial mingling into the Reconstruction South.[42] At the multiracial state constitutional conventions mandated under the first Reconstruction Act in 1867, Black delegates in several states argued for integrated schools. In Virginia, outspoken Norfolk activist Thomas Bayne put forth a resolution to forbid schools from excluding any "child, pupil, or scholar ... on account of race, color, or any invidious distinction."[43] In South Carolina, North Carolina, and Alabama, delegates sought similar language for their constitutions. Republicans did not unite behind these proposals, with most white and many Black policymakers considering them too controversial to pursue. Nonetheless, these delegates achieved a crucial victory, staving off efforts to explicitly require school segregation, leaving the question open for future legislative debate.[44]

The boldest advocacy for mingling happened in Louisiana, where a deep Afro-Creole protest tradition had long complicated white supremacist logics of racial segregation. After the Civil War, activists in this tradition took to the pages of the Black-owned *New Orleans Tribune* to defend school integration and refute the racial logics whites cited to rationalize feelings of fear and disgust.[45] Extending the rhetoric of mingling championed at Black conventions before the war, *Tribune* writers connected interracial mingling to national fellow feeling: "We want to see our children seated on the same benches with the white girls and boys, so that every prejudice of color may disappear from childhood, and the next generation be aroused to a sentiment of fraternity."[46] When the Louisiana convention began in 1867, half of its participants were Black; many were likely *Tribune* readers versed in the Afro-Creole protest tradition. By a 71–6 margin, the convention voted to require integrated schools in the state's constitution—the only Southern state to do so during the nineteenth century.[47] In the process, those delegates helped showcase the appeal of mingling as a rhetoric of Reconstruction.

As white Republican figures embraced education as a Reconstruction policy, the question of extending mingling to race vexed them. For influential Congregational minister Henry Ward Beecher, the Civil War underscored more than ever the need for schools to promote "fellowship and common feeling" among children of disparate religions and national origins.[48] Yet when it came to race, he contradicted this view, claiming that "schools should not be forced to have black and white children" until public sentiments evolved to accept that arrangement.[49] Others, inspired by experiments with interracial democracy in the South, accepted racial integration in schools as a way to make abstractions about sympathetic feeling concrete in the public imagination. In the popular lithograph *Reconstruction*, for instance, artist John Lawrence Giles portrayed an integrated school with Black and white children playing peacefully under the banner of "Universal Education" as one of the institutions keys to realizing the transcendent vision of reunion in the image's center (figures 4.1 and 4.2).

By 1870, as more Republicans turned to schools as a unified solution to national discord, some figures began to fold race into the wider rhetoric of mingling.[50] In *Harper's Magazine*, cartoonist Thomas Nast showcased this synthesis as he critiqued a proposal to allow Catholic schools to access a portion of New York's common school fund (figure 4.3). Should the policy proceed, Nast's cartoon warned, the dancing circle of diverse children in the first frame would be fragmented into a "Methodist School," a "German

Figure 4.1. John Lawrence Giles, *Reconstruction* (New York: Bateman, 1867). Lithograph, Prints and Photographs Division, Library of Congress, LC-DIG-pga-01366.

Figure 4.2. John Lawrence Giles, *Reconstruction* [detail] (New York: Bateman, 1867). Lithograph, Prints and Photographs Division, Library of Congress, LC-DIG-pga-01366.

Figure 4.3. Thomas Nast, "Our Common Schools as They Are and as They May Be," *Harper's Weekly*, February 26, 1870, 140.

School," an "Episcopal School," an "African School," and others, with the once-happy children left to brawl in the streets. Though steeped in anti-Catholic paranoia, Nast's image notably took for granted that race belonged alongside religion, language, and national origin as categories the school mingled together.[51] During the 1870s, whether to include race in the method of mingling—or whether to embrace the logic of mingling at all—thus presented a source of tension for Republican members of Congress.

Schools became part of a wider congressional debate over the racial integration of public spaces. Kirt Wilson notes that the 1860s brought about a remarkable shift in Black political and economic life. Within a decade, many formerly enslaved Black Americans gained the ability to join the Union military, relocate from plantations, exert greater autonomy over their labor, pursue education, join political organizations such as the Union League, vote in elections, and run for elected offices.[52] Although Black rights and power remained circumscribed—often in violent ways—the presence of Black people in so many previously forbidden civic realms led to more frequent interracial contact and new resistance to racial hierarchies. With a greater voice in national politics, Black people and their allies increasingly began to interrogate the logics of racial exclusion that denied them access to public spaces. As the most outspoken Radical Republican in the US Senate, Sumner embraced the cause of desegregation first as a stand-alone bill in 1870, then as an amendment to the Amnesty Act of 1872.[53] The legislation expanded Sumner's antebellum appeals from *Roberts v. Boston* to call for equal access to an array of public spaces. Turning once more to the rhetoric of educational mingling, school integration became a cornerstone of his legislative and rhetorical intervention.

For Sumner and his allies, the moment represented a pivotal opportunity to shape the nascent school systems mandated under newly redrafted Southern state constitutions. Yet the moment also presented a fraught political situation. By 1872, Democrats and a breakaway faction of Liberal Republicans coalesced around a revised rhetoric of public feeling. This discourse framed ongoing sectional resentments as the consequence of Republican policy rather than of Southern recalcitrance. Sumner's civil rights bill provided a key rallying point for their critique, a means of synthesizing feelings of white racist backlash, antifederal resentment, and deepening fatigue after a decade of war and Reconstruction. Against this backdrop, Congress considered the fate of racial integration in schools and with it the whole method of educational mingling as a means of generating sympathy across lines of difference.

"ALL COMMINGLE IN THE COMMON SCHOOL": DEFINING POSITIONS ON MINGLING, JANUARY–MAY 1872

The debate over integration happened amid a wider breakdown in the Republican Party's coalition and vision for Reconstruction. Senator Carl Schurz (R-MO) exemplified the shifting politics of many moderate party leaders. In 1865, General Schurz's postwar report of an "absence of national feeling" in the South helped warrant Radical Republican policies to transform the region.[54] By 1872, Schurz had been elected to Congress and chose to blame lingering hostilities between North and South on his own party's "feverish atmosphere of partisan passion and selfishness." Leading a breakaway faction of Liberal Republicans, Schurz argued that Northern policymakers needed to promote "a new era of good feeling" by extending charity, sympathy, and autonomy to the South.[55] Fulfilling those ends meant removing the postwar policies Liberals viewed as inflaming white Southern anger—that is, policies that penalized leaders of the rebellion and safeguarded Black rights. In 1872, Liberal Republicans and Democrats in Congress pursued an amnesty act that would restore political rights denied to Southern insurrectionists under the Fourteenth Amendment. Senator Arthur I. Boreman (R-WV) endorsed the bill to cease "stirring up bad feeling" in the South and to begin "bringing about a better state of feeling" throughout the nation.[56] For amnesty proponents, the solution to hostile feeling was to treat the emotional tensions responsible for war as having died on the battlefield.

Many Republicans believed that calls for amnesty were premature in a region still marred by white supremacist violence and the suppression of Black rights. Anxious about the sympathetic capacities of white Southerners, a subset of Radical legislators expanded the amnesty debate to encompass issues of education and desegregation. Between January and May 1872, legislators debated amnesty alongside Sumner's Supplementary Civil Rights Bill to require integration in a range of public settings, including schools. The debate underscored serious disagreements over whether mingling based on race or any other category of identity was necessary for schools to fulfill their promise of fostering national fellow feeling. Legislators pursued three separate positions on the question of racial mingling in schools. Sumner and other Radical Republicans touted mingling as a necessity for newly established schools to fulfill their promise for promoting public feeling. Conversely, conservatives, among them Senator Thomas F. Bayard (D-DE), claimed that interracial mingling would evoke such visceral hatred and disgust among white constituents that they would refuse to send their children to school; saving the schools, therefore, meant preventing interracial mingling. Finally, moderate Republicans interrogated the logic of mingling itself, aiming to dissociate schools' sympathetic possibilities from any need for pupils to attend heterogeneous classrooms. Taken together, the perspectives outlined during the 1872 debate situated the question of racial integration within schools as a central point of contention in the wider debate over civil rights. Signaling a deepening acceptance of public education as a national priority, all interlocutors emphasized the need to protect common schools as a promising way to facilitate sectional reunion. They differed over whether interracial mingling enabled or subverted that promise.

The Radical Argument for Mingling in Schools, January-May 1872

Long committed to both education and desegregation, Sumner introduced those subjects as part of the amnesty debate.[57] Believing that the restoration of white rebels' political power posed an acute threat to Black inclusion in public life, he proposed a Supplementary Civil Rights Bill as an amendment to the Amnesty Bill in early 1872. Critics accused Sumner of trying to kill the amnesty measure by fusing it with a cause they thought unable to garner a two-thirds majority in Congress. But for Sumner, the issues of amnesty and integration were inexorably linked. If unrepentant rebels were to be enfranchised despite their clear hostility to their Black neighbors, Black Southerners' full participation in social life needed to be protected by federal power. Sumner viewed integration as a long-term strategy to promote Southerners' fellow feeling and national sentiment. He saw mingling in education as a crucial mechanism to undo the hierarchical culture that sowed prejudice throughout the South. True to his common school movement roots, Sumner rejected any attempt to separate education and integration as causes. The aim of a multiracial society united in common feeling demanded that "all commingle in the common school as in common citizenship." To that end, Sumner situated the common school at the center of his advocacy throughout the 1872 debate. Drawing on the same appeals he had made in *Roberts v. Boston*, the senator once more emphasized that common schools had a loftier aim than teaching a curriculum: "Better even than knowledge is a kindly nature and the sentiment of equality." To segregate the newly founded schools of the South would be to open "a nursery of wrong and injustice," a space in which prejudicial feelings could be recapitulated. "If there is any place from which [caste] ought to be expelled," he emphasized, "it is the school-house."[58]

Supporters of school integration insisted on an urgent need to preempt the formation of prejudicial attitudes among children. To make this point,

Sumner quoted from a letter penned by the trustees of Washington, DC's Black public schools: "Children, naturally, are not affected by this prejudice of race or color. To educate them in separate schools tends to beget and intensify it in their young minds, and so to perpetuate it for future generations." Senator John Sherman (R-OH) similarly appealed to the unique emotional impressibility of children. When some of his state's schools desegregated after the Civil War, he recalled, he "feared that the strong instinct of caste, the feeling of prejudice, would make it difficult to get white and black to go to the same school." Yet his fears were soon assuaged: "Boys and girls are much more sensible, and much more logical, and much more tolerant than men and women.... They are generally better humored, generally kinder." Witnessing these results, Sherman believed that Sumner's civil rights measure would "do as much to preserve kindly feeling in the Southern States as the passage of the amnesty bill."[59] In Sherman's view, the assumption that children would meet each other with hostility was itself a product of racial separation. Once that separation ended, so too did the fear.

Like Sherman, Senator Frederick Frelinghuysen (R-NJ) viewed mingling as an avenue to promote sympathetic habits in the South. He opposed amnesty, believing that the "chasm between love and hatred" that divided Union and Confederacy remained unclosed: "I am not entirely satisfied that the sentiment of hatred has yet entirely died out at the South." To support Sumner's measure without voting for amnesty, Frelinghuysen endorsed desegregation as a way to eliminate the "prejudices incident to [Black people's] being associated with slavery" and to ensure that "every one in the land should be taught the value of [the] principles" reinforced by the Thirteenth, Fourteenth, and Fifteenth Amendments. To this end, he identified desegregation of schooling in particular as vital to the bill's aims.[60] Frelinghuysen's arguments linked the question of national reunion to white Southerners' interracial prejudices: establishing fellow feeling between sections would require first eliminating racial prejudice in the South. Sumner, Sherman, and Frelinghuysen viewed mingling as allowing schools to cultivate faculties of sympathy among the young, a requisite foundation to unite the nation in fellow feeling.

For proponents of school desegregation, the defense of mingling entailed more than just eliminating white Southern prejudices and sectional hatreds. The principle of schooling as a mode of promoting fellow feeling was at risk. Echoing Sumner's arguments from two decades earlier, Senator George F. Edmunds (R-VT) stressed that permitting local schools to reject interracial mingling would entail ceding the whole principle of schooling as a site for contact across lines of difference. Should racial segregation be allowed, he said, "you must remit it to every community to say [that] the foreign born shall be taught in one house by one teacher and the native born in another," that Catholic and Protestant children must be separated, or even that the children of Republican and Democratic parents must attend different schools. In other words, Edmunds feared that accepting practices of racial segregation would mean sacrificing the method of mingling altogether, allowing communities to slice and dice student populations "according to . . . prejudices."[61] For Edmunds, granting communities such authority to break up schools would set a dangerous precedent, hastening the nation's religious fragmentation. Committed to a vision of national identity rooted in Protestantism, Edmunds was perhaps Congress's staunchest critic of both the Catholic and Mormon churches. He worried that Pope Pius IX and Brigham Young held undue emotional sway over the loyalties of the population.[62] In his view, mingling in common schools represented the most effective way to redirect Americans' sentiments away from these divisive influences and to instill fellow feeling toward one another. Any erosion of the principle of mingling thus represented a threat to schools' potential to forge fellow feeling.

Vacillating Critiques of Racial Mingling, January–May 1872

Like antebellum critics of racial integration, congressional opponents of Sumner's bill grounded their objections in visceral accounts of their constituents' feelings of prejudice. Democrats were emphatic that white people would find integration "revolting," reacting in the same way as they would to "small-pox or plague in the schools."[63] Opponents claimed that this impulse of disgust had its ground in self-evident emotional responses that no legislation could change. Representative John T. Harris (D-VA) outright rejected the idea of children as blank slates who lacked the prejudices of adults, contending that even white children would rather not hold a party than allow Black children to attend. Bayard elaborated on these appeals to innate disgust, rationalizing that what Bayard labeled "the instincts of a people and race" were too innate to be corrected through law or institutions: "It is not for men as we would wish them that laws are to be made, it is for men as they are, with all their passions and with all their prejudices." He thus asked his Senate colleagues to search their feelings for what they knew, deep down, to be true: they would not allow their "blue-eyed, fair-haired" children to attend desegregated schools.[64] For Bayard, racial prejudice was bone-deep, self-evident, and unassailable by legislation.

Yet even as critics positioned constituents' untouchable prejudices as a reason to reject the bill, they tacitly acknowledged that childhood contact could alleviate such prejudicial feelings. Bayard pivoted to fears that interracial education would work too well at alleviating visceral feelings. "The object of thus bringing the youth of these two races together," he warned, "is to produce the fusion of the races, the amalgamation of the races." He continued, "by beginning early, the minds of children, ductile and impressible, will be overborne . . . and there may be a mingling" that would eventually lead to the formation of "a mongrel race." Similarly, Harris accompanied his claims about children's innate resistance to interracial contact with a vivid imagining of what contact in school would entail: "They sit on the same seat, learn from the same book, recite the same lesson, drink from the same cup, and in every respect are as social in their relation as brother and sister."[65] The analogy to a familial relationship belied Harris's claim that children possessed an innate resistance to interracial interaction. The school could, in fact, lead children to recognize one another in a manner akin to siblings—and he feared precisely that prospect. For both Bayard and Harris, schooling opened the possibility of a future in which racial distinctions ceased to structure social hierarchies. Paradoxically, that sense of possibility deepened the conviction that fears of interracial mingling had an innate, visceral basis.

Despite such vacillating premises, these critiques of interracial mingling in schools still cited the visceral, unassailable nature of white prejudices as a basis for objecting to the bill: the racial resentments of white constituencies ran too deep for schools to transform through law. Worse, Radical insistence on interracial mingling would backfire, deepening white resentments and causing schools to be shuttered altogether. As Senator Francis Blair (D-MO) put it, the "prejudice against mingling the colored and white children together" would drive "hundreds and thousands" of white children from schools. Though this departure would be voluntary for white families, Blair suggested, the outcome was predictable enough that passing Sumner's bill would amount to Congress willfully "depriving" those children of an education. Worse, according to Blair, the bill would become a "source of agitation and source of antipathy" that would further inflame white Southerners' anger at the federal government and would thus widen rather than narrow the schisms in public feeling.[66]

Democrats were not alone in invoking white backlash as a reason to resist integrating schools. Senator James L. Alcorn (R-MS) claimed that his judgment was informed by the words and deeds of his Black constituents in Mississippi. Both in their efforts to pass the state's constitution and as legislators, he argued, Black voters and their representatives had considered and rejected integrated schools. They did so out of a sober recognition of the depth of white prejudice: "You may say to the passions of the people 'lie down,' but they will not." Claiming to act on behalf of their interests,

Alcorn stressed that the racially separate schools in his state would continue "joyously" as long as they were not "interfered with" by laws mandating integration.[67] Critics of the Supplementary Civil Rights Bill portrayed white resistance as an inevitable reaction that could dismantle the whole postbellum project of common school education.

This framing allowed policymakers who had long critiqued common school movement rhetoric to revise their relationship to the idea of public education. Critics of racial mingling could reposition themselves as the political actors protecting nascent school systems from Radical Republican policies. Invoking the idealistic rhetoric of common school reformers, Bayard contended that his fellow senators had spoken "a great deal upon the importance of education [as] a great moral lever in this country" and as "the universal panacea for every wrong, moral, political, and religious." Given Republicans' paeans to the common school, he was shocked that at such a pivotal, fragile moment they would enact a policy sure to drive white pupils away.[68] Considered alongside Bayard's prior objections to the federal Bureau of Education and an array of other education policies, these remarks read as sarcastic attempts to impugn his rivals as hypocrites. Though disingenuous, Bayard's appeal nonetheless underscored that many of his Republican rivals had invested the common school with deep political hopes that entailed far more than eliminating racial prejudice. Identifying a wedge in Republican educational rhetoric, Bayard found a way to pit the "panacea" of education against the supposed disruptiveness of integration. Many other critics of integration would follow him down this path over the next three years, embracing the idealistic rhetoric of common school reform to frame civil rights as a threat to educational ideals.

Attacks on the Principle of Mingling, January-May 1872

While most critics of the Supplementary Civil Rights Bill cited visceral resistance to racial integration, some adopted a different tactic: interrogating mingling itself. Sympathetic to the aims of the Liberal Republican movement, Senator Orris S. Ferry (R-CT) sought the policy approach least likely to incite partisan tempers in the short term.[69] While he supported common schools and their value to reunion, he disagreed with Sumner's insistence that pupils of different backgrounds needed to learn side by side to promote fellow feeling or equal rights: "It is nonsense, sir, to talk of the necessity of educating youth in the same building in order to give them equal facilities, advantages, immunities, rights." Ferry believed that his colleagues had reversed the relationship between education and the alleviation of prejudice.

If forced together with Black pupils too early, Southerners would reject schooling outright. But if educated first, white pupils' anti-Black prejudices would eventually fade away: "Cultivate the feelings, educate the prejudices, if need be, of the people of the South for another generation," he explained, "and the time will come" for school integration.[70] Ferry's remarks implied that Southern racial prejudices could be eliminated through education even if Black and white children lacked contact in the classroom. The elimination of prejudice was contingent not on proximate contact with difference but on the inculcation of enlightened attitudes through curriculum.

In addition to interrogating the necessity of mingling, other members of Congress questioned whether Republicans like Edmunds truly saw the principle as universal. Senator Eugene Casserly (D-CA) drew on his experiences debating Republicans in his home state to make that case. In California, Republican politicians often wrangled over how and whether to confer legal rights on Black people without also extending them to the state's far larger populations of Native Americans and Chinese immigrants.[71] Like most Democrats of the era, Casserly held a less complicated view: extend legal rights to none of the three groups. Used to decrying double standards in Republican policy, he interrogated the Republicans' selective expectations about mingling. Casserly noted that when slaveholding Cherokee, Chickasaw, and Choctaw peoples in Indian Territory had to accept the Thirteenth Amendment, they were permitted to set aside separate land and schools for those who had been emancipated.[72] Likewise, he alluded to President Ulysses S. Grant's "Peace Policy," which separated Native Americans until they were deemed capable of assimilation into white society.[73] In both cases, Republicans had favored separation rather than integration in Native American education. As Casserly explained, "The policy of having mixed schools, of drawing closer and closer the association of the negro with the white people, does not seem to be the policy which it is thought proper to pursue toward the Indians . . . nor even toward the negroes and the Indians."[74] In critiquing Republicans' inconsistency, Casserly drew attention to how Republican advocacy for universal education tended to rest on racialized distinctions. Proponents of the Supplementary Civil Rights Bill's educational language viewed the common school as a route to a multiracial democracy but did not see all groups as yet capable of taking their first steps onto that pathway.

In the final month of debate, opponents of the Supplementary Civil Rights Bill began to articulate their version of the role that schools—even segregated ones—could play in promoting sympathetic feelings. On May 9, 1872, Ferry called to amend the bill and strike its language regarding schools. Echoing the localist opponents to the Hoar Bill over the previous two years, he staked out a position that was more rather than less devoted to common schooling as instrumental to the formation of fellow feeling. He described schools in his home state of Connecticut as "the dearest object to the hearts of the people" and "the great preserving influence of the community" and attributed this heartfelt conviction to local residents' stake in the generation of the school. To "attach the hearts of the people to [schooling] by power from the outside" could only foster resentments and "endanger the whole system."[75] Like Bayard and other critics of the Supplementary Civil Rights Bill, Ferry believed that federal officials needed to respect local whites' feelings of disgust. Further, he situated these white objections as not just a visceral feeling of racial resentment but also a deeply established emotional tether to schooling as a central element of communal identity. Disgust and hate toward the other could be reframed as love for the sanctity of the neighborhood school.[76] Implicitly, that love of the school as an institutional formation was also not restricted to Ferry's hometown. The school could be re-created in any community where that institution organically sprang up and it could do so with the same intensity of love. Even if communities never knew each other—even if they willfully chose not to know each other—they could still share the conviction that schools provided an emotional anchor, a common attachment, a basis for sympathy across wide expanses.

The Demise of the Supplementary Civil Rights Bill, May 1872

Although Ferry's attempt to strike the school clause narrowly failed, opponents continued to isolate schooling as one of the bill's most controversial and emotion-laden provisions. The fate of the school desegregation clause and Sumner's response to it underscored the emotional investments legislators had made in schools and mingling as an approach. In the dead of night on May 21, 1872, with many legislators, including Sumner, absent from the floor, opponents to the school clause initiated a vote on the Supplementary Civil Rights Bill. Over objections from Sumner's allies, those present narrowly passed an amendment that weakened the bill and removed language regarding juries and schools. Informed of the vote, Sumner rushed back to the Senate chamber, chastising his colleagues for "adopt[ing] an emasculated civil rights bill, with two essential safeguards wanting." He was apoplectic that "the spirit of caste will receive new sanction in the education of children."[77]

With Sumner present, the Senate passed the Amnesty Bill with the weakened version of the civil rights measure attached, but not even the watered-down civil rights bill survived final negotiations in the House.[78] And while Sumner lamented the demise of every facet of the bill, he became most emotional when he spoke about Congress's failures to secure access to public education on equal terms. On his deathbed two years later, he confided to Hoar that Republican failures to affirm a national commitment to equal education had left Sumner "so overcome by his feelings that he burst into tears and left the Senate Chamber."[79]

Sumner was not alone in drawing on the language of feeling to describe the stakes of education policy. By the time the Senate voted in favor of Southern amnesty, both supporters and opponents of Sumner's measure had ascribed a deep emotional valence to schooling as an institutional cornerstone of sectional reunion. Sumner and other Radicals continued to fight for education legislation as a stand-alone bill. They returned to the question of civil rights during the next session of Congress, when they were joined in their advocacy by several of the nation's first Black legislators. By the end of that debate, Congress had affirmed its faith in schooling as a form of sectional amelioration but had also dismissed mingling as a vital element of that faith.

"ONENESS OF FEELING AND SENTIMENT": DISCARDING MINGLING FROM THE CIVIL RIGHTS ACT DEBATE, 1874-1875

When the Forty-Third Congress convened for its first session in December 1873, the Republican majority faced a set of deepening political challenges. Three months earlier, the nation's railroad, banking, and insurance industries had collapsed, triggering a protracted economic depression that exacerbated class, regional, and racial divides within the Republican coalition.[80] Meanwhile in the South, Democrats stoked white supremacy and engaged in violence to wrest control of state governments from Republicans and oust Black politicians.[81] As a consequence of the Amnesty Act, many Democrats who had openly supported the rebellion returned to Congress with an aim of dismantling what remained of Reconstruction. Amplifying the Liberal Republicans' rhetoric of rapid reconciliation, former Confederate vice president and current US representative Alexander Stephens (D-GA) and others insisted that "the passions and prejudices which attended the conflict are fast subsiding and passing away," obviating any need for further federal action in the South.[82]

Yet even amid a racist backlash, a faltering economy, and a fragmenting party, many Republicans recognized that abandoning Reconstruction would mean sacrificing Black political rights. Although the Civil Rights Bill had failed to pass in 1872, many continued to insist on its reconsideration in the next Congress. With Sumner's health failing, Representative

Benjamin Butler (R-MA) emerged as the bill's most energetic advocate. His position was galvanized by the powerful testimony of the nation's first Black members of Congress, including Representatives Robert Elliott (R-SC), Joseph Rainey (R-SC), and Richard H. Cain (R-SC), whose embodied presence on the House floor constituted a powerful argument for racial equality.[83] The bill was reintroduced in December 1873 and debated intensely for the first half of 1874.

Once again, the Civil Rights Bill's clause requiring integrated public schools became its most intensely contested provision as well as part of a deeper interrogation of where schooling fit into visions of national reconciliation. As the debate opened, a flurry of white Southern Democrats seized the narrative to warn that the bill would provoke a visceral white backlash that would destroy the region's school systems. Staking a claim to education as a policy issue, they framed themselves as protecting a fragile system that would be instrumental to processes of sectional reconciliation. Meanwhile, Republicans struggled internally over whether to include education in the legislation. Some, like Senator George S. Boutwell (R-MA), insisted on mingling as instrumental to the formation of a nation sharing sympathies and republican values. Yet others took the South's threats seriously, wrangling over whether removing the education clause would undercut the party's wider educational vision or the aims of the Civil Rights Bill as a whole. For Black legislators, the course of debate and national politics forced a difficult choice between adherence to mingling in principle or preserving education as a space for the assertion of Black pride and dignity. Facing the threat of losing a vote on the entire Civil Rights Bill and the specter of white backlash against public schools, both Black and white Republicans ultimately compromised and removed the school clause. In doing so, they rejected the idea of mingling as part of education's intervention in public feeling.

The Democratic Party's Visceral Educational Blackmail, January–June 1874

Beginning in early January 1874, Democrats centered the visceral depth of white prejudice to portray the Civil Rights Bill as a threat to Southern schools. Harris initiated this argument, insisting that white Southerners' resistance to education was grounded in "a natural prejudice, a prejudice that God himself placed in the hearts of the southern children and the southern people." Such bone-deep feelings could not be expelled, and white parents and children would respond by simply refusing to attend schools. Harris cited a letter from William H. Ruffner, Virginia's superintendent of public instruction, warning that the passage of the Civil Rights Bill would "immediately wipe out, or practically destroy, the public school system of Virginia." Much as Bayard had in 1872, Harris recognized the civil rights bill as providing Democrats an opportunity to claim the mantle of education. Shifting blame for destroying schools away from Virginia's population and onto federal policymakers, Harris accused Republicans of a "driv[ing] the poor children of Virginia and the South from the public schools, expelling the little orphans with fair hair and blue eyes, because they have been taught by God and their mothers that colored children are not their equals." Linking the innocence of (white) children to the fragility of the system, Harris's argument positioned him and his fellow Democrats as protecting the schools from a Republican Party with no regard for innate sentiment. Harris also framed his party as more committed to the cause of national fellow feeling: "The people of my state and its representatives desire to have partisan and factious feeling buried."[84] To bury hostility, Harris counseled respect for prejudice.

To claim the mantle of protector of common schools, Harris and his fellow Virginia Democrats rewrote the state's recent education policy history. Most notably, they claimed that in 1870, the state's conservative-majority legislature—a short-lived coalition of Democrats and disgruntled Republicans—enacted a separate-but-equal common school bill six years earlier than the Radical Republican–approved state constitution required. The result, Harris insisted, was "a free-school system in actual successful operation, which baffles competition anywhere in this country."[85] Harris's narrative ignored the pressure Republicans in Congress exerted to ensure Virginia's conservatives adhered to the state constitution's education provisions. Harris also elided Ruffner's struggles to persuade conservatives to adequately fund the system or support education for Black pupils.[86] Virginia's Democrats were strategic in making these omissions. They recognized the political benefits of pivoting on the issue to galvanize opposition to the Civil Rights Bill. The nascent and segregated school system had already proven popular in the state.[87] That popularity created an opening in which Harris could frame his opposition to the Civil Rights Bill in terms not strictly of deep prejudice but also of love for an institution now regarded as vital to the vaunted goal of sectional reunion. On this point, Harris noted that Thomas Jefferson had consulted with John Adams when designing the University of Virginia, lamenting that policymakers from Massachusetts, "the descendants of Adams," now "come here and seek to break up that institution" by integrating it.[88] Invoking the two former presidents' famed friendship as a synecdoche for interstate relations, Harris's anecdote implied that a future path to national sympathy would entail educational collaboration—without any discussion of racial mingling.

Harris's arguments signaled the Democratic Party's approach to schools throughout the debate. Between January and June 1874, legislators from ten different states echoed Harris's reasoning.[89] They began from the premise that white racism emanated from unalterable emotions rooted in human nature—that "the feeling, the prejudice, the repugnance are universal."[90] This claim frequently morphed into the contradictory position that by fostering "familiar contact," educational mingling would defeat prejudice, "break down the distinctions set up by nature itself," and promote interracial sex and marriage.[91] Ironically, the prospect that prejudices would break down was cited as a reason to respect their permanent inviolability.

The purported consequences of disrespecting such deep feelings would be dire. Should Congress pass the Civil Rights Bill, Representative Milton J. Durham (D-KY) warned, they "will have aroused and embittered the feelings of the Anglo-Saxon race to such an extent that it will be hard to control them." Those uncontrollable feelings would spell the end of the South's fledgling school systems—the equivalent, Representative Roger Q. Mills (D-TX) suggested, of the Black child "enter[ing] a white school like a bombshell, and blow[ing] up the whole concern." Rather than a salve for hostile feelings, Democrats contended, education would become a site of schism. Senator Thomas Norwood (D-GA) argued the bill would "make a battle-ground of the public schools, or drive the poor away from their doors"—effectively reopening the "chasm" of war. In the process, the Republicans would reveal their desire to drag out the acrimony of war as long as possible, pitching measures intended, according to Senator Lewis V. Bogy (D-MO), "not to abate, but to increase, the sectional animosities and race antagonisms" that beset the postbellum republic.[92] In short, Democrats presented a unified argument that (ingenuously or not) portrayed the common school as a public good and ameliorative force that racial integration would destroy.

Republicans countered their rivals' supposed investments in public schools, attempting to correct the historical record. Responding to the recurring argument that Southerners would sooner dismantle their schools than allow racial mingling, Butler scoffed, "'Break up the common school system of the South!' Why, sir, until [Northern Republicans] sent the carpet-baggers down there you had not in fact a common-school system in the South." At stake for Republicans was not merely credit for the popular institution they championed but also whether to believe Southern Democrats' claims to have embraced public schooling as a national project. Representative William Stowell (R-VA) noted the irony that in the name of protecting schools, members of the Virginia General Assembly had openly threatened "that if the Congress of the United States dare to pass the civil-rights bill now under consideration they will close every public school in the State of Virginia." Love for the common school system seemed incompatible with treating that system as an object of legislative blackmail. Yet critics of the Civil Rights Bill saw no hypocrisy in their position. As Representative Ephraim K. Wilson (D-MD) argued, "Destruction of the public-school system of the South would not be the result of spite or retaliation" but would constitute "a spontaneous outgrowth of the principles of human nature."[93] In this way, Democrats used the appeal to innate, visceral prejudice to shield themselves from claims that they did not value schools. Democrats thus placed Republicans in the unfamiliar position of defending their party's specific vision for public schools rather than the principle of public schooling itself.

Republican Schisms over Mingling, January-June 1874

Whereas Democrats crafted a united message, Republicans wrangled over whether integrated schools were necessary for the party's vision for civil rights and education. With Sumner on his deathbed, responsibility for defending mingling largely fell to Boutwell, who had succeeded Mann as the Massachusetts secretary of education, adopting the famed reformer's arguments for bringing together children of disparate backgrounds in school.[94] Though Boutwell had not been outspoken regarding racial integration before the Civil War, during the Civil Rights Bill debate he had echoed Sumner's view that separating students by race would "rob [the] system of public instruction" of a vital pedagogical feature. Education could fulfill its sympathetic mission only if communities "bring together in public schools, during the forming period of life, the children of all classes, and educate them together." By fostering sympathetic relations among children of different identities in a local community, schools would also build children's capacity to imagine themselves as part of a national community of fellow feeling. Mingling would teach children "ideas as to government and the institutions of the country" and "remove the prejudices which exist between persons of different races and different colors, and substitute the idea of human equality."[95] For Boutwell, the schools' influence on public feeling could not be separated from classroom contact between children.

Unlike Sumner in 1872, Boutwell did not find himself flanked by other senators in making the case for mingling, although many legislators shared his commitment to integration and several House members argued for the principle. Making Boutwell's abstractions concrete, legislators cited examples of integration in New Orleans and elsewhere to contest Democrats' apocalyptic portrayal of mingling's potential consequences for schools. Likewise, several

Black members of the House carried forward the integrationist message of the antebellum colored conventions, aligning themselves with Boutwell.[96] For the most part, though, Boutwell found himself isolated. Even defenders of the school clause seldom went as far as Boutwell in defending mingling.

Most Republicans took seriously the prospect of white backlash, opting for a narrower interpretation of the Civil Rights Bill's implications for schools. After listening to Democrats' portents of ruined school systems, Senator Timothy Howe (R-WI) made his feelings clear: "I hear the threat, and I admit I am afraid." He questioned whether the potential gains to be made through students' classroom interactions were worth the political risks should the South indeed abandon public education. He disagreed with Boutwell "that it was necessary to mingle [children] in the school-houses, in order that they might there unlearn this prejudice which separates one color from the other." Howe simply did not believe that the political problem of transforming prejudice belonged with public schools. Senator William M. Stewart (R-NV) similarly argued that "no political consideration can make me vote in a manner which I fear will deny to any child the right to be educated." If a "great moral idea" was at stake in the debate, he argued, it was not racial integration but "education, and nothing else."[97] Deferring to the visceral feelings of white Southerners, these Republicans began to distance themselves from mingling.

Republicans consequently began to argue for a narrower reading of the school clause. Frelinghuysen, an outspoken proponent of Sumner's desegregation views two years earlier, adopted a far less radical position in 1874. In his interpretation, the Civil Rights Bill did not bar states from separating schools based on race but merely affirmed that Black pupils could attend white schools and vice versa if they so wished.[98] This weakened view of the bill's intent would likely make segregated schools the norm through most of the nation, with only rare students seeking to exercise the right to cross racial boundaries. Fretful about white backlash against schools and fearing for their electoral prospects, most of the Civil Rights Bill's proponents adopted this interpretation as the debate unfolded.[99] In the process, they also began to abandon the idea of mingling as a necessary element of schools' emotional intervention.

While some Republicans committed to a weakened version of the school clause, others more explicitly contested the connection between racial mingling and education's potential. The most outspoken figure to take this position was Senator Aaron Sargent (R-CA), who sought to amend the Civil Rights Bill to permit separate schools as long as they were "equal in all respects."[100] Whereas Boutwell treated mingling and education as inseparable parts of the same idea, Sargent dissociated the two.[101] In his view, arguments for mingling were rooted in "abstract ideas or theoretical principles" rather than "the condition of the times." In actual, lived reality, Sargent argued, integration offered "doubtful advantages" while stirring "the irresistible passions of mankind" against the public schools. For Sargent, education could proceed to secure the nation's future even if students did not come into contact with peers from other backgrounds. "The education of the coming generation" was "more important to the people of the United States, to its future, to the future of its institutions" than any other policy. Education's potential was precisely the reason to reject racial integration: "I think it is more important to the colored race and to the white race that the means of education which are now being extended throughout this country . . . shall not be overthrown."[102]

For Republicans who had embraced education as a vehicle for national reconciliation but feared the political fallout of integration, Sargent's appeal offered a compelling model. Further weakening the link between education and integration, Sargent stoked resurgent Republican anxieties about the Catholic Church. Integrated schools might grant Catholics a powerful argument in their "inveterate and determined assaults upon the common-school system."[103] Earlier common school reformers had cited the prospect that Catholics might break up the common school system as an argument in favor of mingling as a universal principle applicable across lines of religion, class, national origin, and race. Now the same fears led Sargent to reject mingling outright as a necessary facet of children's educational experiences. Inverting Sumner's formulation, Sargent argued that similar institutional experiences rather than engagement with other students would foster fellow feeling.

Black Representatives' Dilemma, January 1874-March 1875

As white members of Congress entertained removing education from the Civil Rights Bill, the nation's first Black Representatives negotiated their own educational priorities. While their opinions differed on the school clause, they all understood education—of Black and white people, preferably together—as essential to civil rights. Challenging Southern Democrats' visceral rhetorics, they advocated pedagogical mingling as a way to strike at white prejudice before it could solidify in adulthood. Representative Josiah Walls (R-FL) insisted that the supposedly immutable disgust of white people was in fact a "baseless prejudice" rooted in "the rotten dogmas of the past." Rather than ignite a backlash, "to open the common schools" would "destroy the prejudices which stand in the way of" Black advancement. Mingling would preempt the passing of prejudices from one generation to the next. Where pedagogical mingling had been implemented, Rainey explained, schools had "quieted apprehensions, and contributed largely to remove fears and annihilate that prejudice which has been declared upon this floor should be fostered and respected." Rather than defer to prejudices as natural, Congress needed to adopt "the aim of making more complete the destruction of this uncharitable sentiment" by opening "the public schools to all."[104] For Walls and Rainey, hatred and disgust were not immutable but could be changed through contact and claims to the contrary were a fiction devised to legitimate the white supremacist hierarchy.

On a deeper level, Black legislators recognized that interracial mingling in schools could promote a future polity in which Black and white people shared in community of fellow feeling. Each day in the House, Black legislators embodied the idea that the physical presence of difference could counteract and rebuke prejudice. When the Civil Rights Bill debate commenced, they watched Elliott boldly refute Stephens in a physical enactment of political equality.[105] In the schoolroom, children would encounter similar dynamics of flesh-and-blood equal participation at a more impressionable age. Cain summarized mingling as a force for producing a community bonded by fellow feeling: "It is . . . a law of education to assimilate, to bring together, to harmonize discordant elements, to bring about oneness of feeling and sentiment, to develop similarity of thought, similarity of action, and thus tend to carry forward the people harmoniously."[106] For Cain, the classroom could instill sympathy across lines of race, not merely eliminating white prejudice but preparing all pupils for a future of concerted action as members of a shared community.

In arguing in favor of mingling, Black policymakers advanced a more fundamental point about the future role of Black Americans in public life. Just a decade earlier, prominent white Republicans had entertained the idea of Black emigration to Liberia or to an "internal colony" in South Carolina.[107] And in 1872, Democratic members of Congress had printed a committee report portending "either the exodus or the extinction of" Black Americans, who constituted a "disturbing element in the social and political condition of the more powerful race."[108] Many white policymakers viewed Native Americans and freedpeople in the South as two variations on the same "problem," which could be resolved by holding populations at a remove until some future, undefined point when whites decided that these people were ready to assimilate.[109] For Rainey, integrated schooling provided Congress a way to chart another course for Black Americans, one that presumed equality from the start rather than deferring it until some point at which civic worth and "civilization" had been affirmed. "We do not intend to be driven to the frontier as you have driven the Indian," he informed his white counterparts. "Our purpose is to remain in your midst as an integral part of the body-politic. We are training our children to take our places when we are gone."[110] Mingling in schools would produce a reckoning with the reality of a multiracial democracy, ensuring that children would grow up learning and feeling together with other members of their future civic community. Mingling would affirm that Black children would not be relegated to a separate (and, from white people's perspective, inherently lower) tier of education. If common schools were to constitute the path to participation in a civic community, Black people needed to be in those spaces just as they were in Congress.

While Black legislators embraced mingling to promote equality in public life, they also recognized schools as a bulwark for Black people's sense of dignity and self-definition. Throughout debates on the Civil Rights Bill, Blacks challenged white supremacist legislators' assertions about racial inferiority by substituting a hierarchy based on intelligence.[111] Cain invoked education as a way to assert Black people's status, humanity, and competitiveness in a nation that treated them as subhuman. Drawing on the logics of pedagogical pride and shame codified by the recently established Bureau of Education, Cain challenged imputations of Black ignorance. White South Carolinians had imprisoned freedpeople's teachers, outlawed learning, and destroyed Black schools, he reminded Congress. Yet despite these disadvantages, Black children still had a 12 percent higher literacy rate than white children in the state. "Although there is such disparity between us and [white people] so far as relates to education and resources," Cain concluded, "even now we fear not a comparison in the condition of education."[112] In using statistics to set populations side by side, Cain defended Black dignity on terms that white policymakers had begun to accept as a basis for evaluating civic worth. Moreover, he tapped into Black communities' pride in their postbellum educational achievements. Yet in making this argument, Cain and other legislators drew a double-edged sword. They connected judgments of Black worth to a malleable logic of educational inclusion and exclusion, a logic that had already been deployed to restrict their rights to civic participation.

Cain saw no logical contradiction between these appeals to dissolve prejudice through mingling and affirm racial pride through schools. Schooling could both harmonize Black and white pupils and provide Black people with an argument against those who denigrated them. But the debate over the Civil Rights Bill and its electoral consequences placed Cain and other Black legislators' priorities in tension. The first session of the Forty-Third Congress ended without a vote on the bill, leaving the issue of civil rights an open question during the 1874 midterm elections. In those elections, ninety-two seats in the House of Representatives—nearly a third of the body—swung to the Democrats, costing Republicans control for the first time since the start of the Civil War. Many factors influenced the outcome, including economic depression, a spate of political scandals, and Democratic Redeemers reclaiming power in much of the South. But newspapers and political commentators largely placed blame on white racial backlash against the Civil Rights Bill and especially on controversies regarding the school clause.[113]

When Congress reconvened for its lame-duck session in December, Republicans weighed three approaches to schools: a Senate version of the bill requiring full integration, a House Judiciary Committee revision requiring segregated schools to receive equal resources, and a proposed amendment by Representative Stephen W. Kellogg (R-CT) to remove schools from the bill altogether.[114] These options presented Black legislators with a difficult choice. As a cohort, they had a complex set of educational goals: to instill fellow feeling across the nation, to eliminate white prejudice, to foster the conditions needed for multiracial democracy, and to provide Black people with a vehicle for their advancement, pride, and dignity. Now those aims seemed to be in tension with one another. Even if Black Representatives persuaded fellow Republicans to include integrated schools in the final bill, Congress might reject the measure altogether, eliminating any recourse against civil rights violations in many other areas of public life. If these legislators did not insist on mingling, they could attain a guarantee of equal educational resources for Black schools—no small victory with a hostile Democratic House on the horizon and a racist backlash underway at the polls. Yet they would accede to school segregation in federal law and defer to white Southern Democrats' claims about the visceral, insurmountable nature of white prejudice. There had no good options and reached no clear consensus.[115]

On February 3–4, 1875, Cain spoke on behalf of the third option: removing schools entirely from the bill. Lamenting that Congress could not be persuaded of "those higher conceptions entertained by Mr. Sumner," Cain would prefer to have the school language "struck out entirely" over allowing Congress to introduce an "invidious distinction in the laws of this country." Omitting schools from the bill left the issue open to be settled another day. After an electoral drubbing and amid the South's ongoing threats to dismantle schools for white and Black children, an affirmation of mingling in schools seemed a bridge too far for Congress. But Cain still affirmed the vital role of education in promoting Black people's future in civic life. He implored the Democrats ascendant in the South and in Congress, "Instead of reproaching us with our ignorance, establish schools; let them guarantee to us school-houses in all the hamlets of the country; let them not burn them down, but build them up; let them not hang the teachers, but encourage and protect them; and then we shall have a great change in this country."[116]

As Cain pleaded for states support for Black education, he presented it as a national issue that implicated all people. Absent a method of mingling, he cited an alternative conception of education's influence on fellow feeling that was less specific about how schools would instill common sentiments. "The more the people are educated," he said, "the better citizens they make. If you would have peace, if you would have quiet, if you would have good will, educate the masses of the community."[117] Even in places where laws pulled people apart, giving everyone access to schooling would still somehow bring them together in a spirit of goodwill. No more and no less than an expression of hope for what schools might still accomplish, Cain's rhetoric settled on a vision of national education closer to Sargent's than Sumner's.

By the end of the debate over the Civil Rights Bill, most Republicans accepted Cain's compromise position on the question of schools. Before the vote, Butler, the bill's sponsor, agreed that schools should be removed, citing Southern Democrats' warning of white backlash: "There is such a degree of prejudice in the South that I am afraid that the public-school system, which has never yet obtained any special hold in the South, will be broken up if we put that provision into the bill."[118] With Butler's reluctant blessing, the final tally on the Kellogg Amendment to remove educational language was 128 yeas, 48 nays, and 113 abstentions, numbers that reflected Republicans' anxiety over taking either side of the issue.[119] With that outcome, schools would be removed from the bill. Democratic Party objectors had succeeded in driving a wedge between the issues of education and integration.

Several Republicans decried the decision to omit schools from the Civil Rights Bill as blunting its long-term potential and allowing prejudice to fester at its source. "You now propose by this bill to commence at the very foundation of society with the rising generation in your common schools, and implant in the breast of both races a mutual abhorrence and detestation," Representative Julius C. Burrows (R-MI) intoned. Similarly, Representative Charles G. Williams (R-WI) warned that removing schools would dismantle Republicans' hopes of a multiracial democracy. "We sit with colored men in these Halls without prejudice," he observed, "but we teach our little boys that they are too good to sit with these men's children in the public school-room, thereby nurturing a prejudice they never knew."[120] Even if the Civil Rights Bill alleviated the effects of prejudice among adults, it did nothing to prevent such prejudices from taking shape in future generations. The racial problems before Congress would be reproduced for each subsequent legislature. Among future generations, these legislators feared, there would remain an absence of national feeling.

EDUCATION, SEPARATION, AND RECONCILIATION

With the Civil Rights Bill's most controversial language removed, both houses of Congress passed the legislation, and President Grant signed it into law on March 1, 1875. As a symbolic statement of principle by a party whose power had begun to slip, the law was a significant achievement. In theory, it reinforced core ideas embodied in the Thirteenth and Fourteenth Amendments, granting Black people legal recourse against their discriminatory exclusion from numerous public spaces. In practice, though, the bill had limited means of enforcement and did little to intervene in racial discrimination.[121] By 1883, the Supreme Court declared the legislation unconstitutional in a ruling that limited Congress's ability to pass future laws to carry out those amendments.[122] For the bill's most ardent supporters, the biggest disappointment had occurred earlier, when schools were removed. Even if the school clause would have fared no better than the rest of the measure, its omission foreclosed the possibility of integrated schools during a pivotal decade in the establishment of new Southern school systems and circumscribed legislators' ideas regarding schools' power to shape public feeling. Paving the way for a reconciliationist view of schools, the Civil Rights Act debate represented the tragic climax in the broader story of Reconstruction-era education debates.

Since the 1830s, the principle of mingling had animated a pluralistic vision of education that marginalized groups—including postwar Black activists—adapted to their goals. But at a pivotal moment when the nation had begun to coalesce around a conception of education as a mode of sectional reconciliation, Republican legislators abandoned this key tenet of the common school vision. Black civil rights activist, legal scholar, and future US representative John Mercer Langston made this point in an 1874 speech at Oberlin College, his racially integrated alma mater: "Schools which tend to separate the children of the country in their feelings, aspirations and purposes, which foster and perpetuate sentiments of caste, hatred, and ill-will, which breed a sense of degradation on the one part and of superiority on the other, which beget clannish notions rather than teach and impress an omnipresent and living principle and faith that we are all Americans, in no wise realize our ideal of common schools."[123]

The idea of the school as a pluralistic space drawing together children of all identities to inculcate sentimental attachments across lines of difference was at stake in the Civil Rights Act debate. That Congress rejected that idea represented not only a tragedy for civil rights but also a constraint on arguments about what schools could achieve and what feelings they could change.

The visceral prejudices of white people became the outer boundary of national policymakers' educational vision and remained so for eight decades.

The rejection of mingling as a tenet of common schooling had far-reaching implications for education policy discourse, gutting a central principle of the antebellum reform movement. Proponents would no longer argue that Black and white, Catholic and Protestant, and rich and poor children in the same local geographic area needed to develop fellow feeling. Instead, what mattered was that children in the North felt an emotional connection to those in the South and West and that schools would instill a loyalty to the nation that could paper over the resentments and prejudices born of pervasive racial, religious, and economic tensions.

The demise of mingling as a principle almost immediately changed how Congress debated education reforms on other topics, including religion, the issue where appeals to educational mingling had begun. Throughout 1876, members of Congress debated a constitutional amendment proposed by Representative James G. Blaine (R-ME) to ban public funding of parochial schools. For decades, appeals to mingling (however disingenuous) had been central to common school reformers' resistance to separate Catholic education, but the lengthy Senate debates over the Blaine amendment contained no references to pupils learning together as a virtue of stifling the development of parochial schools.[124] Even Edmunds, who during the Civil Rights Act debate had delivered lengthy paeans to the principle that pupils should learn together, made no such claims when expressing his support for the Blaine amendment. Swept up in the anti-Catholic fervor of the 1876 election, Edmunds and other Republicans may simply have dropped the pretense that their views stemmed from anything other than religious animus.[125] But after the Civil Rights Bill debate, it is also likely that arguments for religious mingling in schools too closely echoed appeals for racial mingling, an idea now deemed threatening to the preservation of good feelings throughout the polity.

For Democrats, the outcome of the school clause debate opened an avenue for the party to claim a stake in education. After decades of resisting state-sponsored and taxpayer-funded education, Virginia's Democrats suddenly claimed a zealous commitment to public education. The popularity of the nascent system—established only after Republicans in the US Senate made its creation nonnegotiable—provided Democrats with a means of galvanizing resistance to the Civil Rights Bill as a whole. Likewise, by painting Republicans as seeking to inflame visceral feelings of white anger, Democrats found a way to claim the mantle of educational protection. Southern Democrats' embrace of segregated schooling paved the way for a wider acquiescence to common schools as an outcome of the North's Civil War victory. As with the Reconstruction Amendments, white Southerners accepted the North's legal and institutional changes in principle and then focused on limiting their effects in practice.

The Civil Rights Bill sought to transform the composition of school systems that had only just begun to take shape. In addition, advocates of the bill sought to cement a national vision of common schools as a microcosm of a wider, multiracial public united by sympathies cultivated as children. In the midst of a shift in the national discourse about the best ways to promote fellow feeling, the debate helped to reify a hollowed-out vision of common schooling as a tool of reconciliation. Southerners would accept the institutional structures and assumptions of New Englanders' common school systems, but the Redeemer Democratic governments would define the composition of classrooms, the allocation of resources, and the shape of curricula. Congress settled on this conception of school governance, converging on terms by which education could be elevated to a national priority. But the schools they enacted would not be common in any meaningful sense of the word.

Conclusion

SCHOOLING AND SENTIMENT
Reconciliation and the Limits of Good Feelings

In the aftermath of the Civil War, a subset of Radical Republicans in Congress imagined education as a way to confront an absence of national feeling in the United States. As policymakers crafted transformative constitutional amendments and laws to protect civil rights, education reformers recognized the limitations of law. Constitutional mechanisms to adjudicate conflict and channel passions had been inadequate to avert war; changes to that instrument alone would neither prevent another war nor guarantee the security of Black people freed into the most hostile of contexts. "Character is not changed in a day," Senator Charles Sumner (R-MA) warned in 1865. "That 'Southern heart,' which was 'fired' against the Union, still preserves its vindictive violence. Even if for a moment controlled, who can tell how long it will continue in this mood?"[1] For him and his fellow Radicals, Reconstruction sought a transformation of hearts, of moods, of feeling. But within a decade after the war's end, this bold idea had given way to a reconciliationist rhetoric of education in which schools were conceived as promoting tranquil feelings of love for the nation without reckoning with underlying causes of prejudice, resentment, and anger.

This reconciliationist vision of education played a significant role in the Republican Party's abandonment of Reconstruction and the nation's retreat from protecting Black civil rights. Moreover, legislators' consequent adaptation of the antebellum rhetoric of common schooling not only played a major role in shaping debates about national identity and civic inclusion in the postbellum United States but also continues to severely limit schools' potential to change society today.

"DROWN OUT THE VOICE OF ANGRY PASSIONS": THE FORMATION OF THE RECONCILIATIONIST VISION

By 1877, most members of Congress saw education's role as institutionally reinforcing the reconciliation of North and South, thereby making schools part of what David W. Blight calls "the spirit of reconciliation as a method of forgetting"—a means of selectively refusing engagement with past injustices to preserve sympathetic relations among a privileged white majority in the present.[2] Rather than seeking to change an aristocratic and racist culture, schools would emphasize maintaining feelings of love for the nation while perpetuating hierarchies of class and race.

The pivot to education as a mode of reconciliation aligned with wider shifts in the Republican Party's political philosophy. By the start of the 1870s, the sense of nationalist optimism and hopeful altruism that had underpinned Radical Republicans' efforts began to subside, and a chorus of economic, religious, and political leaders began to pressure the party to scale back the federal presence in the South, cease efforts on behalf of Black civil rights, and forgive those responsible for secession.[3] As white Northern support for Reconstruction waned, Republicans altered their educational approaches in ways that diverged further and further from Radicals' interpretation of the common school tradition. Legislators began to avoid talk of schooling as an overt intervention in Southern culture. Likewise, they shifted their rhetoric to avoid any imputation that education might be used for political ends, especially if those ends entailed enhancing the political agency of freedpeople. An acceptance of schools as fragile spaces easily shattered by politics (particularly the politics of race) dovetailed with a belief that schools ought to soothe public feeling between sections rather than try to alter the social conditions or hierarchies that had generated those hostile feelings.

As the Republican Party discarded Radical education arguments, Southern Democrats became more amenable to the model of taxpayer-funded common schools, a shift that resulted in part from schools' popularity among white Southerners. But Democrats also expressed emotional investments in common schools as a way to rouse opposition to the Civil Rights Bill. With schools established on segregated terms, Democrats could stoke fears that Republican policies aimed to inflame white racial hatreds and destroy a (newly) cherished institution. By 1876, a Democratic National Committee campaign pamphlet touted Southern school systems not as a ruthless imposition by Republicans but as a long-term Southern Democratic project.[4] Alongside acceptance of the three Reconstruction Amendments, Democrats' embrace of Republicans' long-cherished public school policy became a way to signal a symbolic commitment to reconciliation as well as to constrain the role that public education would play in altering Southern life.

Southern Democrats were prepared to accept education policy solely on their own terms, which included the insistence that schools' capacity to promote fellow feeling extended only to the visceral boundary of white hatred and disgust. Democrat Gilbert C. Walker won Virginia's 1869 gubernatorial election using campaign rhetoric intimating that he intended to undercut the education provisions of Virginia's new constitution.[5] Yet just a few months after taking office, he rebranded himself as an advocate of education, taking credit for "one of the most comprehensive and practical free-school laws in existence" and claiming to have implemented it seven years faster than Republicans had required.[6] He later favored federal support for common schools, making that a centerpiece of his 1874 campaign for the House of Representatives.[7] As a member of the House, he proposed a version of the Perce Bill to fund public education through funds generated by selling public lands.[8]

Walker's reconciliationist vision of education departed from the Radicals in a crucial way: he placed an overt and uncompromising emphasis on white supremacy. He hoped that schools could unite "the numerous offshoots of the Caucasian race" in the United States, "melt[ing] together and mold[ing] these diverse elements into one united, harmonious, homogenous people."[9] The conspicuous inclusion of *Caucasian* underscored that idea that not all children would be included in this feeling of harmony and that not all schools would lead to it. The boundaries of civic inclusion in the reconciled republic would be demarcated by whiteness, and schools would not allow those boundaries to be crossed.

This compromised vision of common schooling fostered a shared amnesia about the causes and outcome of the Civil War. By necessity, the Radical Republicans' initial educational vision demanded a thorough reckoning with the sins of slavery and its brutal, bloody consequences for the republic. Forging fellow feeling meant changing how white Southerners were acculturated and subverting the feelings of bitterness toward the Union and hatred toward Black bodies. Calls for education as a mode of sectional reconciliation, conversely, dispensed with acknowledging that history. Speaking in support of Walker's legislation in July 1876, Representative Augustus Cutler (D-NY) portrayed schools as a way of forgetting:

> The people recognize the fact that the war of the rebellion is at an end and that the past is history; they are willing the dead past shall bury its dead; they are anxious that the veil of forgetfulness shall be cast over that unfortunate and unhappy past.... Being thus solicitous

that the past shall be buried, let the children know the present. Teach them the lesson that there is but one country; that that country is but one and indivisible, and never can be separated or torn asunder; ... the innocent prattle of children will drown out the voice of angry passions and sectional strife.[10]

The most dispiriting legacy of Reconstruction-era education debates is that Cutler's call for educational forgetting came to pass. In the classrooms made by Reconstruction, the Lost Cause would be taught and Jim Crow would become cultural common sense. This co-optation of schools' purpose may have facilitated a sort of fellow feeling between Northern and Southern whites, but it did so only by excluding those populations deemed unable to feel as white people felt.

The rhetoric of educational reconciliation reverberated into the next decade, affecting how legislators debated efforts led by Senator Henry W. Blair (R-NH) to pass an educational aid bill. A committed adherent of many of the New England common school movement's ideals, Blair believed that the Constitution's Guarantee Clause implied a right to education.[11] During the 1880s, he fought to obtain US Treasury funds to support state school systems.[12] His bill would have required an equal per-pupil distribution of funds for Black and white children and included strict reporting requirements to hold states to those obligations. In 1890, with Republicans in control of the House, the Senate, and the presidency, Blair believed that his bill would finally become law after three failed attempts.[13]

Blair thought wrong. Several Southern Democrats abandoned the bill, foregoing funds for their states to avoid federal oversight of their schools. For their part, Republican defectors decided that Southerners had proven their desire and ability to support education for both races. Shrugging off the prospect that the South would fail to sustain education for all its citizens, Senator John Sherman (R-OH) said that the region was "making fair and reasonable efforts to educate its illiterates."[14] In the end, Southern Democrats' nominal commitments to education went hand in hand with credulous Republicans' calls to leave the bad feelings of the past behind and allow white Southerners to enact the policies they saw fit. The demise of the Blair Bill closed the door for significant federal education policy until well into the twentieth century and eased the transition to an unequal Jim Crow education system in the South.[15]

Blair's rhetorical task was complicated by Reconstruction-era rhetorical and policy decisions. Members of Congress deferred to traditions of local control, allowing serious contemplation of a national school system to fizzle without a vote. They defined the scope of the Bureau of Education in the narrowest terms, constricting federal authority to the circulation of reports to stoke pride and shame. They offered freedpeople less than a decade of federal support for their schools and downplayed Congress's role in doing so. And they removed school desegregation from the Civil Rights Act of 1875, accepting white disgust as an impenetrable barrier to policy. Congress thus rejected the profound possibilities of the moment, giving subsequent reformers little ground on which to build.

But the tragedy of Reconstruction-era education policy lies not merely in Congress's failure to enact more robust policies but also in its successes, which occurred largely through rhetorical adaptations and innovations. Legislators cemented education as a central theme of national reunion and ensured that public education systems would be established throughout the South. They laid the foundation for the construction of a vast cultural infrastructure for shaping the feelings and ideals of a nation. But they allowed white supremacist governments in the South to fund and administer those schools.

"INDOCTRINATED WITH THE NECESSITY OF PUBLIC SCHOOLS": THE RHETORIC OF EDUCATION AT THE END OF RECONSTRUCTION

By the end of Reconstruction, legislators had accepted many of the guiding ideas of the antebellum common school movement, including the basic institutional structures of the classroom, the view of the classroom as an extension of the domestic sphere, and the idea that schooling should be universally accessible and was a government responsibility to be funded by taxpayer money and coordinated by state superintendents. But they had jettisoned other principles, among them direct federal supervision of education and mingling, and ceded most responsibilities to promote education to actors outside of government.

Untethered from the burdens of defending specific policies, national politicians could posit schools as the solution to a range of social problems without wading into the complexities of policymaking. As with appeals to union and patriotism, appeals to the moral influence of educational institutions became at once a hollow platitude and a way of asserting a commitment to a common value. Espousing support for the common school became a shorthand way for political leaders to espouse a love of the United States. Further, postbellum policymakers discovered in the reconciliationist rhetoric of education a potent way to negotiate questions of school promotion, national identity, and civic inclusion. Although Congress did not craft the rhetoric of education on its own, and its almost exclusively male, white, elite members did not truly represent the nation, their power enabled them to play an outsized role in perpetuating a collection of policy ideas, educational tropes, and assumptions. The emotional logics of legislators' educational rhetoric facilitated the national expansion of public schools while providing policymakers a malleable way to adjudicate questions of civic belonging.

Statistical Shame, Gendered Hope, and the Path to a National System

By 1876, localists embraced the argument that the virtues of common schools were so self-evident, so close to people's hearts, that communities would establish and maintain the institutions without federal requirements. As Senator Theodore F. Randolph (D-NJ) told his colleagues, "So certainly have our people been indoctrinated with the *necessity* of public schools that if every State system were abandoned to-morrow, there would promptly arise a local one" in its place.[16] This argument presented proponents of federal policies with a paradox they would not overcome until the next century. The better federal politicians were at convincing the public that education mattered deeply to public feeling, the more easily localists could claim that the communal desire for schooling negated any need for federal intervention.

Members of Congress dispensed with Radicals' calls for a federal education system but nonetheless articulated a persuasive logic of school reform predicated on the circulation of feelings about education. According to Representative James A. Garfield (R-OH), the circulation of such feelings among local, state, and associational actors provided the basis of a diffuse but "great American system of education."[17] In many ways, Garfield proved correct. As historian Tracy L. Steffes argues, by the early twentieth century, the United States possessed a remarkably cohesive network of schools that spanned every state and that had arisen not through direct federal coordination but through efforts at persuasion and emulation undertaken by state- and local-level policymakers. Despite these origins, the result was "so uniform, both structurally and functionally, that many Americans perceived and spoke of a national 'system' in their midst."[18] In subsequent decades, policymaking through comparison and ranking became a significant way for federal and state governments to persuade local governments to voluntarily adopt policy changes.[19] The logic of emotional influence underpinning the Bureau of Education provided a way to forge a national system where a federal one did not exist.

In the waning years of Reconstruction, logics of seeing and shaming exerted considerable influence over state-level policymakers. For example, the planners of the 1876 Centennial Exposition in Philadelphia sought to showcase post–Civil War reconciliation and progress to a global audience and consequently invited all state-level education leaders to design exhibits showcasing their jurisdictions' educational progress. But Pennsylvania superintendent of public instruction James Pyle Wickersham worried that a side-by-side comparison with European exhibits would cast shame on the United States. After years of "boasting of our systems of free schools," school leaders might embarrass themselves by presenting a disorganized "mass of miscellaneous articles" that revealed the absence of federal leadership.[20] Bureau of Education commissioner John Eaton Jr. addressed these concerns, sending circulars to state superintendents outlining the types of information that should be included. State leaders followed his recommendations, preparing small libraries of school statistics, student work, curricular reports, and other documents selected to impress global education leaders (and of course to outshine other states).[21] The event captured how national ecologies of pride and shame, stoked by and responded to by a federal leader, indirectly motivated uniformity among state policymakers.

In addition, the reconciliationist rhetoric of education amplified the feelings of hope associated with the domesticity of women teachers. Congress invoked such feelings to warrant the renewal of the Freedmen's Bureau, citing a need to protect women teachers and their schoolhouses from surrounding ecologies of white hostility. Throughout these debates, women teachers found themselves in a paradoxical position. Their educational influence depended on their apolitical invisibility—a removal into domestic space from which pupils with proper emotions might emerge. Yet those intimate labors were publicized by policymakers who sought to promote national reforms. Individual teachers thus were engaged in unavoidably politicized work of educating Black children in the South but had to present their work as maternal, intimate, and apolitical. Those contradictions also made the Freedmen's Bureau vulnerable to allegations that teachers had veered into the political realm, impressing radical ideas on their emotionally susceptible pupils.

Even after the Freedmen's Bureau was shuttered and aid associations scaled back their work in the South, the linkage of schooling with maternal feelings continued to shape the national expansion of education. At the Centennial Exposition, Ruth Burritt taught a live classroom of Philadelphia children with exposition attendees in observance (figure 5.1).[22] Relegated to a separate Women's Building by the event's male planners, the "lovely spectacle" of Burritt's classroom nonetheless garnered large audiences and received far more press attention than the data-filled libraries the male superintendents had promoted.[23] Modeling maternal intimacy in a public

Figure 5.1. "The Instruction of Children in the Kindergarten Cottage, Under the Auspices of the Women's Department," in *Frank Leslie's Historical Register of the United States Centennial Exposition, 1876*, ed. Frank H. Norton (New York: Leslie's, 1876), 118.

fishbowl, Burritt's semiprivate teaching had an outsized influence on a swirling national controversy about when to begin children's first years of education. After Reconstruction, teachers continued to occupy this conflicted position, with the tranquil feelings generated in domestic space amplified to promote schools' public intervention.

Literacy, Exclusion, and the Dual Character of Education Policy Rhetoric

By the start of the 1870s, members of Congress recognized Reconstruction as a process that encompassed incorporating not just the South but also the West into a burgeoning national empire.[24] They began to consider public education among the strategies for managing the demographic complexity and conflicting feelings that the incorporation of new territories and states would introduce. As typified by the arguments of Representative William F. Prosser (R-TN), that appeal had a dual character. Education offered a way to align the feelings of populations estranged by race, religion, national origin, and language. Yet the apparent uniformity of education relied on racialized assumptions about feeling that rendered some groups as more educable than others. The rhetoric of education provided policymakers a way to negotiate the felt dimensions of identification and division. Beyond defining *us* versus *them*, education adjudicated who among many *thems* could join *us* and on what terms.

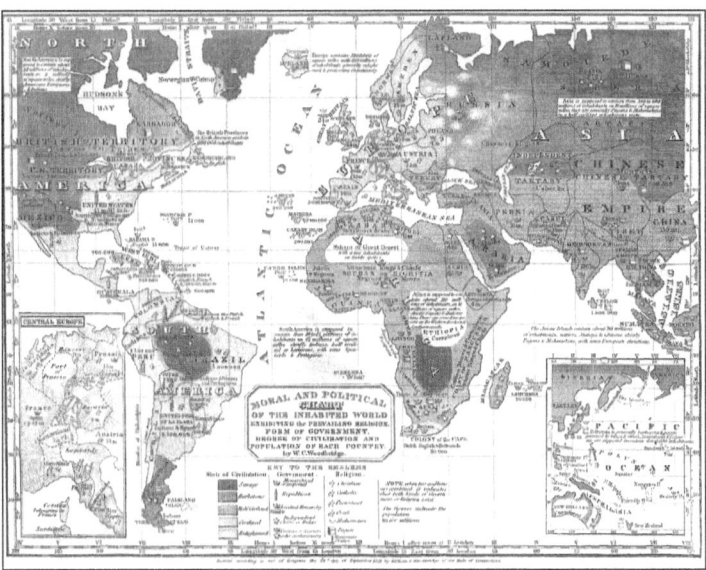

Figure 5.2. William Channing Woodbridge, "Moral and Political Chart of the World," in *Woodbridge's School Atlas: An Improved Edition* (Hartford, CT: Cooke, 1833), 3.

The codification of literacy helped to reinforce the dual character of education. Literacy offered a shorthand way of discerning whether a person had been acculturated to participate in an emotional community. Knowing whether people were literate—however that construct was defined or measured—was understood as a proxy for whether they could manage their feelings in accordance with society's emotional norms. The illusory objectivity of literacy made it a potent tool for maintaining civic boundaries even as legal definitions of citizenship became more inclusive. Once people widely accepted the premise that illiteracy rendered a group a threat to public feeling, only creatively devised and subjectively administered exams would be required to rationalize that group's exclusion from the ballot box.[25] Prominent Republicans in Congress foresaw this possibility during the Fifteenth Amendment debate, proposing language that would bar states from creating educational qualifications for voting.[26] These calls went unheeded, paving the way for Jim Crow literacy exams and efforts to make literacy a condition for immigration to the United States.[27]

An 1875 speech by Representative James Monroe (R-OH) underscored how literacy discourses legitimized racial and hierarchical conceptions of citizenship.[28] Speaking to a meeting of Ohio teachers and school administrators, he recalled examining a map in one of his childhood textbooks that portrayed "the relative enlightenment of the different nations of our planet" through a gradient, ranging from the bright whiteness of America "into the blackness of Africa" (figure 5.2). Decades later, the introduction of literacy

Figure 5.3. Francis A. Walker, "Map Showing the Illiteracy of the Aggregate Population," in *Statistical Atlas of the United States Based on the Results of the Ninth Census, 1870* (New York: Bien, 1874), 29.

as a measurable and visualizable logic reinforced Monroe's long-internalized mental picture of a world shaded by gradations of intelligence. He noted that the 1870 US Census report included a map "intended to picture the relative degrees of illiteracy in different states by darker or lighter shadings" (figure 5.3) and described himself as "startled by the black cloud that rests upon the South."[29] Monroe warned that the lack of public education would leave those darkened portions of the map susceptible to demagogues who would exploit the untamed passions of residents of those areas. The visual grammar of educational shaming—a logic that underpinned congressional arguments for the Bureau of Education—reified the conceptual relationships among race, education, and emotional capacities for civic participation.

As Reconstruction-era education debates reified literacy as an exclusionary tool, they also revealed how logics of emotional impressibility could be invoked in malleable ways to adjudicate which populations could be educated and toward what ends.[30] During the Civil War, missionary groups and members of Congress had treated freedpeople's education as an experiment to prove that Black feeling could be molded for productive economic and sometimes civic participation. Discourses about Black children and adults eagerly seizing educational opportunities circulated widely, grounding hopeful visions of a multiracial republic. Yet with each subsequent expansion of Black political rights, opponents of Black civic inclusion turned the logic of emotional impressibility against freedpeople, raising the specter of their rapid indoctrination into radical feelings and ideas. After the passage of the Fifteenth Amendment, Republicans began to cast doubt on Black capacities for emotional control and to insist that freedpeople needed to prove their worthiness to exercise their new right. Over the next twenty years, white elites who had endorsed Black suffrage reframed that effort as well-intentioned but premature, a privilege bestowed on a population not yet morally, intellectually, or emotionally prepared for it.[31]

After accepting schools as a preparatory space within which future citizens would learn fellow feeling, legislators turned to the question of who would be included in those schools. At stake in the debate over racial mingling was the matter of civic belonging. What did people need to learn to live together, to feel together, to work through ideas and become literate in the company of others? Who would be part of this semiprivate, quasipublic space created to inculcate people into a sympathetic national community? As Black participants in the Civil Rights Bill debate fully recognized, omission of children from this preparatory space would surely warrant their later omission from other forms of civic participation on the grounds that they lacked preparation. That legislators refused to extend the Civil Rights Act of 1875 to include schools exposed the dual character of education. That political choice legitimated whites' visceral feelings as an immovable object around which public policy would have to work. It ratified the view that children could be divided from one another, sorted into hierarchies, and somehow still learn to share a common attachment to the nation. It laid the foundation for children to learn not merely in separate spaces but in divergent ways dictated by their presumed racial capacities. In common schools, white children would learn to be citizens; in colonial and apartheid schools, children on the margins would be taught to subsist and labor until at some ill-defined point generations away they might be deemed competent to join a community of fellow feeling.[32]

THE LIMITS OF GOOD FEELINGS

The tradition of public address scholarship needs to talk about feelings. Despite Ernest J. Wrage's early observation that rhetorical analyses provide "an index to the history of man's values and goals, his hopes and fears, his aspirations and negations," scholars have shied from theorizing the ways that those hopes, fears, and other feelings underwrite public discourse.[33] Beyond traditional approaches to examining pathos in texts, public address scholars have generally abstained from the "affective turn" in the humanities. In part, this aversion has stemmed from rhetoricians' deep sensitivity about the limitations of discerning textual effects and the epistemic quandaries of knowing how people felt at any given moment.[34] To the extent that public address scholars have contemplated questions of affect and feeling, they often concentrate on episodes from recent decades.[35] Observers tend to feel more confident making claims about the circulation of affect and emotion when they are immersed in ecologies of feeling. These hesitancies are understandable, but they also delimit the scope of scholarship in troubling ways.

The aversion to theories about feeling and to critical perspectives more broadly reflects the field's historical insularity, whiteness, and resistance to critique. As Jay Childers puts it, the discipline's "old assumptions about discourse, reason, and persuasion simply do not match the reality of how rhetoric moves people" through the orchestration of feeling.[36] Following scholars such as Christa J. Olson and Lisa M. Corrigan, I have sought to capture the virtue of attending closely to feelings as a part of public address inquiry.[37] I initially noticed legislators' references to feeling only in passing, concentrating my energies more on the abstract philosophical dialogues evident in these texts. Only after engaging with scholars of affect theory and emotions history did I recognize how deeply these nineteenth-century rhetors' worlds were structured by assumptions about feeling. Attention to feeling subsequently revealed the complex ways these discourses of education, often banal on their face, transformed questions of national identity and civic exclusion during the most tumultuous period in US history.

In the end, Congress's Reconstruction debates should prompt a careful reevaluation of the relationship between education and feeling. For the most radical voices at the time, education represented an appealing societal intervention precisely because it could engage with the sources of prejudice and hatred at their roots in childhood. As Representative Josiah T. Walls (R-FL) argued, if "public sentiment" led to discrimination, then "such public sentiment needs penal correction, and should be regulated by law."[38] Walls, Sumner, and others understood education's impact on feelings as substantive and believed that schools would level the aristocratic culture of the South by introducing alternative ideas that children did not receive at home. From this perspective, flesh-and-blood interactions were seen as dispelling prejudices. These Radicals recognized that merely enlightening members of the public to read, speak, or write well would not automatically lead them to discard ingrained feelings of superiority and resentment—that what schools taught mattered in effecting durable transformations of public feeling.

Representative George Frisbie Hoar (R-MA) initially shared this outlook. But after the failure of his bill for a national system of education, his perspective shifted. He adopted a more neutral view of what schools would do and how they would teach. Somehow, though, this neutrality accompanied an even deeper conviction that schools could transform society for the better. In the midst of the Perce Bill debate, he made perhaps his most naive comment: if every state in the Union had a strong system of public schools, he "would be contented that the wand of power might be held by my political opponents for a century."[39] Hoar believed that the moral and sympathetic power of education was so inherent, so intrinsic to the institution, that the substance of Democratic rivals' ideas would change if their constituents attended schools.

Beneath Hoar's claim rested an assumption that an educated society would be egalitarian, unprejudiced, deliberative, and calm, that such a society would restrain its passions and place domestic tranquility before all other civic aims. If Hoar is taken at his word, he believed that education would enable people to arrive at beliefs and policy conclusions that he would find amenable. He believed that members of the public would be so aligned in feeling that their priorities would never diverge enough to result in a violent conflict. And he believed this to be true no matter how those schools were organized and no matter what they taught. He believed in education without hesitation, without question, as though enlightened people cannot be unjust, as though schooled societies cannot be undemocratic.

Largely through the unreflective faith in education settled on by figures like Hoar, Reconstruction-era education policy rhetoric shifted from an affirmative vision of social change to an ameliorative acceptance of an inegalitarian order. Schooling became about the promotion of good feelings, no matter the causes of social discontent. In a nation where half a million people had just died on a battlefield, this goal may have seemed worthy. With the benefit of hindsight, it is now clear that such a conception of education failed in many respects, benefited only some Americans, and inflicted generations of harm on others. A conception of education as a neutral salve for hostile sentiment may foster superficial feelings of sympathy among those people it does not silence or expel. But it cannot make a nation more just.

NOTES

PREFACE

1. Wendy Kopp, "Building the Movement to End Educational Inequity," *Phi Delta Kappan* 89, no. 10 (2008): 734-36.

2. Barack Obama, "Proclamation 8363—National Volunteer Week, 2009," April 21, 2009, *American Presidency Project*, https://www.presidency.ucsb.edu/documents/proclamation-8363-national-volunteer-week-2009.

3. I reflected on this experience in Michael J. Steudeman, "Ignoring the Ghost of Horace Mann: A Reflective Critique of Teach For America's Solipsistic Pedagogy," in *Teach For America Counter-Narratives: Alumni Speak Up and Speak Out*, ed. T. Jameson Brewer and Kathleen Demarrais (New York: Lang, 2015), 47–54.

4. See, e.g., Lisa A. Flores, "Between Abundance and Marginalization: The Imperative of Racial Rhetorical Criticism," *Review of Communication* 16, no. 1 (2016): 17.

INTRODUCTION - EDUCATION AND ESTRANGEMENT

1. Carl Schurz, *The Reminiscences of Carl Schurz* (New York: McClure, 1907), 2:48; Carl Schurz, *The Condition of the South: Extracts from the Report of Major-General Carl Schurz, on the States of South Carolina, Georgia, Alabama, Mississippi and Louisiana; Addressed to the President* (Philadelphia, 1865), 7, 17, 6.

2. In the words of Mark Wahlgren Summers, many Republicans "fear[ed] that the war had settled nothing, that the Union still lay in peril, . . . and [that] the enemies of republican government were more resilient and cunning than normal mortals" (*A Dangerous Stir: Fear, Paranoia, and the Making of Reconstruction* [Chapel Hill: University of North Carolina Press, 2009], 4). See also Michael E. Woods, *Emotional and Sectional Conflict in the Antebellum United States* (New York: Cambridge University Press, 2014), 21–34, 119–205; Nina Silber, *The Romance of Reunion: Northerners and the South, 1865–1900* (Chapel Hill: University of North Carolina Press, 1997), 39–70.

3. For a sense of the comparative significance of these terms, a text search of the complete joint committee report shows that the word *union* appears 936 times. For examples of this language, see US Congress, *Report of the Joint Committee on Reconstruction at the*

First Session Thirty-Ninth Congress (Washington, DC: Government Printing Office, 1866), pt. 1 [Tennessee], pp. 105, 108, 112, pt. 2, [Virginia, North Carolina, South Carolina], pp. 11, 14, 18, 20, 22, 25.

4. US Congress, *Report of the Joint Committee*, p. xxi, pt. 2, pp. 11, 4, 246, 32, pt. 4 [Florida, Louisiana, Texas], p. 124.

5. *The Nineteenth Annual Report of the American Society for Colonizing the Freedpeople of Color of the United States, with the Proceedings of the Annual Meeting, December 15, 1835* (Washington, DC: Dunn, 1836), 3.

6. On the implications of the colonization movement for the Civil War and Reconstruction, see Nicholas Guyatt, *Bind Us Apart: How Enlightened Americans Invented Racial Segregation* (New York: Oxford University Press, 2016), 328–30. On the popularity of colonization among elites and education leaders, see Craig Steven Wilder, *Ebony & Ivy: Race, Slavery, and the Troubled History of America's Universities* (New York: Bloomsbury, 2013), 265–73. On the core arguments advanced by colonization advocates, see Bjørn F. Stillion Southard, *Peculiar Rhetoric: Slavery, Freedom, and the American Colonization Movement* (Jackson: University Press of Mississippi, 2019), 26–35.

7. Cox added that the Black and white copresence in the South "prevents that homogeneity of institutions and manners, North and South, which I have said I believe to be the only sure foundation of permanent peace" ("Important Document: The Oberlin Letter of Gen. Cox," *Cincinnati Enquirer*, August 2, 1865).

8. On Republican attitudes toward the South at the start of the Thirty-Ninth Congress, see Eric Foner, *Reconstruction: America's Unfinished Revolution, 1863–1877* (1988; New York: Perennial Classics, 2002), 241–46. On the emotional expectations imposed on freedpeople during Reconstruction, see Saidiya V. Hartman, *Scenes of Subjection: Terror, Slavery, and Self-Making in Nineteenth-Century America* (New York: Oxford University Press, 1997), 115–63.

9. Heather Cox Richardson, *West from Appomattox: The Reconstruction of America After the Civil War* (New Haven: Yale University Press, 2007), 113–20.

10. Anti-Catholic sentiment played a significant role in shaping Republican postwar education politics, emerging by the mid-1870s as a dominant theme in the party's campaign rhetoric. See Ward M. McAfee, *Religion, Race, and Reconstruction: The Public School in the Politics of the 1870s* (Albany: State University of New York Press, 1998), 27–78. On how anxieties about religious difference motivated Republican policymakers especially in the West, see Joshua Paddison, *American Heathens: Religion, Race, and Reconstruction in California* (Berkeley: University of California Press, 2012), 24–25.

11. See, e.g., Joshua Paddison, "Race, Religion, and Naturalization: How the West Shaped Citizenship Debates in the Reconstruction Congress," in *Civil War Wests: Testing the Limits of the United States*, ed. Adam Arenson (Berkeley: University of California Press, 2015), 181–201.

12. For the federal government's constrained involvement in education policy up to 1860, see Donald R. Warren, *To Enforce Education: A History of the Founding Years of the United States Office of Education* (Detroit: Wayne State University Press, 1974), 25–57; Lee W. Anderson, *Congress and the Classroom: From the Cold War to "No Child Left Behind"* (University Park: Penn State University Press, 2007), 29–38; David Tyack, Thomas James, and Aaron Benavot, *Law and the Shaping of Public Education, 1785–1954* (Madison: University of Wisconsin Press, 1987), 13–126.

13. *Cong. Globe*, 41st Cong., 2nd sess., appendix, 486 (1870).

14. A few significant works that have examined federal education policy during Reconstruction include Goodwin Liu, "Education, Equality, and National Citizenship," *Yale Law Journal* 116 (2006): 330–410; Ward M. McAfee, "Reconstruction Revisited: The Republican Education Crusade of the 1870s," *Civil War History* 42 (1996): 133–53; McAfee, *Religion, Race, and Reconstruction*; Gordon Canfield Lee, *The Struggle for Federal Aid, First Phase: A History of Attempts to Obtain Federal Aid for the Common Schools, 1870–1890* (New York: Teachers College, Columbia University, 1949); William Preston Vaughn, *Schools for All: The Blacks and Public Education in the South, 1865–1877* (Lexington: University Press of Kentucky, 1974). Other key works on Reconstruction-era education include Michael David Cohen, *Reconstructing the Campus: Higher Education and the American Civil War* (Charlottesville: University of Virginia Press, 2012); Ronald E. Butchart, *Schooling the Freed People: Teaching, Learning, and the Struggle for Black Freedom, 1861–1876* (Chapel Hill: University of North Carolina Press, 2013); Hilary Green, *Educational Reconstruction: African American Schools in the Urban South, 1865–1890* (New York: Fordham University Press, 2016); Warren, *To Enforce Education*.

15. "Dockery, Oliver Hart," *Biographical Directory of the United States Congress*, https://bioguide.congress.gov/search/bio/D000386, accessed November 3, 2024.

16. *Cong. Globe*, 41st Cong., 2nd sess., 2320 (1870).

17. James Jasinski, "A Constitutive Framework for Rhetorical Historiography: Toward an Understanding of the Discursive (Re)constitution of 'Constitution' in *The Federalist Papers*," in *Doing Rhetorical History: Concepts and Cases*, ed. Kathleen J. Turner (Tuscaloosa: University of Alabama Press, 1998), 83. In distinguishing the analysis of "discrete moments" and "over time," I am borrowing the distinction between synchronic and diachronic forms of analysis. See David Zarefsky, "Four Senses of Rhetorical History," in *Doing Rhetorical History*, ed. Turner, 32.

18. Williamjames Hull Hoffer, *To Enlarge the Machinery of Government: Congressional Debates and the Growth of the American State, 1858–1891* (Baltimore: Johns Hopkins University Press, 2007), 8. On the *Globe*'s importance in documenting the challenges facing the postwar United States, see W. E. B. Du Bois, *Black Reconstruction in America: An Essay Toward a History of the Part Which Black Folk Played in the Attempt to Reconstruct Democracy in America, 1860–1880* (1935; New York: Free Press, 1998), 723.

19. Elizabeth Gregory McPherson, "Reporting the Debates of Congress," *Quarterly Journal of Speech* 28, no. 2 (1942): 141–48.

20. Zornitsa Keremidchieva, "The U.S. *Congressional Record* as a Technology of Representation: Toward a Materialist Theory of Institutional Argument," *Journal of Argumentation in Context* 3, no. 1 (2014): 78.

21. James Jasinski, "The Status of Theory and Method in Rhetorical Criticism," *Western Journal of Communication* 65, no. 3 (2001): 256.

22. Kirt H. Wilson, "The Racial Contexts of Public Address: Interpreting Violence During the Reconstruction Era," in *The Handbook of Rhetoric and Public Address*, ed. Shawn J. Parry-Giles and J. Michael Hogan (Chichester, UK: Blackwell, 2010), 213.

23. Robert Asen, "Reflections on the Role of Rhetoric in Public Policy," *Rhetoric & Public Affairs* 13, no. 1 (2010): 135.

24. Jasinski, "Constitutive Framework," 73.

25. See, e.g., Melissa Gregg and Gregory J. Seigworth, eds., *The Affect Theory Reader* (Durham, NC: Duke University Press, 2010).

26. See, e.g., Debbie Hawhee, "Rhetoric's Sensorium," *Quarterly Journal of Speech* 101, no. 1 (2015): 2–17; Jay Childers, "Reimagining Public Address," *Rhetoric and Public Affairs* 24, nos. 1–2 (2021): 397–412.

27. Jenny Edbauer Rice, "The New 'New': Making a Case for Critical Affect Studies," *Quarterly Journal of Speech* 94, no. 2 (2008): 206. See also Erin J. Rand, "Review: Bad Feelings in Public: Rhetoric, Affect, and Emotion," *Rhetoric and Public Affairs* 18, no. 1 (2015): 161–76.

28. For an example of this work, see Brian Massumi, *Parables for the Virtual: Movement, Affect, Sensation* (Durham, NC: Duke University Press, 2002).

29. Lisa Corrigan, *Black Feelings: Race and Affect in the Long Sixties* (Jackson: University Press of Mississippi, 2020), xxiii. I deliberately choose to use *feeling* as a far-reaching and flexible term. I do so for two reasons. First, this echoes what I found in the historical record: nineteenth-century arguers used *feeling* in an array of flexible ways, and I want to capture the complexity of meanings they associated with the term. The second reason is conceptual. Like Ann Cvetkovich, I find that an open-ended usage of *feeling* helps to explain the ways feelings slide between individuated and social registers in ordinary speech. See Ann Cvetkovich, *Depression: A Public Feeling* (Durham, NC: Duke University Press, 2012), 4–5.

30. Throughout this book, I use *emotion* and *feeling* interchangeably for stylistic reasons. I use *sentiment* when doing so is consistent with the language used in the discourse itself.

31. Barbara H. Rosenwein, "Worrying About Emotions in History," *American Historical Review* 107, no. 3 (2002): 842. Rosenwein's work is a foundational text in a historical subfield, emotions history, that informs my perspective on this project. See, e.g., Peter N. Stearns and Jan Lewis, eds., *An Emotional History of the United States* (New York: New York University Press, 1998); Jan Plamper, William Reddy, Barbara Rosenwein, and Peter Stearns, "The History of Emotions: An Interview," *History and Theory* 49, no. 2 (2010): 237–65; Susan J. Matt and Peter N. Stearns, eds., *Doing Emotions History* (Urbana: University of Illinois Press, 2014).

32. On reading first-person accounts of emotion as historical evidence, see William M. Reddy, *The Navigation of Feeling: A Framework for the History of Emotions* (New York: Cambridge University Press, 2004), 100–101, 105–7.

33. Mark Seymour, "Emotional Arenas: From Provincial Circus to National Courtroom in Late Nineteenth-Century Italy," *Rethinking History* 16, no. 2 (2012): 179.

34. My phrasing here is an allusion to Benedict Anderson, *Imagined Communities*, rev. ed. (New York: Verso, 2006), 6.

35. For example, Maurice Charland bases his account of constitutive rhetoric on Kenneth Burke's theory of identification. See Maurice Charland, "Constitutive Rhetoric: The Case of the *Peuple Québécois*," *Quarterly Journal of Speech* 73, no. 2 (1987): 133–50.

36. Kenneth Burke, *A Rhetoric of Motives* (Berkeley: University of California Press, 1969), xiii–xv, 19–23; Kenneth Burke, *Attitudes Toward History*, 3rd ed. (Berkeley: University of California Press, 1984), 263–73.

37. Ersula J. Ore, *Lynching: Violence, Rhetoric, and American Identity* (Jackson: University Press of Mississippi, 2019), 32.

38. From the onset, Kenneth Burke recognized that identification had a significant emotional dimension: it can occur *"spontaneously, intuitively,* even *unconsciously"* (*Language as Symbolic Action: Essays on Life, Literature, and Method* [Berkeley: University of California Press, 1966], 301).

39. Danielle S. Allen, *Talking to Strangers: Anxieties of Citizenship Since Brown v. Board of Education* (Chicago: University of Chicago Press, 2004).

40. Sara Ahmed, *The Cultural Politics of Emotion* (New York: Routledge, 2004), 4, 45.

41. Sara Ahmed, "Collective Feelings: Or, the Impressions Left by Others," *Theory, Culture & Society* 21, no. 2 (2004): 26, 32–34.

42. For a nuanced discussion of these distinctions and their function in postwar debate, see Kirt H. Wilson, *The Reconstruction Desegregation Debate: The Politics of Equality and the Rhetoric of Place, 1870–1875* (East Lansing: Michigan State University Press, 2002), 77–120.

43. K. H. Wilson, *Reconstruction Desegregation Debate*, 115.

44. Asen, "Reflections," 124.

45. Ahmed, *Cultural Politics of Emotion*, 12.

46. On the role of institutionalism as an idea guiding nineteenth-century reformers' interventions in the interior lives of the polity, see Christopher Castiglia, *Interior States: Institutional Consciousness and the Inner Life of Democracy in the Antebellum United States* (Durham, NC: Duke University Press, 2008), 5–8, 26–34. For historical perspective on institutions' role in generating emotional norms, see Peter N. Stearns and Carol Z. Stearns, "Emotionology: Clarifying the History of Emotions and Emotional Standards," *American Historical Review* 90 (1985): 813–36.

47. On mourning and pain, see Drew Gilpin Faust, *This Republic of Suffering: Death and the American Civil War* (New York: Vintage, 2008). On despair, depression, and the disintegration of family ties, see David Silkenat, *Moments of Despair: Suicide, Divorce, and Debt in Civil War Era North Carolina* (Chapel Hill: University of North Carolina Press, 2011). On wartime trauma, see Diane Miller Sommerville, *Aberration of Mind: Suicide and Suffering in the Civil War-Era South* (Chapel Hill: University of North Carolina Press, 2018). On homesickness and nostalgic longing, see Susan J. Matt, *Homesickness: An American History* (New York: Oxford University Press, 2011), 75–140; Frances Clark, "So Lonesome I Could Die: Nostalgia and Debates over Emotional Control in the Civil War North," *Journal of Social History* 41, no. 2 (2007): 253–82.

48. Abraham Lincoln, "First Inaugural Address, Final Text, March 4, 1861" in *The Collected Works of Abraham Lincoln*, ed. Roy P. Basler (Ann Arbor: University of Michigan Digital Library Production Services, 2001), 4:271.

49. Jenell Johnson, "'A Man's Mouth Is His Castle': The Midcentury Fluoridation Controversy and the Visceral Public," *Quarterly Journal of Speech* 102, no. 1 (2016): 1–20.

50. Carl Schurz, "The Need of Reform and a New Party," in *Speeches, Correspondence and Political Papers of Carl Schurz*, ed. Frederic Bancroft (New York: Putnam's, 1913), 2:300, 306.

51. Woods, *Emotional and Sectional Conflict*, 238; David W. Blight, *Race and Reunion: The Civil War in American Memory* (Cambridge: Harvard University Press, 2001), 60–63.

52. *Cong. Globe*, 39th Cong., 1st sess., 3046 (1866), 41st Cong., 3rd sess., appendix, 192 (1871), 1074 (1871). For the textbook, see J. S. Blackburn, *A Southern School History of the United States of America: From the Earliest Discoveries to the Present Time* (Baltimore: Lycett, 1869).

53. Asen, "Reflections," 130.

54. Chris Beneke, "The Idea of Integration in the Age of Horace Mann," in *Inequity in Education: A Historical Perspective*, ed. Debra Meyers and Burke Miller (Lanham, MD: Lexington, 2009), 101–14.

55. Horace Mann, *Annual Reports on Education* (Boston: Lee and Shepard, 1872), 669–70.

56. See, e.g., Jane Lydon, *Imperial Emotions: The Politics of Empathy Across the British Empire* (New York: Cambridge University Press, 2020); Harald Fischer-Tiné and Christine Whyte, "Introduction: Empires and Emotions," in *Anxieties, Fear and Panic in Colonial Settings: Empires on the Verge of a Nervous Breakdown*, ed. Harald Fischer-Tiné (New York: Cambridge University Press, 2016), 1–23.

57. On the cultivation of the fellow feeling concept, see Elizabeth Barnes, *States of Sympathy: Seduction and Democracy in the American Novel* (New York: Columbia University Press, 1997), 20–22; Andrew Burstein, "The Political Character of Sympathy," *Journal of the Early Republic* 21, no. 4 (2001): 611–17.

58. Adam Smith, *The Theory of Moral Sentiments*, pt. 1, *Of the Propriety of Action* (London: Bohn, 1853), 3–30.

59. Xine Yao, *Disaffected: The Cultural Politics of Unfeeling in Nineteenth-Century America* (Durham, NC: Duke University Press, 2021), 13.

60. Noah Webster, Chauncey A. Goodrich, and Noah Porter, *An American Dictionary of the English Language* (Springfield, MA: Merriam, 1865), 503.

61. Abram Van Engen, *Sympathetic Puritans: Calvinist Fellow Feeling in Early New England* (New York: Oxford University Press, 2015), 90, 282 n. 21.

62. James Axtell, *The School upon a Hill: Education and Society in Colonial New England* (New York: Norton, 1974), 12–24.

63. Rogan Kersh, *Dreams of a More Perfect Union* (Ithaca: Cornell University Press, 2001), 26–38.

64. Woods, *Emotional and Sectional Conflict*, 21.

65. Courtney A. Weikle-Mills, *Imaginary Citizens: Child Readers and the Limits of American Independence, 1640–1868* (Baltimore: Johns Hopkins University Press, 2012), 36.

66. Webster, Goodrich, and Porter, *American Dictionary*, 429.

67. Quoted in Henry Barnard, ed., *Pestalozzi and Pestalozzianism: Life, Educational Principles, and Methods of John Henry Pestalozzi* (New York: Brownell, 1859), 178.

68. Sara Ahmed, *The Promise of Happiness* (Durham, NC: Duke University Press, 2010), 54.

69. Joel Perlmann and Robert A. Margo, *Women's Work?: American Schoolteachers, 1650–1920* (Chicago: University of Chicago Press, 2001), 48.

70. Jo Anne Preston, "Domestic Ideology, School Reformers, and Female Teachers: Schoolteaching Becomes Women's Work in Nineteenth-Century New England," *New England Quarterly* 66, no. 4 (1993): 531–51. For a detailed analysis of the complex reasons for the feminization of teaching, see Geraldine J. Clifford, *Those Good Gertrudes: A Social History of Women Teachers in America* (Baltimore: Johns Hopkins University Press, 2014), 45–95; Nancy Hoffman, *Woman's "True" Profession: Voices from the History of Teaching*, 2nd ed. (Cambridge: Harvard Education Press, 2003), 1–78.

71. Catharine Beecher, *A Treatise on Domestic Economy for the Use of Young Ladies at Home and at School*, rev. ed. (New York: Harper, 1868), 137.

72. Dana Luciano, *Arranging Grief: Sacred Time and the Body in Nineteenth-Century America* (New York: New York University Press, 2007), 58–60; Elizabeth Maddock Dillon, *The Gender of Freedom: Fictions of Liberalism and the Literary Public Sphere* (Stanford, CA: Stanford University Press, 2004), 19.

73. Jessica Enoch, "A Woman's Place Is in the School: Rhetorics of Gendered Space in Nineteenth-Century America," *College English* 70 (2008): 284; Horace Mann, "Report of the Secretary of the Board of Education on the Subject of Schoolhouses (Supplementary to His First Annual Report)," in *Lectures and Annual Reports, on Education*, ed. Mary Peabody Mann (Boston: Rand & Avery, 1867), 433–92; William W. Cutler III, "Cathedral of Culture: The Schoolhouse in Educational Thought and Practice Since 1820," *History of Education Quarterly* 29, no. 1 (1989): 1–40.

74. Ahmed, *Promise of Happiness*, 123–33.

75. Beneke, "Idea of Integration," 101–14. On the relationship between proximity and emotions of hate, see Ahmed, *Cultural Politics of Emotion*, 49–54. On the schoolroom as a sanctuary space, see Enoch, "Woman's Place," 282–84.

76. Rita Koganzon, "'Producing a Reconciliation of Disinterestedness and Commerce': The Political Rhetoric of Education in the Early Republic," *History of Education Quarterly* 52, no. 3 (2012): 403–29.

77. Quoted in James Pyle Wickersham, *A History of Education in Pennsylvania* (Lancaster, PA: Inquirer Publishing, 1886), 312.

78. Kathleen Edgerton Kendall, "Education as the 'Balance Wheel of the Social Machinery': Horace Mann's Arguments and Proofs," *Quarterly Journal of Speech* 54, no. 1 (1968): 13–21.

79. Chris Beneke, "'Mingle with Us': Religious Integration in Eighteenth and Nineteenth-Century American Education," *American Educational History Journal* 33, no. 1 (2006): 31–32.

80. W. S. Dutton, "The Proposed Substitution of Sectarian for Public Schools," *Common School Journal* 10, no. 11 (1848): 168–69; Stephen Macedo, *Diversity and Distrust: Civic Education in a Multicultural Democracy* (Cambridge: Harvard University Press, 2003), 54. On this theme's role in Horace Mann's rhetoric, see Steven K. Green, *The Bible, the School, and the Constitution: The Clash That Shaped Modern Church-State Doctrine* (New York: Oxford University Press, 2012), 26–29; Massachusetts Department of Education, *Twelfth Annual Report of the Board of Education, Together with the Twelfth Annual Report of the Secretary of the Board* (Boston: Dutton and Wentworth, 1849), 131.

81. S. K. Green, *Bible, the School, and the Constitution*, 33–36.

82. S. K. Green, *Bible, the School, and the Constitution*, 77–78.

83. Massachusetts Department of Education, *Eighth Annual Report of the Board of Education, Together with the Eighth Annual Report of the Secretary of the Board* (Boston: Dutton and Wentworth, 1845), 51.

84. K. H. Wilson, *Reconstruction Desegregation Debate*, 69, 138–39.

85. On the notion of *sympathy* as referring to a "community of feeling," see John Corrigan, *Business of the Heart: Religion and Emotion in the Nineteenth Century* (Berkeley: University of California Press, 2002), 235.

86. Abraham Lincoln, "Address Before the Wisconsin State Agricultural Society, Milwaukee, Wisconsin, September 30, 1859," in *The Collected Works of Abraham Lincoln*,

ed. Roy P. Basler (Ann Arbor: University of Michigan Digital Library Production Services, 2001), 3:480.

87. Ahmed, *Promise of Happiness*, 41–42, 129.

88. Kyla Schuller, *The Biopolitics of Feeling: Race, Sex, and Science in the Nineteenth Century* (Durham, NC: Duke University Press, 2018), 8.

89. David Wallace Adams, *Education for Extinction: American Indians and the Boarding School Experience, 1875–1928* (Lawrence: University Press of Kansas, 1995), 12–24.

90. Hilary J. Moss, *Schooling Citizens: The Struggle for African American Education in Antebellum America* (Chicago: University of Chicago Press, 2009), 193.

91. In 1846 the School Committee of Boston justified segregated schools on the grounds that Black children's "peculiar physical, mental, and moral structure, requires an educational treatment, different, in some respects, from that of white children" (*Report to the Primary School Committee, June 15, 1846, on the Petition of Sundry Colored Persons, for the Abolition of the Schools for Colored Children* [Boston: Eastburn, 1846], 29).

92. Kirk Branch, "'A Mockery in the Name of a Barrier': Literacy Test Debates in the Reconstruction Era Congress, 1864–1869," *Literacy in Composition Studies* 3 (2015): 44–65.

93. On the development of these educational tiers as part of broader post-Reconstruction imperial projects, see Clif Stratton, *Education for Empire: American Schools, Race, and the Paths of Good Citizenship* (Oakland: University of California Press, 2016).

94. Castiglia, *Interior States*, 5.

95. Lauren Berlant, *The Queen of America Goes to Washington City: Essays on Sex and Citizenship* (Durham, NC: Duke University Press, 1997), 25–54. For nineteenth-century applications of this concept, see Karen Sánchez-Eppler, *Dependent States: The Child's Part in Nineteenth-Century American Culture* (Chicago: University of Chicago Press, 2005), xxii–xxvi; Weikle-Mills, *Imaginary Citizens*, 20–21.

96. James Pyle Wickersham, "Education as an Element in Reconstruction," in National Teachers' Association, *Proceedings and Lectures of the Sixth Annual Meeting* (Hartford, CT: Office of the *American Journal of Education*, 1865), 290.

97. Robert Dale Owen, James McKaye, and Samuel G. Howe, *Preliminary Report Touching the Condition and Management of Emancipated Refugees; Made to the Secretary of War, by the American Freedmen's Inquiry Commission, June 30, 1863* (New York: Trow, 1863), 23.

98. Nancy Beadie, "The Limits of Standardization and the Importance of Constituencies: Historical Tensions in the Relationship Between State Authority and Local Control," in *Balancing Local Control and State Responsibility for K–12 Education*, ed. Neil D. Theobald and Betty Malen (Larchmont, NY: Eye on Education, 2000), 57–61.

99. Mark Groen, "The Whig Party and the Rise of Common Schools, 1837–1854," *American Educational History Journal* 35, no. 2 (2008): 251–60. There were exceptions to the dominance of Whig leadership on educational issues. For example, Democratic governor George Wolf of Pennsylvania strongly defended that state's first common school law.

100. Sun Go and Peter Lindert, "The Uneven Rise of American Public Schools to 1850," *Journal of Economic History* 70, no. 1 (2010): 3–4.

101. Nancy Beadie, "'Hidden' Governance or Counterfactual Case?: The US Failure to Pass a National Education Act, 1870–1940," in *School Acts and the Rise of Mass Schooling: Education Policy in the Long Nineteenth Century*, ed. Johannes Westberg, Lukas Boser, and Ingrid Brühwiler (Cham, Switzerland: Palgrave Macmillan, 2019), 327–28.

102. Carl L. Bankston III and Stephen J. Caldas, *Public Education: America's Civil Religion; A Social History* (New York: Teachers College Press, 2009), 30. For other remarks on the disparate development of education systems before the Civil War, see David Tyack and Elisabeth Hansot, *Managers of Virtue: Public School Leadership in America, 1820–1980* (New York: Basic Books, 1982), 83; Carl F. Kaestle, *Pillars of the Republic: Common Schools and American Society, 1780–1860* (New York: Hill and Wang, 1983), 207.

103. Lyman Beecher, *A Plea for the West* (Cincinnati: Truman and Smith, 1835), 16.

104. George S. Boutwell, *Thoughts on Educational Topics and Institutions* (Boston: Phillips, Sampson, 1859), 220.

105. Wickersham, "Education as an Element," 296.

106. David F. Labaree, *The Making of an American High School: The Credentials Market and the Central High School of Philadelphia, 1838–1939* (New Haven: Yale University Press, 1988), 13, 26–28, 173–82; Martin Ridge, *Ignatius Donnelly: The Portrait of a Politician* (Chicago: University of Chicago Press, 1962), 5.

107. *Cong. Globe*, 39th Cong., 1st sess., 60 (1865).

108. Henry J. Perkinson, *The Imperfect Panacea: American Faith in Education*, 4th ed. (Boston: McGraw-Hill, 1995); Thomas C. Hunt, *The Impossible Dream: Education and the Search for Panaceas* (New York: Lang, 2002).

109. James A. Garfield, "The National Bureau of Education," in *President Garfield and Education: Hiram College Memorial*, ed. Burke A. Hinsdale (Boston: Osgood, 1882), 212.

110. Record of the Business Transacted by the Committee on Education and Labor of the House of Representatives, During the 2nd Session of the 41st Congress, Commencing on Dec. 6, 1869, 6–7, RG 233, Records of the Committee on Education and Labor, 40th–48th Congresses (1867–1883), Records of the US House of Representatives, 1789–1989, National Archives, Washington, DC.

111. In his three-volume history of American education, Lawrence A. Cremin writes that the postwar period "reflected an emerging national consensus" in support of common schooling (*American Education: The National Experience, 1783–1876* [New York: Harper & Row, 1980], 520).

112. *Cong. Globe*, 39th Cong., 1st sess., 5 (1865). See also William H. Barnes, *History of the Thirty-Ninth Congress of the United States* (New York: Harper, 1868), 21.

113. *Cong. Globe*, 39th Cong., 1st sess., 3050 (1866).

114. On visceral rhetorics of emotion, see Jenell Johnson, "'A Man's Mouth Is His Castle': The Midcentury Fluoridation Controversy and the Visceral Public," *Quarterly Journal of Speech* 102, no. 1 (2016): 1–20.

115. See Cyril Outerbridge Packwood, *Joseph Hayne Rainey: Detour—Bermuda, Destination—U.S. House of Representatives* (Hamilton, Bermuda: Island Press, 1977); Committee on House Administration of the US House of Representatives, *Black Americans in Congress, 1870–2007* (Washington, DC: Government Printing Office, 2008), 62–67.

116. Committee on House Administration, *Black Americans in Congress*, 62–67.

117. Emily Edson Briggs, *The Olivia Letters: Being Some History of Washington City for Forty Years as Told by the Letters of a Newspaper Correspondent* (New York: Neale, 1906), 276.

118. *Cong. Globe*, 42nd Cong., 2nd sess., appendix, 16 (1872).

CHAPTER ONE - FEDERALISM AND FEELING

1. As Nancy Beadie notes, these schools were established according to local pacts and subscription agreements, taking on a public character despite not being formal government projects (*Education and the Creation of Capital in the Early American Republic* [New York: Cambridge University Press, 2010], 20–32).

2. Campbell F. Scribner, *The Fight for Local Control: Schools, Suburbs, and American Democracy* (Ithaca: Cornell University Press, 2016), 16.

3. David Tyack and Elisabeth Hansot, "Conflict and Consensus in American Public Education," *Daedalus* 110, no. 3 (1982): 6.

4. On Sumner's involvement in the common school movement, see William J. Reese, *Testing Wars in the Public Schools: A Forgotten History* (Cambridge: Harvard University Press, 2013), 138–53.

5. Charles Sumner, *The National Security and the National Faith; Guarantees for the National Freedman and the National Creditor: Speech of Hon. Charles Sumner at the Republican State Convention, in Worcester, September 14, 1865* (Boston: Wright & Potter, 1865), 6.

6. George Frisbie Hoar, "*Claims of the Free Institute of Industrial Science: Necessity of Technical Education for the Development of Our Manufacturing Interests*," February 11, 1869, 4, box 174, Pamphlets: 1855–1879 folder, George Frisbie Hoar Papers, Massachusetts Historical Society, Boston. On the development of the Hoar Bill, see George Frisbie Hoar, *Autobiography of Seventy Years* (New York: Scribner's, 1903), 1:166–67, 195.

7. David Zarefsky and Victoria J. Gallagher, "From 'Conflict' to 'Constitutional Question': Transformations in Early American Public Discourse," *Quarterly Journal of Speech* 76, no. 3 (1990): 258.

8. Malcolm M. Feeley and Edward Rubin, *Federalism: Political Identity & Tragic Compromise* (Ann Arbor: University of Michigan Press, 2011), 43, 50.

9. Lauren Berlant, *The Anatomy of National Fantasy: Hawthorne, Utopia, and Everyday Life* (Chicago: University of Chicago Press, 1991), 13.

10. On the development of stratified tiers of civic education, see Clif Stratton, *Education for Empire: American Schools, Race, and the Paths of Good Citizenship* (Oakland: University of California Press, 2016).

11. Despite the expansion of federal powers, Kurt T. Lash notes, Congress refused to "significantly undermine the dualist conception of American government" (*The Fourteenth Amendment and the Privileges and Immunities of American Citizenship* [New York: Cambridge University Press, 2014], 6).

12. George Thomas, *The Founders and the Idea of a National University: Constituting the American Mind* (New York: Cambridge University Press, 2015), 6; David Tyack, "Forming the National Character: Paradox in the Educational Thought of the Revolutionary Generation," *Harvard Educational Review* 36, no. 1 (1966): 29–41.

13. Charles de Secondat Montesquieu, *The Spirit of the Laws*, trans. and ed. Anne M. Cohler, Basia Carolyn Miller, and Harold Samuel Stone (1748; New York: Cambridge University Press, 1989), 35–56.

14. George Washington, "Eighth Annual Address to Congress, December 7, 1796," *American Presidency Project*, https://www.presidency.ucsb.edu/node/200398; Thomas, *Founders and the Idea*, 32.

15. On the Founders' foiled education projects, see Lorraine Smith Pangle and Thomas L. Pangle, *The Learning of Liberty: The Educational Ideas of the American Founders* (Lawrence: University Press of Kansas, 1993), 125–52.

16. Pangle and Pangle, *Learning of Liberty*, 4–6.

17. James Jasinski, "Rhetoric and Judgment in the Constitutional Ratification Debate of 1787–1788: An Exploration of the Relationship Between Theory and Critical Practice," *Quarterly Journal of Speech* 78, no. 2 (1992): 208.

18. Some Antifederalists did accept a limited role for federal promotion of education as a means to teach Christian morality. See, e.g., Charles Turner's remarks in *Debates and Proceedings in the Convention of the Commonwealth of Massachusetts, Held in the Year 1788, and Which Finally Ratified the Constitution of the United States* (Boston: White, 1856), 275–76; Herbert J. Storing, *What the Anti-Federalists Were For: The Political Thought of the Opponents of the Constitution* (Chicago: University of Chicago Press, 1981), 21–23.

19. Thomas, *Founders and the Idea*, 63–70.

20. Jasinski, "Rhetoric and Judgment," 203; Richard K. Matthews, *If Men Were Angels: James Madison and the Heartless Empire of Reason* (Lawrence: University Press of Kansas, 1995); András Sajó, *Constitutional Sentiments* (New Haven: Yale University Press, 2011), 120–21.

21. James Madison, "No. 46: The Influence of the State and Federal Governments Compared" (1788), in *The Federalist Papers*, ed. Charles R. Kesler (New York: Signet Classics, 2003), 291. As Alison L. LaCroix argues, this view was central to Madison's conception of federalism, which viewed "political authority as capable of enduring division between levels of government based on subject matter" (*The Ideological Origins of American Federalism* [Cambridge: Harvard University Press, 2010], 6).

22. Doni Gewirtzman, "Our Founding Feelings: Emotion, Commitment, and Imagination in Constitutional Culture," *University of Richmond Law Review* 43 (2009): 623–83.

23. Rogan Kersh, *Dreams of a More Perfect Union* (Ithaca: Cornell University Press, 2001), 76–77.

24. Drew R. McCoy, *The Last of the Fathers: James Madison and the Republican Legacy* (New York: Cambridge University Press, 1991), 199–206.

25. James Madison, "Public Opinion," in *The Papers of James Madison*, ed. William T. Hutchinson and William M. E. Rachal (Charlottesville: University Press of Virginia, 1983), 14:170; Colleen A. Sheehan, *The Mind of James Madison: The Legacy of Classical Republicanism* (New York: Cambridge University Press, 2017), 77–80; Kersh, *Dreams*, 79.

26. James Madison, *The Writings of James Madison, Comprising His Public Papers and His Private Correspondence*, ed. Gaillard Hunt (New York: Putnam's, 1900), 9:107.

27. "No. 203: Civilization of the Indians, Communicated to the House of Representatives, March 23, 1824," in *American State Papers: Class II, Indian Affairs* (Washington, DC: Gales and Seaton, 1834), 2:458.

28. Lori J. Daggar, "The Mission Complex: Economic Development, 'Civilization,' and Empire in the Early Republic," *Journal of the Early Republic* 36, no. 3 (2016): 467–91.

29. Adam Dahl, *Empire of the People: Settler Colonialism and the Foundations of Modern Democratic Thought* (Lawrence: University Press of Kansas, 2018), 37–40.

30. Even during the convention, Madison conceded, the "task of marking the proper line of partition" had been "arduous," complicated by the ambiguities of language (James Madison, "No. 37: Concerning the Difficulties of the Convention in Devising a Proper Form of Government" [1788], in *Federalist Papers*, ed. Kesler, 223–25).

31. Quoted in Michael T. Bernath, *Confederate Minds: The Struggle for Intellectual Independence in the Civil War South* (Chapel Hill: University of North Carolina Press, 2010), 53.

32. Feeley and Rubin, *Federalism*, 105.

33. Michael E. Woods, *Emotional and Sectional Conflict in the Antebellum United States* (New York: Cambridge University Press, 2014), 29–31.

34. Steeped in the Transcendentalist movement, with its emphasis on the perfectibility of human souls, Boston's civic leaders were engaged in a wide range of programs of moral improvement beyond just education. See Octavius Brooks Frothingham, *Transcendentalism in New England: A History* (New York: Putnam's, 1876), 105–83. On the cultural milieu surrounding Sumner and Mann, see Anne-Marie Taylor, *Young Charles Sumner and the Legacy of the American Enlightenment, 1811–1851* (Amherst: University of Massachusetts Press, 2001), 126–63.

35. As Christopher Castiglia writes, the era's reform movements situated "the vectors of social inequality and dissent in proximity to normative character," framing political conflict as a product of internal affective states (*Interior States: Institutional Consciousness and the Inner Life of Democracy in the Antebellum United States* [Durham, NC: Duke University Press, 2008], 101). On the democratic anxieties specific to the common school movement, see Brian W. Dotts, "'Making Rome Appear More Roman': Common Schooling and the Whig Response to Jacksonianism," *Journal of Philosophy & History of Education* 62, no. 1 (2012): 207–26; Michael J. Steudeman, "Horace Mann, 'The Necessity of Education in a Republican Government' (Fall 1839)," *Voices of Democracy* 8 (2014): 1–22; Rogers Smith, *Civic Ideals: Conflicting Visions of Citizenship in U.S. History* (New Haven: Yale University Press, 1997), 216–20.

36. Mary Peabody Mann, *Life of Horace Mann* (Boston: Walker, Fuller, 1865), 74–75, 95.

37. David Hogan, "Modes of Discipline: Affective Individualism and Pedagogical Reform in New England, 1820–1850," *American Journal of Education* 99, no. 1 (1990): 12–15.

38. Horace Mann, *Annual Reports on Education* (Boston: Lee and Shepard, 1872), 669–70; Kathleen Edgar Kendall, "Education as the 'Balance Wheel of the Social Machinery': Horace Mann's Arguments and Proofs," *Quarterly Journal of Speech* 54, no. 1 (1968): 13–21.

39. Karl-Ernst Jeismann, "American Observations Concerning the Prussian Educational System in the Nineteenth Century," in *German Influences on Education in the United States to 1917*, ed. Henry Geitz, Jürgen Heideking, and Jurgen Herbst (New York: Cambridge University Press, 1995), 21–42.

40. Christopher Clark, *Iron Kingdom: The Rise and Downfall of Prussia, 1600–1947* (New York: Penguin, 2007), 332. Mann had a particularly rosy view of Prussia's internal politics, which would explode into revolutionary conflict in 1848.

41. Horace Mann, "Seventh Annual Report of the Secretary of the Board of Education," *Common School Journal* 6 (1844): 84.

42. Horace Mann, *An Oration Delivered Before the Authorities of the City of Boston,, July 4, 1842*, 5th ed. (Washington, DC: Library of Congress, 1842), 29.

43. Hilary J. Moss, *Schooling Citizens: The Struggle for African American Education in Antebellum America* (Chicago: University of Chicago Press, 2009), 149–63.

44. Association of Masters of the Boston Public Schools, *Remarks on the Seventh Annual Report of the Hon. Horace Mann, Secretary of the Massachusetts Board of Education* (Boston: Little and Brown, 1844), 25.

45. Whereas educators abroad could count on the "strong power of Prussian school authority" to underwrite their punishments, American teachers needed their pupils "to recognize and obey rightful authority wherever it exists in the great chain." Association of Masters, *Remarks*, 120, 129.

46. Allison Speicher, *Schooling Readers: Reading Common Schools in Nineteenth-Century American Fiction* (Tuscaloosa: University of Alabama Press, 2016), 59–62; Jean Baker, "From Belief into Culture: Republicanism in the Antebellum North," *American Quarterly* 37, no. 4 (1985): 543–44. On the various forms of local resistance, see Michael B. Katz, *Reconstructing American Education* (Cambridge: Harvard University Press, 1989), 24–57.

47. "Dedication of the Statue of Hon. Horace Mann," *Massachusetts Teacher* 18 (August 1865): 272.

48. Charles Brooks, *Some Reasons for the Immediate Establishment of a National System of Education for the United States* (New York: Loyal Publication Society, 1865), 17, 21.

49. Leonard Glenn Smith, "A History of the United States Office of Education, 1867–1967" (PhD diss., University of Oklahoma, 1967), 7–9.

50. Edward L. Pierce, *Memoir and Letters of Charles Sumner* (Boston: Roberts, 1881), 2:223. Sumner and Mann already had a close affiliation at this time, having worked in the same legal offices at 4 Court Street in Boston during the 1830s (A.-M. Taylor, *Young Charles Sumner*, 85–86).

51. Charles Sumner, "Mr. Mann's Report on Education Abroad," *Boston Advertiser*, March 12, 1844; Charles Sumner, "Mr. Mann's Report," *Boston Advertiser*, March 21, 1844; Reese, *Testing Wars*, 57–68; Stanley K. Schultz, *The Culture Factory: Boston Public Schools, 1789–1860* (New York: Oxford University Press, 1973), 138–53.

52. *Roberts v. City of Boston*, 59 Mass. 198, 5 Cush. 198 (1849).

53. *Cong. Globe*, 39th Cong., 1st sess., 673 (1866).

54. Charles Sumner, *Are We a Nation?: Address of Hon. Charles Sumner, Before the New York Young Men's Republican Union, at the Cooper Institute, Tuesday Evening, Nov. 19, 1867* (New York: Young Men's Republican Union, 1867), 36.

55. Andrew Johnson, "First Annual Message," December 4, 1865, *American Presidency Project*, https://www.presidency.ucsb.edu/node/201985.

56. Eric Foner, *Reconstruction: America's Unfinished Revolution, 1863–1877* (1988; New York: Perennial Classics, 2002), 224–27.

57. Sumner, *National Security and the National Faith*, 21.

58. Charles Sumner, "Our Domestic Relations; or, How to Treat the Rebel States," *Atlantic Monthly*, September 1863, 528.

59. See Charles Sumner, *The One Man Power vs. Congress!: Address of Hon. Charles Sumner, at the Music Hall, Boston, October 2, 1866* (Boston: Wright & Potter, 1866).

60. On Sumner's rhetorical background and Ciceronian inspirations, see A.-M. Taylor, *Young Charles Sumner*, 48–51. On the affective dimensions of sensus communis in the rhetorical tradition, see John D. Schaeffer, *Sensus Communis: Vico, Rhetoric, and the Limits of Relativism* (Durham, NC: Duke University Press, 1990), 75–76.

61. Sumner, "Our Domestic Relations," 519–20.

62. Sumner, *National Security and the National Faith*, 15; Charles Sumner, *Validity and Necessity of Fundamental Conditions on States: Speech of Hon. Charles Sumner, of Massachusetts, in the Senate of the United States, June 10, 1868* (Washington, DC: Library of Congress, 1870), 5.

63. Janis L. McDonald, "The Republican Revival: Revolutionary Republicanism's Relevance for Charles Sumner's Theory of Equality and Reconstruction," *Buffalo Law Review* 38, no. 2 (1990): 465–514; William M. Wiecek, *The Guarantee Clause of the U.S. Constitution* (Ithaca: Cornell University Press, 1972), 193–98; Pierce, *Memoir and Letters*, 4:259.

64. Sumner, *National Security and the National Faith*, 13, 18, 17. On the popular reception of Sumner's address in Massachusetts, see David Herbert Donald, *Charles Sumner and the Rights of Man* (1970; New York: Da Capo, 1996), 226–28; Pierce, *Memoir and Letters*, 4:258.

65. *Cong. Globe*, 39th Cong., 2nd sess., 1626 (1867).

66. *Cong. Globe*, 40th Cong., 1st sess., 51 (1867).

67. Sumner's ideas on education thus reflected the nineteenth-century discourse of "impressibility," which presumed that populations were more or less capable of regulating their emotions properly based on the "accumulation of sensory impressions" over generations. See Kyla Schuller, *The Biopolitics of Feeling: Race, Sex, and Science in the Nineteenth Century* (Durham, NC: Duke University Press, 2018), 3.

68. *Cong. Globe*, 40th Cong., 1st sess., 167, 170, 581 (1867).

69. Heather Andrea Williams, *Self-Taught: African American Education in Slavery and Freedom* (Chapel Hill: University of North Carolina Press, 2005), 72–79.

70. *Proceedings of the Colored People's Convention of the State of South Carolina, Held in Zion Church, Charleston, November 1865* (Charleston: South Carolina Leader Office, 1865), 10.

71. For instance, Henry E. Hayne defended a compulsory attendance provision on grounds that "the system has worked well in Germany and Massachusetts" (*Proceedings of the Constitutional Convention of South Carolina, Held at Charleston, S.C., Beginning January 14th and Ending March 17th, 1868* [Charleston, SC: Denny & Perry, 1868], 685).

72. *Proceedings of the Constitutional Convention*, 694.

73. Derek W. Black, "The Constitutional Compromise to Guarantee Education," *Stanford Law Review* 70 (2018): 780.

74. Gordon B. McKinney, "Southern Mountain Republicans and the Negro, 1865–1900," *Journal of Southern History* 41, no. 4 (1975): 496–97.

75. Foner, *Reconstruction*, 422–44.

76. Jane Dailey, *Before Jim Crow: The Politics of Race in Postemancipation Virginia* (Chapel Hill: University of North Carolina Press, 2000), 19–21, 27–28; Richard Lowe, "Another Look at Reconstruction in Virginia," *Civil War History* 32, no. 1 (1986): 74–76.

77. "The Campaign; Our Candidates at Woodstock: Speeches by Colonel Walker, John H. Lewis, J. H. Williams, and Moses Walton; Shenandoah Aroused," *Richmond Daily Dispatch*, June 10, 1869, 1.

78. "No Difference," *Staunton Spectator and General Advertiser*, June 1, 1869, 2.

79. *Cong. Globe*, 41st Cong., 2nd sess., 325 (1870).

80. Sumner read this quotation from a pamphlet allegedly circulated by Walker's campaign; the senator may have embellished the speech's contents. Nonetheless, Sumner's rhetoric and the Senate's response illustrate Republican concerns about Southern commitments to carrying out public school provisions. See *Cong. Globe*, 41st Cong., 2nd sess., 546 (1870). On Walker's rise in Virginia, see Foner, *Reconstruction*, 413.

81. *Cong. Globe*, 41st Cong., 2nd sess., 565, 546 (1870).

82. *Cong. Globe*, 41st Cong., 2nd sess., 643 (1870).

83. D. W. Black, "Constitutional Compromise," 783.

84. *Cong. Globe*, 41st Cong., 2nd sess., 418, appendix, 480 (1870).

85. Record of the Business Transacted by the Committee on Education and Labor of the House of Representatives, During the 2nd Session of the 41st Congress, Commencing on Dec. 6, 1869, 6–7, RG 233, Records of the Committee on Education and Labor, 40th–48th Congresses (1867–1883), Records of the US House of Representatives, 1789–1989, National Archives, Washington, DC.

86. *Cong. Globe*, 41st Cong., 2nd sess., 759, 3302, 765 (1870).

87. Stacey L. Smith, "Beyond North and South," *Journal of the Civil War Era* 6, no. 4 (2016): 571–73.

88. On postwar white Northerners' tendency to reason "by analogy across populations" in the West and South, see Cathleen Cahill and Crystal N. Feimster, "Interlude 2: Racial Dimensions," in *Reconstruction and Mormon America*, ed. Clyde A. Milner II and Brian Q. Cannon (Norman: University of Oklahoma Press, 2019), 113–14; Brett D. Dowdle, "'To Merge Them into More Wholesome Elements': The Greater Reconstruction and Its Place in Utah," in *Reconstruction and Mormon America*, ed. Milner and Cannon, 150–80.

89. Heather Cox Richardson, *West from Appomattox: The Reconstruction of America After the Civil War* (New Haven: Yale University Press, 2007), 113–20.

90. Kevin Bruyneel, *Settler Memory: The Disavowal of Indigeneity and the Politics of Race in the United States* (Chapel Hill: University of North Carolina Press, 2021), 50–51.

91. S. B. McCormick, "Cambria Co.: Educational Survey of the County," *Pennsylvania School Journal* 4 (December 1855): 167–68. On Prosser's background teaching in Cambria County, Pennsylvania, see *History of the Pacific Northwest: Oregon and Washington* (Portland, OR: North Pacific History Company, 1889), 2:527–29.

92. *Cong. Globe*, 41st Cong., 2nd sess., 763, 762 (1870). For context regarding Republican political leaders' anti-Mormon anxieties, see Dowdle, "To Merge Them into More Wholesome Elements," 173.

93. *Cong. Globe*, 41st Cong., 2nd sess., 764, 763 (1870).

94. *Cong. Globe*, 41st Cong., 2nd sess., 762 (1870); Judith A. Boughter, *Betraying the Omaha Nation, 1790–1916* (Norman: University of Oklahoma Press, 1998), 61. As Jason Edward Black writes, it is important to question the authenticity of statements allegedly made by Native Americans through the rhetorical frame and language of colonizers. The translator of this letter, Commissioner of Indian Affairs William P. Dole, was particularly enamored of the Great Father mythology and its educational implications and easily could have inserted such language into the letter. See Jason Edward Black, "Native Resistive Rhetoric and the Decolonization of American Indian Removal Discourse," *Quarterly Journal of Speech* 95, no. 1 (2009): 71–72; Francis Paul Prucha, *The Great Father: The United States Government and the American Indians* (Lincoln: University of Nebraska Press, 1984), 465.

95. *Cong. Globe*, 41st Cong., 2nd sess., 764, 762, 765, 763 (1870).

96. *Cong. Globe*, 41st Cong., 2nd sess., appendix, 486 (1870).

97. *Cong. Globe*, 41st Cong., 2nd sess., appendix, 480 (1870).

98. *Cong. Globe*, 41st Cong., 2nd sess., appendix, 484, 485 (1870).

99. Carl Schurz, "Address to the People of Missouri, Sept. 10, 1870," in *Speeches, Correspondence and Political Papers of Carl Schurz*, ed. Frederic Bancroft (New York: Putnam's, 1913), 1:518, 512.

100. Ward M. McAfee, *Religion, Race, and Reconstruction: The Public School in the Politics of the 1870s* (Albany: State University of New York Press, 1998), 105–10.

101. Henry Wilson, "New Departure," *Atlantic Monthly* 21 (1871): 120, 119, 109–10.

102. See Feeley and Rubin, *Federalism*, 40–43.

103. *Cong. Globe*, 41st Cong., 3rd sess., appendix, 78 (1871).

104. *Cong. Globe*, 41st Cong., 3rd sess., appendix, 80 (1871).

105. *Memorial Addresses on the Life and Character of Michael Crawford Kerr, Speaker of the House of Representatives of the United States* (Washington, DC: Government Printing Office), 54.

106. *Cong. Globe*, 41st Cong., 3rd sess., 1371, 1372 (1871).

107. *Cong. Globe*, 41st Cong., 3rd sess., appendix, 94 (1871).

108. When Illinois held a state constitutional convention in 1862, McNeely served as a delegate. In that role, he proposed to eliminate language requiring a superintendent of public instruction. This position placed McNeely in a distinct minority, and his proposal was voted down, 49–8. See *Journal of the Constitutional Convention of the State of Illinois, Convened at Springfield, January 7, 1862* (Springfield, IL: Lanphier, 1862), 870–71.

109. *Cong. Globe*, 41st Cong., 3rd sess., appendix, 94, 95 (1871).

110. *Cong. Globe*, 41st Cong., 3rd sess., appendix, 96 (1871).

111. See, e.g., Charles Brooks, *Two Lectures—I: History of the Introduction of State Normal Schools in America; II: A Prospective System of National Education for the United States* (Boston: Wilson, 1864), 18; Carl F. Kaestle, "Social Change, Discipline, and the Common School in Early Nineteenth-Century America," *Journal of Interdisciplinary History* 9 (1978): 9–10.

112. Multiple Republicans indicated that they supported a federal intervention in schools but echoed concerns about the bill going too far. See, e.g., Representative William Lawrence (R-OH), *Cong. Globe*, 41st Cong., 3rd sess., 1244 (1871); Representative Oliver H. Dockery (R-NC), *Cong. Globe*, 41st Cong., 3rd sess., appendix, 241 (1871).

113. *Cong. Globe*, 41st Cong., 3rd sess., appendix, 189 (1871).

114. John Eaton to George Frisbie Hoar, February 2, 1871, box 12, February 1–15, 1871, folder, Hoar Papers.

115. *Cong. Globe*, 41st Cong., 3rd sess., 1042 (1871).

116. *Cong. Globe*, 41st Cong., 3rd sess., appendix, 79, 95 (1871).

117. *Cong. Globe*, 41st Cong., 3rd sess., appendix, 95, 80 (1871).

118. Doni Gewirtzman, "'Vital Tissues of the Spirit': Constitutional Emotions in the Antebellum United States," in *The Routledge Research Companion to Law and Humanities in Nineteenth-Century America*, ed. Nan Goodman and Simon Stern (New York: Routledge, 2017), 334.

119. *Cong. Globe*, 41st Cong., 3rd sess., appendix, 98 (1871).

CHAPTER TWO - A SYSTEM OF SHAME

1. Walter J. Frazer Jr. "John Eaton, Jr., Radical Republican: Champion of the Negro and Federal Aid to Southern Education, 1869–1882," *Tennessee Historical Quarterly* 25, no. 3 (1966): 240.

2. John Eaton with Ethel Osgood Mason, *Grant, Lincoln and the Freedmen: Reminiscences of the Civil War* (New York: Longmans, Green, 1907), 248–60.

3. John Eaton, *The Relation of the National Government to Public Education* (Philadelphia: Educational Gazette Publishing, 1870), 9, 7, 10.

4. David Tyack, "The Kingdom of God and the Common School: Protestant Ministers and the Educational Awakening in the West," *Harvard Educational Review* 32, no. 4 (1966): 450. On the regional distinctions between Northwestern and Northeastern common school development, see David Tyack and Elisabeth Hansot, *Managers of Virtue: Public School Leadership in America, 1820–1980* (New York: Basic Books, 1982), 44–56; Carl F. Kaestle, *Pillars of the Republic: Common Schools and American Society, 1780–1860* (New York: Hill and Wang, 1983), 182–217.

5. On shame in nineteenth-century classrooms, see Peter N. Stearns, *Shame: A Brief History* (Urbana: University of Illinois Press, 2017), 77–81. On the dynamics of shame in education more generally, see Margaret Werry and Róison O'Gorman, "Shamefaced: Performing Pedagogy, Outing Affect," *Text and Performance Quarterly* 27, no. 3 (2007): 213–30.

6. James C. Scott, *Seeing Like a State: How Certain Schemes to Improve the Human Condition Have Failed* (New Haven: Yale University Press, 1998), 2, 11–19, 89–90. On American policymakers' shift toward a rational, social scientific language of politics, see Daniel T. Rodgers, *Contested Truths: Keywords in American Politics Since Independence* (Cambridge: Harvard University Press, 1998), 144–45.

7. For a detailed history of the Bureau of Education's development, see Donald R. Warren, *To Enforce Education: A History of the Founding Years of the United States Office of Education* (Detroit: Wayne State University Press, 1974). On the rise of statistics in Reconstruction-era education policy, see Andrew Donnelly, "The Yankee Leviathan Collects Statistics: Federal Education Policy During Reconstruction," *Harvard Data Science Review* 3, no. 4 (2021), https://doi.org/10.1162/99608f92.d35b59a0.

8. This transitional period in congressional policymaking is recounted in Williamjames Hull Hoffer, *To Enlarge the Machinery of Government: Congressional Debates and the Growth of the American State, 1858–1891* (Baltimore: Johns Hopkins University Press, 2007).

9. *Cong. Globe*, 39th Cong., 1st sess., 653 (1866).

10. Peter S. Onuf, *Statehood and Union: A History of the Northwest Ordinance* (Bloomington: Indiana University Press, 1987), 21–43; Jeffrey Ostler, "'Just and Lawful War' as Genocidal War in the (United States) Northwest Ordinance and Northwest Territory, 1787–1832," *Journal of Genocide Research* 18, no. 1 (2016): 1–20.

11. Gordon T. Stewart, "The Northwest Ordinance and the Balance of Power in North America," in *The Northwest Ordinance: Essays on Its Formulation, Provisions, and Legacy*, ed. Frederick D. Williams (East Lansing: Michigan State University Press, 1989), 21–38.

12. Edward Carrington to James Monroe, August 7, 1787, in *Letters of Delegates to Congress, 1774–1789*, ed. Paul H. Smith (Washington, DC: Library of Congress, 1976), 24:391.

13. Robert S. Hill, "Federalism, Republicanism, and the Northwest Ordinance," *Publius* 18 (1988): 41–52.

14. Northwest Ordinance, July 13, 1787, RG 360, Miscellaneous Papers of the Continental Congress, 1774–1789, Records of the Continental and Confederation Congresses and the Constitutional Convention, 1774–1789, National Archives, Washington, DC. Regarding the Northwest Ordinance forming new states on equal terms with existing states, see Adam Dahl, *Empire of the People: Settler Colonialism and the Foundations of Modern Democratic Thought* (Lawrence: University Press of Kansas, 2018), 37–38.

15. Brian Balogh, *A Government Out of Sight: The Mystery of National Authority in Nineteenth-Century America* (New York: Cambridge University Press, 2009), 185; Timothy L. Smith, "Protestant Schooling and American Nationality, 1800–1850," *Journal of American History* 53, no. 4 (1967): 691–92.

16. Timothy L. Smith, "The Ohio Valley: Testing Ground for America's Experiment in Religious Pluralism," *Church History* 60, no. 4 (1991): 461–62.

17. Connecticut reverend E. F. Chapin quoted in William S. Kennedy, *The Plan of Union; or, A History of the Presbyterian and Congregational Churches of the Western Reserve* (Hudson, OH: Pentagon, 1856), 24. For other examples of religious leaders anxious about the absence of organized schooling in Illinois, Indiana, Wisconsin, and Ohio, see T. L. Smith, "Protestant Schooling and American Nationality," 691–94.

18. Neil Meyer, "Falling for the Lord: Shame, Revivalism, and the Origins of the Second Great Awakening," *Early American Studies* 9, no. 1 (2011): 153–54.

19. John F. Wakefield, "'Whosoever Will, Let Him Come': Evangelical Millennialism and the Development of American Public Education," *American Educational History Journal* 39, no. 2 (2012): 290–91; T. L. Smith, "Protestant Schooling and American Nationality," 691–92; Tyack, "Kingdom of God and the Common School," 448–50.

20. Alexander Campbell, "On Common Schools," in *Popular Lectures and Addresses*, 247–71 (Philadelphia: Challen, 1863), 270.

21. Campbell, "On Common Schools," 270.

22. Stearns, *Shame*, 77–81; Peter N. Stearns and Clio Stearns, "American Schools and the Uses of Shame: An Ambiguous History," *History of Education* 46, no. 1 (2017): 66–68.

23. Although major Northwestern cities adopted the change soon after their Northwestern counterparts, in the rural Northwest the shift toward evaluations came later. See William J. Reese, *Testing Wars in the Public Schools: A Forgotten History* (Cambridge: Harvard University Press, 2013), 173–77. On the cultural roles of student exhibitions as a mode of assessment, see Allison Speicher, *Schooling Readers: Reading Common Schools in Nineteenth-Century American Fiction* (Tuscaloosa: University of Alabama Press, 2016), 50.

24. Sara Ahmed, *The Cultural Politics of Emotion* (New York: Routledge, 2004), 107; Margaret Werry and Róison O'Gorman, "Shamefaced: Performing Pedagogy, Outing Affect," *Text and Performance Quarterly* 27, no. 3 (2007): 213–30.

25. "Love of Applause," in *McGuffey's New Fifth Eclectic Reader: Selected and Original Exercises for Schools*, ed. William H. McGuffey, 234–37 (Cincinnati: Smith, 1857), 234; Stearns and Stearns, "American Schools and the Uses of Shame," 66. At least 47 million copies of the *Readers* were in use across Ohio, Indiana, and the broader Midwest by 1870. See John A. Nietz, "Why the Longevity of the McGuffey Readers?" *History of Education Quarterly* 4, no. 2 (1964): 119–25.

26. William Slocomb, "School Government," *Ohio Educational Monthly* 18, no. 1 (1868): 3–5.

27. Paul Theobald, "Country School Curriculum and Governance: The One-Room School Experience in the Nineteenth-Century Midwest," *American Journal of Education* 101, no. 2 (1993): 125–26.

28. See, e.g., Lyman Beecher, *A Plea for the West* (Cincinnati: Truman and Smith, 1835), 145. On the "pervasive quality of dissent" against centralized authority among Protestant denominations, see Nathan O. Hatch, *The Democratization of American Christianity* (New Haven: Yale University Press, 1989), 206–9. On the tenuous Protestant compromise favoring nondenominational moral education, see T. L. Smith, "Protestant Schooling and American Nationality," 694–95; R. Laurence Moore, "Bible Reading and Nonsectarian Schooling: The Failure of Religious Instruction in Nineteenth-Century Public Education," *Journal of American History* 86, no. 4 (2000): 1581–99.

29. Calvin E. Stowe, "Prussian System of Public Instruction, Part II: Applicability of the System to the United States," *Common School Advocate* 1, no. 3 (1837): 18.

30. David Tyack and Elisabeth Hansot, "Conflict and Consensus in American Public Education," *Daedalus* 110, no. 3 (1981): 5; Tyack, "Kingdom of God and the Common School," 454, 448–51. On the publications established throughout the Northwest to promote educational causes, see Sheldon Emmor Davis, *Educational Periodicals During the Nineteenth Century* (Washington, DC: Government Printing Office, 1919).

31. Samuel Lewis, "Common Schools: Address of the Superintendent of Ohio to the County," *Western Academician and Journal of Education and Science* 1, no. 7 (1837): 384.

32. Mary E. Stuckey, "FDR, the Rhetoric of Vision, and the Creation of a National Synoptic State," *Quarterly Journal of Speech* 98, no. 3 (2012): 301.

33. Onuf, *Statehood and Union*, 38.

34. See, e.g., William Cronon, *Nature's Metropolis: Chicago and the Great West* (New York: Norton, 1991), 101–2.

35. Warren, *To Enforce Education*, 70–76; Lawrence A. Cremin, *American Education: The National Experience, 1783–1876* (New York: Harper & Row, 1980), 335–52; Lee S. Duemer, "The Agricultural Origins of the Morrill Land Grant Act of 1862," *American Educational History Journal* 34, no. 1 (2007): 135–46.

36. William G. W. Lewis, *Biography of Samuel Lewis, First Superintendent of Common Schools for the State of Ohio* (Cincinnati: Thompson, 1857), 196.

37. Wakefield, "Whosoever Will, Let Him Come," 298.

38. Alan I. Marcus, *Agricultural Science and the Quest for Legitimacy: Farmers, Agricultural Colleges, and Experiment Stations, 1870–1890* (Ames: Iowa State University Press, 1985), 12–13; T. Swann Harding, *Two Blades of Grass: A History of Scientific Development in the U.S. Department of Agriculture* (Norman: University of Oklahoma Press, 1947), 18–19.

39. On the rapid growth of school systems in Ohio and the deep commitments that schooling generated, see Johann N. Neem, "Path Dependence and the Emergence of Common Schools: Ohio to 1853," *Journal of Policy History* 28, no. 1 (2016): 48–80.

40. "Memorial on Behalf of the Ohio University," in *Journal of the Senate of the State of Ohio: For the Second Session of the Fifty-Fourth General Assembly* (Columbus, OH: Nevins, 1861), 50.

41. Kyla Schuller, *The Biopolitics of Feeling: Race, Sex, and Science in the Nineteenth Century* (Durham, NC: Duke University Press, 2018), 81.

42. On the role of missions in the Northwest Territory, see Lori J. Daggar, "The Mission Complex: Economic Development, 'Civilization,' and Empire in the Early Republic," *Journal of the Early Republic* 36, no. 3 (2016): 467–91; on the "civilizing" ideology of the missions, see Francis Paul Prucha, *The Great Father: The United States Government and the American Indians* (Lincoln: University of Nebraska Press, 1984), 135–58.

43. James B. Finley, *History of the Wyandott Mission at Upper Sandusky, Ohio* (Cincinnati: Thompson, 1840), 206. On the way the Wyandots received this discourse of literacy, see Michael Leonard Cox, "The Ohio Wyandots: Religion and Society on the Sandusky River, 1765–1843" (PhD diss., University of California, Riverside, 2016), 268–72.

44. David Wallace Adams, *Education for Extinction: American Indians and the Boarding School Experience, 1875–1928* (Lawrence: University Press of Kansas, 1995), 5–27.

45. See, e.g., Nikki Marie Taylor, *Frontiers of Freedom: Cincinnati's Black Community, 1802–1868* (Athens: Ohio University Press, 2004), 161–74.

46. *Minutes of the State Convention, of the Colored Citizens of Ohio, Convened at Columbus, Jan. 15th, 16th, 17th, and 18th, 1851* (Columbus, OH: Glover, 1851), 17.

47. On the complexity of evolving attitudes about race in Ohio, see Paul Finkelman, "The Strange Career of Race Discrimination in Antebellum Ohio," *Case Western Reserve Law Review* 55, no. 2 (2004): 375. On literacy as a rationale for subordinating Black citizens in the antebellum North, see Hilary J. Moss, *Schooling Citizens: The Struggle for African American Education in Antebellum America* (Chicago: University of Chicago Press, 2009), 4.

48. Other Northwestern states had similarly oppressive policies. Illinois did not formally allow Black students to have access to public education until the Civil War era. See Davison M. Douglas, "The Limits of Law in Accomplishing Racial Change: School Segregation in the Pre-Brown North," *UCLA Law Review* 44 (1997): 692–97.

49. Peter S. Onuf, "The Northwest Ordinance and Regional Identity," *Wisconsin Magazine of History* 72 (1989): 293–304.

50. Jurgen Herbst, "The Development of Public Universities in the Old Northwest," in *Northwest Ordinance*, ed. F. D. Williams, 111. The universities established under the Morrill Act were themselves part of a legacy of colonial dispossession of Native American lands. See Margaret A. Nash, "Entangled Pasts: Land-Grant Colleges and American Indian Dispossession," *History of Education Quarterly* 59, no. 4 (2019): 437–67.

51. For accounts of Garfield's lecture on the "Theory and Practice of Teaching," endorsement of professional education journals, support from educational associations, and reputation as a "teacher at Institutes," see "Intelligence: Cuyahoga Co. Teachers' Institute," *Ohio Journal of Education* 8, no. 6 (1859): 187–88; editorial, *Ohio Journal of Education* 8, no. 9 (1859): 286; editorial, *Ohio Journal of Education* 8, no. 11 (1859): 349.

52. "A Republican," *Colonel Mark H. Dunnell: A Few Chapters of His Personal Military and Political History* (n.p., 1867), Wilson Library, University of Minnesota, Minneapolis.

53. Andrew Jackson Rickoff, "A National Bureau of Education," in *National Teachers' Association: Proceedings and Lectures of the Sixth Annual Meeting, Held at Harrisburg, on the 16th, 17th, and 18th of August, 1865* (Hartford, CT: Office of the *American Journal of Education*, 1865), 303.

54. *Cong. Globe*, 39th Cong., 1st sess., 60 (1865).

55. Emerson E. White, "National Bureau of Education," *American Journal of Education* 16, no. 4 (1866): 180.

56. Hoffer, *To Enlarge the Machinery*, 92; Allan Peskin, "The Short, Unhappy Life of the Federal Department of Education," *Public Administration Review* 33, no. 6 (1973): 572–75.

57. John Clark Ridpath, *The Life and Work of James A. Garfield: Twentieth President of the United States* (Cincinnati: Jones, 1881), 217–18.

58. *Cong. Globe*, 39th Cong., 1st sess., 3045 (1866).

59. In Scott's terms, the impetus was for the "chaotic, disorderly, changing social reality" to become "something more closely resembling the administrative grid of observations" (*Seeing Like a State*, 82).

60. *Cong. Globe*, 39th Cong., 1st sess., 3045 (1866).

61. Anna Koivusalo, "'He Ordered the First Gun Fired & He Resigned First': James Chesnut, Southern Honor, and Emotion," in *The Field of Honor: Essays on Southern Character and American Identity*, ed. John Mayfield (Columbia: University of South Carolina Press, 2017), 197.

62. David Leverenz, *Honor Bound: Race and Shame in America* (New Brunswick, NJ: Rutgers University Press, 2012), 67.

63. John Mayfield, "The Marketplace of Values: Honor and Enterprise in the Old South," in *Field of Honor*, ed. Mayfield, 7–12.

64. *Cong. Globe*, 39th Cong., 1st sess., 587, 2968 (1866).

65. *Cong. Globe*, 39th Cong., 1st sess., 3047, 3048 (1866).

66. *Cong. Globe*, 39th Cong., 1st sess., 2969, 2968 (1866).

67. *Cong. Globe*, 39th Cong., 1st sess., 3050, 3049 (1866).

68. *Cong. Globe*, 39th Cong., 1st sess., 3050 (1866).

69. *Cong. Globe*, 39th Cong., 1st sess., 3049 (1866).

70. *Cong. Globe*, 39th Cong., 1st sess., 3050 (1866).

71. *Cong. Globe*, 39th Cong., 1st sess., 3051, 3269–70, 1842–45, 1893, 1949 (1866); Warren, *To Enforce Education*, 89.

72. Edith Nye MacMullen, *In the Cause of True Education: Henry Barnard and Nineteenth-Century School Reform* (New Haven: Yale University Press, 1991), 259.

73. *Cong. Globe*, 40th Cong., 2nd sess., 1139, 1141, 3703 (1868).

74. Thaddeus Stevens, *The Famous Speech of Hon. Thaddeus Stevens of Pennsylvania in Opposition to the Repeal of the Common School Law of 1834* (Philadelphia: Thaddeus Stevens Memorial Association, 1904), 6–7. On Stevens's subsequent support for public education, see Christopher Shepard, "Making No Distinctions Between Rich and Poor: Thaddeus Stevens and Class Equality," *Pennsylvania History: A Journal of Mid-Atlantic Studies* 80, no. 1 (2013): 37–50.

75. *Cong. Globe*, 39th Cong., 1st sess., 3050–51 (1866).

76. *Cong. Globe*, 40th Cong., 2nd sess., 3704 (1868).

77. Kaestle, *Pillars of the Republic*, 187.

78. *Cong. Globe*, 40th Cong., 2nd sess., 3704 (1868).

79. *Cong. Globe*, 40th Cong., 3rd sess., 1542 (1869), 40th Cong., 2nd sess., 3705 (1868), 41st Cong., 2nd sess., 1491 (1870).

80. The population of Chicago grew nearly 900 percent in twenty years, going from 29,963 in 1850 to 109,260 in 1860 to 298,977 in 1870 (US Census Bureau, *Seventh Census of the United States: 1850: Volume IV, Compendium, Part VI, Population of Cities, Towns, &c.* [Washington, DC: Armstrong, 1853], 347; US Census Bureau, *Eighth Census of the United States, 1860*, vol. 1, *Population*, pt. 2, *Florida–Illinois* [Washington, DC: Government Printing Office, 1864], 90; US Census Bureau, *Ninth Census of the United States, 1870*, vol. 1, *Population* [Washington, DC: Government Printing Office, 1872], 110).

81. Shepherd Johnston, *Historical Sketches of the Public School System of the City of Chicago, to the Close of the Year 1878–79* (Chicago: Clark & Edwards, 1880), 39–41.

82. Allan Peskin, *Garfield* (Kent, OH: Kent State University Press, 1999), 296; *Cong. Globe*, 40th Cong., 2nd sess., 1139 (1868), 40th Cong., 3rd sess., 1542 (1869); Werry and O'Gorman, "Shamefaced."

83. Anticipating congressional criticism, Barnard's introduction tried to account for his difficulties in synthesizing the disparate material. See *Report of the Commissioner of Education, with Circulars and Documents Accompanying the Same . . . 1868* (Washington, DC: Government Printing Office, 1868), x–xi; Warren, *To Enforce Education*, 113–14.

84. *Cong. Globe*, 40th Cong., 3rd sess., 1796 (1869), 41st Cong., 2nd sess., 3356 (1870).

85. *Report of the Commissioner of Education Made to the Secretary of the Interior for the Year 1870* (Washington, DC: Government Printing Office, 1870), 5; MacMullen, *In the Cause of True Education*, 278; Eaton with Mason, *Grant, Lincoln and the Freedmen*, 258.

86. Stephen J. Sniegoski, *John Eaton, U.S. Commissioner of Education, 1870–1886* (Washington, DC: Office of Educational Research and Improvement, 1995).

87. *Report of the Commissioner of Education . . . 1870*, 1–80.

88. *Report of the Commissioner of Education . . . 1870*, 482–502. See also Susan Schulten, *Mapping the Nation: History and Cartography in Nineteenth-Century America* (Chicago: University of Chicago Press, 2012), 157–59.

89. *Cong. Globe*, 41st Cong., 3rd sess., 1131, 1133 (1871); *Report of the Commissioner of Education . . . 1870*, 103.

90. *Cong. Globe*, 41st Cong., 3rd sess., 1418 (1871); *Report of the Commissioner of Education . . . 1870*, 103.

91. *Cong. Globe*, 41st Cong., 3rd sess., 1133, 1134–35 (1871).

92. On the growing discontent with Hoar's approach to reform, see Ward M. McAfee, *Religion, Race, and Reconstruction: The Public School in the Politics of the 1870s* (Albany: State University of New York Press, 1998), 113–21.

93. Record of the Business Transacted by the Committee on Education and Labor of the House of Representatives, During the 2nd Session of the 42nd Congress, Commencing on Dec. 4, 1871, 52, RG 233, Records of the Committee on Education and Labor, 40th–48th Congresses (1867–1883), Records of the US House of Representatives, 1789–1989, National Archives, Washington, DC.

94. *Cong. Globe*, 42nd Cong., 2nd sess., 567 (1872).

95. *Cong. Globe*, 42nd Cong., 2nd sess., 852, 567 (1872).

96. *Cong. Globe*, 42nd Cong., 2nd sess., 859–60 (1872).

97. *Cong. Globe*, 42nd Cong., 2nd sess., 794 (1872).

98. *Cong. Globe*, 42nd Cong., 2nd sess., 592 (1872).
99. *Cong. Globe*, 42nd Cong., 2nd sess., 566 (1872).
100. Kirt H. Wilson, *The Reconstruction Desegregation Debate: The Politics of Equality and the Rhetoric of Place, 1870–1875* (East Lansing: Michigan State University Press, 2002), 10–16.
101. *Cong. Globe*, 42nd Cong., 2nd sess., appendix, 15–16 (1872).
102. Susan Zaeske, "'The South Arose as One Man': Gender and Sectionalism in Antislavery Petition Debates, 1835–1845," *Rhetoric & Public Affairs* 12, no. 3 (2009): 358.
103. *Cong. Globe*, 42nd Cong., 2nd sess., appendix, 15–16 (1872).
104. *Cong. Globe*, 42nd Cong., 2nd sess., 800, 801, appendix, 38 (1872). For similar remarks by Representative Henry D. McHenry (D-KY), see *Cong. Globe*, 42nd Cong., 2nd sess., 788–89 (1872).
105. On Storm's educational background, see, e.g., C. R. Coburn, *Report of the Superintendent of Common Schools of the Commonwealth of Pennsylvania for the Year Ending June 5, 1865* (Harrisburg, PA: Singerly & Myers, 1866), 155–57.
106. *Cong. Globe*, 42nd Cong., 2nd sess., 857, 858, 799 (1872).
107. *Cong. Globe*, 42nd Cong., 2nd sess., 569 (1872). The Southern Democrats were Abraham E. Garrett (D-TN), Edward Golladay (D-TN), Abraham E. Garrett (D-TN), James M. Leach (D-NC), and James Harper (D-NC). See *Cong. Globe*, 42nd Cong., 2nd sess., 882, 903 (1872).
108. *Cong. Globe*, 42nd Cong., 2nd sess., 882, 903, 860 (1872).
109. George Frisbie Hoar, *Autobiography of Seventy Years* (New York: Scribner's, 1903), 1:265; Hoffer, *To Enlarge the Machinery*, 116.
110. *Cong. Globe*, 41st Cong., 3rd sess., 492 (1871).
111. *Cong. Globe*, 42nd Cong., 2nd sess., 861 (1872).
112. Brian Balogh, *The Associational State: American Governance in the Twentieth Century* (Philadelphia: University of Pennsylvania Press, 2015), 201.
113. Hoffer, *To Enlarge the Machinery*, xi, 89–103.
114. *Cong. Globe*, 42nd Cong., 2nd sess., 859–60 (1872).
115. The logics that underwrote the Perce Bill—of statistical influence, detailed social scientific reporting, and inducing rather than enforcing state activity—continued to appeal to Congress well into the Gilded Age. The Perce Bill framework became a foundational model for the most significant post-Reconstruction attempt to create a federal education program: New Hampshire Republican senator Henry William Blair's bill for a national education fund, which was debated repeatedly throughout the 1880s. The Blair Bill approached funding in a more ambitious way than the Perce Bill, seeking to draw funds directly from the US Treasury. But it also shared the key concessions that Perce Bill drafters made. It allowed racial segregation, allocated funds based on states' illiteracy rates, and left states in control of how to spend their funds (albeit with extensive reporting requirements to prove effective and fair distribution of the money). That legislation also won over an unusual bipartisan coalition of Northern Republicans and Southern Democrats, passing the Senate three times but faltering in a House committee. See Gordon B. McKinney, *Henry W. Blair's Campaign to Reform America: From the Civil War to the U.S. Senate* (Lexington: University Press of Kentucky, 2013), 95–99, 119.

116. Kirk Branch, "'A Mockery in the Name of a Barrier': Literacy Test Debates in the Reconstruction Era Congress, 1864–1869," *Literacy in Composition Studies* 3, no. 2 (2015): 59–61.

117. W. E. B. Du Bois, *Black Reconstruction in America* (1935; New York: Free Press, 1998), 648.

CHAPTER THREE - AN ATMOSPHERE OF ALTRUISM

1. C. Anna Harwood attended Illinois State Normal University from January 3, 1859, until the end of her third year. See Office of the University Registrar, "University Enrollment Ledger, 1857–1867," *Illinois State University ReD: Research and eData*, 46–47, https://ir.library.illinoisstate.edu/enrl/1.

2. "Mississippi: Record of Rebel Crime—Assassination of Lieutenant Blonding [sic]—The Ordeal for Northern Men and Women," *Philadelphia Inquirer*, May 30, 1866, 2. A publication from the Congregational Church attended by Segur and Harwood wrote that the two had a "copartnership in their lives which continued unbroken until the death of Miss Segar [sic], September, 1920, a period of over fifty years." See Ella Warren Harrison, Pauline Schenk, Jessie A. Phelps, Carrie Dunbar, Olive Pierce, F. W. Stewart, and S. T. Brigham, eds., *The Hampshire Colony Congregational Church: Its First Hundred Years, 1831–1931* (Princeton, IL: Bureau County Record, 1931), 85.

3. "Mississippi, Grenada," *American Missionary* 32, no. 9 (1878): 275.

4. The story printed in the *Philadelphia Inquirer* was reprinted in other outlets across the country. See, e.g., "Mississippi—A Record of Violence—What Does It Mean?" *Delaware Republican*, June 11, 1866, 1; "From Mississippi—A Record of Violence—What Does It Mean?" *New York Tribune*, May 29, 1866, 7; "From Mississippi—A Record of Violence," *Daily Iowa State Register*, June 8, 1866, 3.

5. J. W. Alvord, *Report on Schools and Finances of Freedmen: For July, 1866* (Washington, DC, 1866), 12, 20–21. The report also discussed Blanding's assassination and the events documented in *The Philadelphia Inquirer* and elsewhere.

6. On the fervent nationalism at the peak of the Civil War, see Melinda Lawson, *Patriot Fires: Forging a New American Nationalism in the Civil War North* (Lawrence: University Press of Kansas, 2002), 11.

7. Linda Warfel Slaughter, *Freedmen of the South* (Cincinnati: Elm Street, 1869), 114.

8. Jessica Enoch, "A Woman's Place Is in the School: Rhetorics of Gendered Space in Nineteenth-Century America," *College English* 70, no. 3 (2008): 284–87.

9. Kyla Schuller, *The Biopolitics of Feeling: Race, Sex, and Science in the Nineteenth Century* (Durham, NC: Duke University Press, 2018), 13–14.

10. Elizabeth Maddock Dillon, *The Gender of Freedom: Fictions of Liberalism and the Literary Public Sphere* (Stanford, CA: Stanford University Press, 2004), 18.

11. "Words from a Freedmen's Teacher," *Monthly Religious Magazine* 35, no. 6 (1866): 402.

12. Robert Harrison, "New Representations of a 'Misrepresented Bureau': Reflections on Recent Scholarship on the Freedmen's Bureau," *American Nineteenth Century History* 8, no. 2 (2007): 206.

13. Jacqueline Jones, *Soldiers of Light and Love: Northern Teachers and Georgia Blacks, 1865–1873* (Athens: University of Georgia Press, 1992), 94–96; George R. Bentley, *A History of the Freedmen's Bureau* (Philadelphia: University of Pennsylvania Press, 1955), 62–75.

14. Jessica Enoch, *Refiguring Rhetorical Education: Women Teaching African American, Native American, and Chicano/a Students, 1865–1911* (Carbondale: Southern Illinois University Press, 2008), 67–68; J. Jones, *Soldiers of Light and Love*, 103–4; Amanda Claybaugh, "Public Education and the Welfare State: The Case of the Freedmen's Schools," *Occasion: Interdisciplinary Studies in the Humanities* 2 (2010): 8.

15. On education as an "orientation device" for affect, see Sara Ahmed, *The Promise of Happiness* (Durham, NC: Duke University Press, 2010), 54.

16. US Congress, House, Committee on Education and Labor, *Charges Against General Howard*, 41st Cong., 2nd sess., 1870, H. Doc. 121, 50.

17. Chandra Manning, "Contraband Camps and the African American Refugee Experience During the Civil War," *Oxford Research Encyclopedia of American History* (New York: Oxford University Press, 2020), https://oxfordre.com/americanhistory/americanhistory/abstract/10.1093/acrefore/9780199329175.001.0001/acrefore-9780199329175-e-203.

18. Freedmen's Aid Society leaders to Representative Thomas D. Eliot (R-MA), December 1, 1863, printed in *Cong. Globe*, 38th Cong., 2nd sess., 690 (1865).

19. On the deliberate ambiguity of the bureau legislation, see Williamjames Hull Hoffer, *To Enlarge the Machinery of Government: Congressional Debates and the Growth of the American State, 1858–1891* (Baltimore: Johns Hopkins University Press, 2007), 68.

20. Michael E. Woods, *Emotional and Sectional Conflict in the Antebellum United States* (New York: Cambridge University Press, 2014), 51–62; Eric Foner, *Free Soil, Free Labor, Free Men: The Ideology of the Republican Party Before the Civil War* (1970; New York: Oxford University Press, 1995), 50.

21. Oliver Otis Howard, "Education of the Colored Man" [ca. 1868], 51–52, Oliver Otis Howard Papers, box 43, folder 50, George J. Mitchell Department of Special Collections & Archives, Bowdoin College, Brunswick, Maine. I thank Jessica Lu for sharing this document.

22. Saidiya V. Hartman, *Scenes of Subjection: Terror, Slavery, and Self-Making in Nineteenth-Century America* (New York: Oxford University Press, 1997), 125–30; Eric Foner, *Reconstruction: America's Unfinished Revolution, 1863–1877* (1988; New York: Perennial Classics, 2002), 68, 236–37.

23. White Northerners and Southerners alike interpreted newly emancipated slaves' late-1865 resistance to signing labor contracts with their former masters as a sign of an impending insurrection. See Dan T. Carter, "The Anatomy of Fear: The Christmas Day Insurrection Scare of 1865," *Journal of Southern History* 42, no. 3 (1976): 359–60. See also Heather Cox Richardson, *The Death of Reconstruction: Race, Labor, and Politics in the Post–Civil War North, 1865–1901* (Cambridge: Harvard University Press, 2009), 61–65.

24. Hartman, *Scenes of Subjection*, 127.

25. Schuller, *Biopolitics of Feeling*, 21, 18.

26. See, e.g., Lucy Chase, "Letter from Lucy Chase, April 01, 1863," in *Dear Ones at Home: Letters from Contraband Camps*, ed. Henry L. Swint (Nashville, TN: Vanderbilt University Press, 1966), 56. On the role of imitation in shaping racist assumptions of literacy and

learning after the Civil War, see Kirt H. Wilson, "The Racial Politics of Imitation in the Nineteenth Century," *Quarterly Journal of Speech* 89, no. 2 (2003): 94–99.

27. Christopher Castiglia, *Interior States: Institutional Consciousness and the Inner Life of Democracy in the Antebellum United States* (Durham, NC: Duke University Press, 2008), 103. Schuller describes this attitude as crucial to the reform project of "biophilanthropy," through which philanthropic associations aimed to shape the senses of populations to assimilate them into logics of contract labor (*Biopolitics of Feeling*, 161).

28. Edward L. Pierce, *The Freedmen of Port Royal, South Carolina* (New York: Rebellion Record, 1863), 304, 312.

29. On freedpeople's efforts to support their own education, see Hilary Green, *Educational Reconstruction: African American Schools in the Urban South, 1865–1890* (New York: Fordham University Press, 2016), 17–18. On missionary interpretations of Black educational enthusiasm, see Kevin Dougherty, *The Port Royal Experiment: A Case Study in Development* (Jackson: University Press of Mississippi, 2016), 54–68; Akiko Ochiai, "The Port Royal Experiment Revisited: Northern Visions of Reconstruction and the Land Question," *New England Quarterly* 74, no. 1 (2001): 94–117.

30. Enoch, "Woman's Place," 284–87.

31. Dana Luciano, *Arranging Grief: Sacred Time and the Body in Nineteenth-Century America* (New York: New York University Press, 2007), 58.

32. On efforts to inculcate the Northern white "separate spheres" ideology into freedpeople, see Amy Dru Stanley, *From Bondage to Contract: Wage Labor, Marriage, and the Market in the Age of Slave Emancipation* (New York: Cambridge University Press, 1998), 44–52; Mary Farmer-Kaiser, *Freedwomen and the Freedmen's Bureau: Race, Gender, and Public Policy in the Age of Emancipation* (New York: Fordham University Press, 2010), 14–34. On Northern white philanthropists' bias against hiring Black women teachers, see Geraldine J. Clifford, *Those Good Gertrudes: A Social History of Women Teachers in America* (Baltimore: Johns Hopkins University Press, 2014), 158–59; Heather Andrea Williams, *Self-Taught: African American Education in Slavery and Freedom* (Chapel Hill: University of North Carolina Press, 2005), 115.

33. Ronald E. Butchart's database of freedpeople's teachers during Reconstruction shows that the AMA supported roughly as many Black Southern men as white Northern women (*Schooling the Freed People: Teaching, Learning, and the Struggle for Black Freedom, 1861–1876* [Chapel Hill: University of North Carolina Press, 2013], 80–82).

34. Enoch, *Refiguring Rhetorical Education*, 35–41; Jacqueline Jones, "Women Who Were More Than Men: Sex and Status in Freedmen's Teaching," *History of Education Quarterly* 19, no. 1 (1979): 50.

35. Susan M. Ryan, *The Grammar of Good Intentions: Race and the Antebellum Culture of Benevolence* (Ithaca: Cornell University Press, 2003), 144, 110.

36. On the circulation of teacher narratives, see Amy F. Morsman, "Reporting from the South: Massachusetts Teachers and Freedmen's Education," in *Massachusetts and the Civil War*, ed. Matthew Mason, Katheryn P. Viens, and Conrad Edick Wright (Amherst: University of Massachusetts Press, 2015), 249–74. I am adopting a distinction from Sara Ahmed's work on philanthropic affect: aid narratives tend to invite people to "feel sad *about* [the Other's] suffering" while centering "the charity, aligned *with*" readers and their sense of empowerment (*The Cultural Politics of Emotion* [New York: Routledge, 2004], 21–22).

37. Clifford, *Those Good Gertrudes*, 289–91.

38. Kathleen Weiler, "Women's History and the History of Women Teachers," *Journal of Education* 171, no. 3 (1989): 16–19; J. Jones, *Soldiers of Light and Love*, 104. On teachers' self-sacrifice as a form of affective labor, see Jenny Edbauer Rice, "The New 'New': Making a Case for Critical Affect Studies," *Quarterly Journal of Speech* 94, no. 2 (2008): 207–8.

39. Caroline Faulkner, *Women's Radical Reconstruction: The Freedmen's Aid Movement* (Philadelphia: University of Pennsylvania Press, 2004), 32.

40. J. Jones, *Soldiers of Light and Love*, 10.

41. Louise Michele Newman, *White Women's Rights: The Racial Origins of Feminism in the United States* (New York: Oxford University Press, 1999), 96.

42. Thomas D. Eliot, *Speech of Thomas D. Eliot, of Massachusetts, Delivered in the House of Representatives Feb. 10, 1864, on the Bill for the Establishment of a Bureau of Freedmen's Affairs* (Washington, DC: Polkinhorn, 1864), 16; *US Statutes at Large*, vol. 13 (Boston: Little, Brown, 1866), 507–9.

43. Robert C. Lieberman, "The Freedmen's Bureau and the Politics of Institutional Structure," *Social Science History* 18, no. 3 (1994): 415–16; Andrew Johnson, "Proclamation 134—Granting Amnesty to Participants in the Rebellion, with Certain Exceptions," May 29, 1865, *American Presidency Project*, https://www.presidency.ucsb.edu/node/203492.

44. Ronald E. Butchart, *Northern Schools, Southern Blacks and Reconstruction* (Westport, CT: Greenwood, 1980), 97–107.

45. Foner, *Reconstruction*, 68, 236–37. See also Stanley, *From Bondage to Contract*, 36; Lea S. VanderVelde, "The Labor Vision of the Thirteenth Amendment," *University of Pennsylvania Law Review* 138, no. 2 (1989): 438.

46. J. W. Alvord, *First Semi-Annual Report on Schools and Finances of Freedmen, January 1, 1866* (Washington, DC: Government Printing Office, 1868), 11, 13–14.

47. "Speech of General Howard," *Liberator*, September 1, 1865, 35.

48. "Speech of General Howard," 14.

49. "Rev. Henry Ward Beecher in the House of Representatives, Washington," *Freed-Man*, February 1866, 158.

50. *Cong. Globe*, 39th Cong., 1st sess., 340 (1866).

51. *Cong. Globe*, 39th Cong., 1st sess., 321–22, 396, 340 (1866).

52. *Cong. Globe*, 39th Cong., 1st sess., 514, 517 (1866). Eliot's reformer connections included his brother, William Greenleaf Eliot, an influential Unitarian minister, abolitionist, and common school advocate as well as the founder of Washington University in St. Louis. In their correspondence, William provided Thomas insight into Western reform currents and urged his brother's to act on issues related to emancipation throughout the 1860s. See Adam Arenson, *The Great Heart of the Republic: St. Louis and the Cultural Civil War* (Columbia: University of Missouri Press, 2011), 47–64; Charlotte C. Eliot, *William Greenleaf Eliot: Minister, Educator, Philanthropist* (Boston: Houghton, Mifflin, 1904), 92–93, 183–87.

53. *Cong. Globe*, 39th Cong., 1st sess., 517 (1866).

54. *Cong. Globe*, 39th Cong., 1st sess., 95 (1866).

55. *Cong. Globe*, 39th Cong., 1st sess., 914, 1017 (1866). In a similar appeal, Representative Josiah Grinnell (R-IA) argued that if unreconstructed rebels were freed from the constraints imposed by the bureau in Kentucky, "that statute may now be enforced which imprisoned

a northern lady teacher in a penitentiary many years for pointing a negro to the north star" (*Cong. Globe*, 39th Cong., 1st sess., 651 [1866]).

56. *Cong. Globe*, 39th Cong., 1st sess., appendix, 79, 637 (1866). See also remarks of Representative Burwell C. Ritter (D-KY), *Cong. Globe*, 39th Cong., 1st sess., 636 (1866).

57. Andrew Johnson, "Veto Message," February 19, 1866, *American Presidency Project*, https://www.presidency.ucsb.edu/documents/veto-message-437.

58. John H. Abel and LaWanda Cox, "Andrew Johnson and His Ghost Writers: An Analysis of the Freedmen's Bureau and Civil Rights Veto Messages," *Mississippi Valley Historical Review* 48, no. 3 (1961): 460–79.

59. On the widespread newspaper coverage of these events throughout the North, see Steven Ash, *A Massacre in Memphis: The Race Riot That Shook the Nation One Year After the Civil War* (New York: Hill and Wang, 2013), 176–77.

60. Campbell F. Scribner, "Surveying the Destruction of African American Schoolhouses in the South, 1864–1876," *Journal of the Civil War Era* 10, no. 4 (2020): 469–94.

61. "Interesting Letter from the South," *Iowa State Daily Register*, May 20, 1866, 2.

62. "The Anniversaries: Addresses of General Howard and Henry Ward Beecher Before the American Missionary Association," *New York Herald*, May 9, 1866, 10.

63. US House of Representatives, *Memphis Riots and Massacres, July 25, 1866*, (Report 101, 39th Cong., 1st sess.), 33, 20.

64. *Cong. Globe*, 39th Cong., 1st sess., 2772 (1866).

65. Beginning in the summer of 1866, the bureau's provisions of rations to freedpeople plummeted from 1,400,000 meals in June to only 200,000 in October even as the bureau gained more secure funding sources (Lieberman, "Freedmen's Bureau," 417–18).

66. *Cong. Globe*, 39th Cong., 1st sess., 2773, 3838–42 (1866). Other provisions of the legislation also reinforced the protection theme. For instance, the bill strengthened the bureau's system of courts to better enforce the Civil Rights Act of 1866 in unadmitted Southern states.

67. *Cong. Globe*, 39th Cong., 1st sess., appendix, 68 (1866).

68. Foner, *Reconstruction*, 275–77.

69. Foner, *Reconstruction*, 275–77.

70. *Cong. Globe*, 40th Cong., 2nd sess., 1825 (1868).

71. *Cong. Globe*, 40th Cong., 2nd sess., 3054 (1868). See also remarks of Representatives George M. Adams (D-KY) and Lawrence S. Trimble (D-KY), *Cong. Globe*, 40th Cong., 2nd sess., appendix, 294 1815 (1868).

72. H. C. Richardson, *Death of Reconstruction*, 52–67.

73. Michael Les Benedict, "The Rout of Radicalism: Republicans and the Elections of 1867," *Civil War History* 18, no. 4 (1972): 341–42.

74. J. W. Alvord, *Bureau of Refugees, Freedmen, and Abandoned Lands—1867: Fourth Semi-Annual Report on Schools for Freedmen, July 1, 1867* (Washington, DC: Government Printing Office, 1867), 79.

75. S. C. Armstrong to Thomas D. Eliot, December 30, 1867, Virginia File, Letters Received by Thomas D. Eliot, Chairman of the House Committee on Freedmen's Affairs, December 1867–February 1868, RG 105, Records of the Bureau of Refugees, Freedmen, and Abandoned Lands, National Archives, Washington, DC. On Armstrong's racial philosophy

of education and its influence, see James D. Anderson, *The Education of Blacks in the South, 1860–1935* (Chapel Hill: University of North Carolina Press, 1988), 33–78.

76. *Cong. Globe*, 39th Cong., 1st sess., 2773 (1866).

77. Erik Mathisen, *The Loyal Republic: Traitors, Slaves, and the Remaking of Citizenship in Civil War America* (Chapel Hill: University of North Carolina Press, 2018), 90–91, 144, 147–48.

78. *Cong. Globe*, 39th Cong., 1st sess., 685 (1866).

79. Mathisen, *Loyal Republic*, 145–66.

80. Armstrong to Eliot, December 30, 1867.

81. *Cong. Globe*, 40th Cong., 2nd sess., 1816 (1868).

82. *Cong. Globe*, 40th Cong., 2nd sess., 700 (1868).

83. *Cong. Globe*, 40th Cong., 2nd sess., 703 (1868).

84. "Speech of Senator Doolittle at Bridgeport, March 26," *World*, March 28, 1868, 4..

85. Most leagues were initially established by white Northerners, including an array of bureau officers, but by 1868, Black members had asserted their own political prerogatives. See Michael W. Fitzgerald, *The Union League Movement in the Deep South: Politics and Agricultural Change During Reconstruction* (Baton Rouge: Louisiana State University Press, 1989), 58–65.

86. Mark Wahlgren Summers, *A Dangerous Stir: Fear, Paranoia, and the Making of Reconstruction* (Chapel Hill: University of North Carolina Press, 2009), 63. For an illustration of the false equivalences drawn between the violence of the White Leagues and the Union Leagues, see Nicholas Lemann, *Redemption: The Last Battle of the Civil War* (New York: Farrar, Straus and Giroux, 2007), 80–92.

87. *Cong. Globe*, 40th Cong., 2nd sess., 3054, 4004, 4006, 4005, 2166 (1868).

88. *Cong. Globe*, 40th Cong., 2nd sess., 4006 (1868).

89. *Cong. Globe*, 40th Cong., 2nd sess., 4006, 1816 (1868).

90. *Cong. Globe*, 40th Cong., 2nd sess., 1816, 4479 (1868).

91. J. W. Alvord, *Ninth Semi-Annual Report on Schools for Freedmen, January 1, 1870* (Washington, DC: Government Printing Office, 1870), 5. For example, the American Missionary Association, the largest contributor to freedpeople's education, "began the 1870s with a $78,000 debt and a declining field for collections" (Joe M. Richardson, *Christian Reconstruction: The American Missionary Association and Southern Blacks, 1861–1890* [Athens: University of Georgia Press, 1986], 102).

92. *Cong. Globe*, 40th Cong., 3rd sess., 1029 (1869).

93. Kirk Branch, "'A Mockery in the Name of a Barrier': Literacy Test Debates in the Reconstruction Era Congress, 1864–1869," *Literacy in Composition Studies* 3, no. 2 (2015): 44–65.

94. On Republican concerns about the Fifteenth Amendment, see Foner, *Reconstruction*, 446–48; H. C. Richardson, *Death of Reconstruction*, 77–81.

95. O. O. Howard, *Report of Brevet Major General O. O. Howard, Commissioner, Bureau of Refugees, Freedmen and Abandoned Lands, to the Secretary of War, October 20, 1869* (Washington, DC: Government Printing Office, 1869), 16. On the gradual elimination of federal war powers and downsizing of the military in the South between late 1868 and early 1871, see Gregory P. Downs, *After Appomattox: Military Occupation after the Civil War* (Cambridge: Harvard University Press, 2015), 211–36.

96. Ulysses S. Grant, "Special Message," March 30, 1870, *American Presidency Project*, https://www.presidency.ucsb.edu/documents/special-message-1360.

97. *Cong. Globe*, 41st Cong., 2nd sess., 2295 (1870).

98. *Cong. Globe*, 41st Cong., 2nd sess., 2320, 2322 (1870).

99. *Cong. Globe*, 41st Cong., 2nd sess., 2320 (1870).

100. Mark Wahlgren Summers, *The Era of Good Stealings* (New York: Oxford University Press, 1993), x–xi.

101. *Cong. Globe*, 41st Cong., 2nd sess., 2317, 2318 (1870).

102. *Cong. Globe*, 41st Cong., 2nd sess., 2319 (1870).

103. On Wood's reputation, censure, and allegations against Howard, see Jerome Mushkat, *Fernando Wood: A Political Biography* (Kent, OH: Kent State University Press, 1990), 170–71, 186.

104. *Cong. Globe*, 41st Cong., 2nd sess., 2461 (1870).

105. *Cong. Globe*, 41st Cong., 2nd sess., 2461 (1870).

106. Learning that the bureau distributed copies of Protestant AMA newspapers, McNeely was especially concerned with identifying whether teachers had received "directions to instruct the children there . . . in the peculiar doctrines of any sect." He and Wood likewise interrogated teachers about where their salaries originated. See US House of Representatives, *Charges Against General Howard* (Report 121, 41st Cong., 2nd sess., 1870), 245–47, 378.

107. US House of Representatives, *Charges Against General Howard*, 47, 53, 50.

108. US House of Representatives, *Charges Against General Howard*, 5.

109. US House of Representatives, *Charges Against General Howard*, 16.

110. US House of Representatives, *Charges Against General Howard*, 5, 16, 21–22.

111. US House of Representatives, *Charges Against General Howard*, 20.

112. Butchart, *Schooling the Freed People*, 104.

113. Brian Balogh, *A Government Out of Sight: The Mystery of National Authority in Nineteenth-Century America* (New York: Cambridge University Press, 2009), 293.

114. R. Harrison, "New Representations," 212.

115. W. E. B. Du Bois, *Black Reconstruction in America: An Essay Toward a History of the Part Which Black Folk Played in the Attempt to Reconstruct Democracy in America, 1860–1880* (1935; New York: Free Press, 1998), 667.

116. Hilary Green traces the struggles faced by Black community members in Mobile, Alabama, after the departure of the Freedmen's Bureau, noting their unreliable partnerships with entities such as the Peabody Fund (*Educational Reconstruction*, 130–56, 174–84).

117. On the Peabody Fund as the "first modern foundation," see Olivier Zunz, *Philanthropy in America: A History* (Princeton: Princeton University Press, 2012), 10. On these foundations' formation of "interstitial collaborations . . . intended to substitute for the lack of federal or state leadership in education-policy development," see Joan Malczewski, *Building a New Educational State: Foundations, Schools, and the American South* (Chicago: University of Chicago Press, 2016), 44.

CHAPTER FOUR - THE METHOD OF MINGLING

1. *Proceedings of the Colored People's Convention of the State of South Carolina, Held in Zion Church, Charleston, November 1865* (Charleston: South Carolina Leader Office, 1865), 24.

2. Joe M. Richardson, "Francis L. Cardozo: Black Educator During Reconstruction," *Journal of Negro Education* 48, no. 1 (1979): 75.

3. Cardozo also recognized apprehensions within Black communities about the dissolution of their schools and with it their autonomy in guiding their children's education. See David Tyack and Robert Lowe, "The Constitutional Moment: Reconstruction and Black Education in the South," *American Journal of Education* 94, no. 2 (1986): 248.

4. *Proceedings of the Constitutional Convention of South Carolina, Held at Charleston, S.C., Beginning January 14th and Ending March 17th, 1868* (Charleston, SC: Denny and Perry, 1868) 900–901.

5. Chris Beneke, "The Idea of Integration in the Age of Horace Mann," in *Inequity in Education: A Historical Perspective*, ed. Debra Meyers and Burke Miller (Lanham, MD: Lexington, 2009), 101–22; Stephen Macedo, *Diversity and Distrust: Civic Education in a Multicultural Democracy* (Cambridge: Harvard University Press, 2003), 52–54.

6. Massachusetts Department of Education, *Eighth Annual Report of the Board of Education, Together with the Eighth Annual Report of the Secretary of the Board* (Boston: Dutton and Wentworth, 1849), 51.

7. Hilary J. Moss, *Schooling Citizens: The Struggle for African American Education in Antebellum America* (Chicago: University of Chicago Press, 2009), 160–61.

8. Xine Yao, *Disaffected: The Cultural Politics of Unfeeling in Nineteenth-Century America* (Durham, NC: Duke University Press, 2021), 12–15.

9. Informative histories of the Civil Rights Act debate include Kirt H. Wilson, *The Reconstruction Desegregation Debate: The Politics of Equality and the Rhetoric of Place, 1870–1875* (East Lansing: Michigan State University Press, 2002); Alan Friedlander and Richard Allan Gerber, *Welcoming Ruin: The Civil Rights Act of 1875* (Boston: Brill, 2019). For specific analyses of education debates, see Alfred H. Kelly, "The Congressional Controversy over School Segregation, 1867–1875," *American Historical Review* 44, no. 3 (1959): 537–63; Ward M. McAfee, "Reconstruction Revisited: The Republican Public Education Crusade of the 1870s," *Civil War History* 42, no. 2 (1996): 133–53.

10. K. H. Wilson, *Reconstruction Desegregation Debate*, 1–16.

11. K. H. Wilson, *Reconstruction Desegregation Debate*, 69, 138–39.

12. Michael E. Woods, *Emotional and Sectional Conflict in the Antebellum United States* (New York: Cambridge University Press, 2014), 232–39.

13. Representative Roger Q. Mills (D-TX) quoted in *Cong. Globe*, 43rd Cong., 1st sess., 385 (1874). For a similar remark by Senator Eugene Casserly (D-CA), see *Cong. Globe*, 42nd Cong., 2nd sess., 3248.

14. On the concept of visceral rhetoric, see Jenell Johnson, "'A Man's Mouth Is His Castle': The Midcentury Fluoridation Controversy and the Visceral Public," *Quarterly Journal of Speech* 102, no. 1 (2016): 1–20.

15. On the role of anxieties about interracial marriage and "amalgamation" during the Massachusetts school integration debates of the 1840s, see Kyle G. Volk, *Moral Minorities and the Making of American Democracy* (New York: Oxford University Press, 2014), 101–31.

16. James Pyle Wickersham, *A History of Education in Pennsylvania* (Lancaster, PA: Inquirer Publishing, 1886), 180.

17. Chris Beneke, "'Mingle with Us': Religious Integration in Eighteenth and Nineteenth-Century American Education," *American Educational History Journal* 33, no. 1 (2006): 32–35.

18. Noah Webster, Chauncey A. Goodrich, and Noah Porter, *An American Dictionary of the English Language* (Springfield, MA: Merriam, 1865), 840.

19. Massachusetts Board of Education, *Eleventh Annual Report of the Board of Education, together with the Eleventh Annual Report of the Secretary of the Board* (Boston: Dutton and Wentworth, 1848), 88. See also Beneke, "Idea of Integration"; Chris Lubienski, "Redefining 'Public' Education: Charter Schools, Common Schools, and the Rhetoric of Reform," *Teachers College Record* 103, no. 4 (2001): 650–51.

20. While common school advocates generally supported gender-based mingling, they did so on different terms: by describing the classroom as an extension of the home, a space in which children grew up in harmony as brothers and sisters. See David Tyack and Elisabeth Hansot, "Silence and Policy Talk: Historical Puzzles about Gender and Education," *Educational Researcher* 17, no. 3 (1988): 36.

21. Calvin E. Stowe, *Wisdom and Knowledge: The Nation's Stability: An Address Delivered at Crawfordsville, Indiana, July 7, 1840* (Crawfordsville, IN: Euphonean Society of Wabash College, 1840), 14.

22. Stowe, *Wisdom and Knowledge*, 14.

23. Moss, *Schooling Citizens*, 153–81.

24. "Meeting of Colored Citizens," *Liberator*, August 10, 1849, 127.

25. Debates over abolishing the Smith School and the merits of integrated schooling had been underway in Boston's Black community for several years, furnishing rationales on which Morris and Sumner relied when arguing before the Massachusetts Supreme Court. See Stephen Kendrick and Paul Kendrick, *Sarah's Long Walk: The Free Blacks of Boston and How Their Struggle for Equality Changed America* (Boston: Beacon, 2004), 117–71.

26. Sumner, *Equality Before the Law: Unconstitutionality of Separate Colored Schools in Massachusetts: Argument of Charles Sumner, Esq., Before the Supreme Court of Massachusetts in the Case of Sarah C. Roberts vs. the City of Boston, December 4, 1849* (Washington: Rives and Bailey, 1870), 15.

27. Sumner, *Equality Before the Law*, 13.

28. On the significant and long understudied role of the colored conventions movement in shaping antebellum Black political culture, see P. Gabrielle Foreman, Jim Casey, and Sarah Lynn Patterson, eds., *The Colored Conventions Movement: Black Organizing in the Nineteenth Century* (Chapel Hill: University of North Carolina Press, 2021).

29. For a powerful example of Black advocates recognizing and rejecting the duplicitous ways white leaders employed the logics of educational gatekeeping, see "An Appeal to the Colored Citizens of Pennsylvania," in *Minutes of the State Convention of the Coloured Citizens of Pennsylvania, Convened at Harrisburg, December 13th and 14th, 1848* (Philadelphia: Merrihew and Thompson, 1849), 12–22.

30. "Cazenovia Fugitive Slave Law Convention, August 21–22, 1850," in *The Proceedings of the Black State Conventions, 1840–1865*, ed. Philip S. Foner and George E. Walker (Philadelphia: Temple University Press, 1979), 1:46. For a similar argument in New York, see *Proceedings of the State Convention of Colored People, Held at Albany, New-York, on the 22d, 23d, 24th of July, 1851* (Albany, NY: Van Benthuysen, 1851), 33.

31. See, e.g., Reverend Charles W. Gardner's insistence that schools "educate male and female, white and colored, rich and poor, together, and so teach them that they are all human beings, united in a common brotherhood of universal love" (*Proceedings of the Colored National Convention, Held in Franklin Hall, Sixth Street, Below Arch, Philadelphia, October 16th, 17th, and 18th, 1855* [Salem, NJ: National Standard Office, 1856], 39).

32. For example, one Boston antislavery editor "narrated a colorphobia incident" in which a Black child in Vermont gained admission to a white school and gradually became "faithful and zealous friends" with children who had previously "taunted her complexion." See "Meetings of the Friends of Equal School Rights," *The Liberator*, November 9, 1849. On defining prejudice in terms of fear and phobias, see Don James McLaughlin, "Dread: The Phobic Imagination in Antislavery Literature," *J19: The Journal of Nineteenth-Century Americanists* 7, no. 1 (2019): 21–48.

33. *Minutes and Address of the State Convention of the Colored Citizens of Ohio, Convened at Columbus, January 10th, 11th, 12th, & 13th, 1849* (Oberlin, OH: J. M. Fitch's Power Press, 1849), 23.

34. J. Johnson, "A Man's Mouth Is His Castle," 4.

35. B. P. Aydelott, *Prejudice Against Colored People* (Cincinnati: American Reform Tract and Book Society, 1863), 16–17.

36. Mark M. Smith, *How Race Is Made: Slavery, Segregation, and the Senses* (Chapel Hill: University of North Carolina Press, 2006), 29–47.

37. J. Johnson, "A Man's Mouth Is His Castle," 5.

38. *Roberts v. City of Boston*, 59 Mass. 198, 5 Cush. 198 (1850), 209.

39. "Negroes in the Boston Primary Schools," *Boston Olive Branch*, June 21, 1845, 2; "The Schools for Colored Children," *Boston Courier*, July 10, 1845.

40. M. M. Smith, *How Race Is Made*, 37–39; Volk, *Moral Minorities*, 101–31; Katharine Nicholson Ings, "Between Hoax and Hope: Miscegenation and Nineteenth-Century Interracial Romance," *Literature Compass* 3 (2006): 648–57; Jane Dailey, *Before Jim Crow: The Politics of Race in Postemancipation Virginia* (Chapel Hill: University of North Carolina Press, 2000), 94–96.

41. For example, opponents of emancipation made *miscegenation*—a newly coined term for the mixing of races—into an 1864 presidential campaign controversy, underscoring how anxieties about interracial contact and sex intensified after emancipation. See Elise Lemire, *"Miscegenation": Making Race in America* (Philadelphia: University of Pennsylvania Press, 2002), 115–44.

42. Black efforts to pursue integration also continued in the North. See Hugh Davis, *"We Will Be Satisfied with Nothing Less": The African American Struggle for Equal Rights in the North During Reconstruction* (Ithaca: Cornell University Press, 2011), 72–96.

43. *Journal of the Constitutional Convention of the State of Virginia, Convened in the City of Richmond, December 3, 1867* (Richmond, VA: New Nation, 1867), 333; Michael Hucles,

"Many Voices, Similar Concerns: Traditional Methods of African-American Political Activity in Norfolk, Virginia, 1865–1875," *Virginia Magazine of History and Biography* 100, no. 4 (1992): 554–55.

44. Tyack and Lowe, *Constitutional Moment*, 246–48; William Preston Vaughn, *Schools for All: The Blacks and Public Education in the South, 1865–1877* (Lexington: University Press of Kentucky, 1974), 55–78.

45. Kristi Richard Melancon and Petra Munro Hendry, "'Listen to the Voice of Reason': The *New Orleans Tribune* as Advocate for Public, Integrated Education," *History of Education* 44, no. 3 (2015): 303.

46. Quoted in Melancon and Hendry, "Listen to the Voice of Reason," 310.

47. Vaughn, *Schools for All*, 78; Melancon and Hendry, "Listen to the Voice of Reason," 311–12; Mary Niall Mitchell, *Raising Freedom's Child: Black Children and Visions of the Future After Slavery* (New York: New York University Press, 2008), 208–9.

48. Henry Ward Beecher, "National Unity: Thanksgiving Day Sermon—Thursday Morning, Nov. 18, 1869," in *The Sermons of Henry Ward Beecher in Plymouth Church, Brooklyn*, vol. 3, September 1869–March 1870 (New York: Ford, 1870), 171.

49. Quoted in Thomas W. Handford, ed., *Beecher: Christian Philosopher, Pulpit Orator, Patriot and Philanthropist* (Chicago: Belford, Clarke, 1887), 128–29.

50. On the complex relationship between race and education throughout this period, see Ward M. McAfee, *Religion, Race, and Reconstruction: The Public School in the Politics of the 1870s* (Albany: State University of New York Press, 1998), 125–202.

51. On Nast's anti-Catholic illustrations, see Benjamin Justice, "Thomas Nast and the Public School of the 1870s," *History of Education Quarterly* 45, no. 2 (2005): 171–206.

52. K. H. Wilson, *Reconstruction Desegregation Debate*, 11–12.

53. Patrick O. Gudridge, "Privileges and Permissions: The Civil Rights Act of 1875," *Law and Philosophy* 8, no. 1 (1989): 87–88.

54. Carl Schurz, *The Condition of the South: Extracts from the Report of Major-General Carl Schurz, on the States of South Carolina, Georgia, Alabama, Mississippi and Louisiana; Addressed to the President* (Philadelphia, 1865), 7.

55. Carl Schurz, "The Need of Reform and a New Party," in *Speeches, Correspondence and Political Papers of Carl Schurz*, ed. Frederic Bancroft (New York: Putnam's), 2:300, 306; Woods, *Emotional and Sectional Conflict*, 238; David W. Blight, *Race and Reunion: The Civil War in American Memory* (Cambridge: Belknap Press of Harvard University Press, 2001), 60–63.

56. *Cong. Globe*, 42nd Cong., 2nd sess., 3180–81 (1872).

57. Although Sumner briefly joined the Liberal Republican movement, he ultimately distanced himself out of commitments to Reconstruction and civil rights. See Andrew L. Slap, *The Doom of Reconstruction: The Liberal Republicans in the Civil War Era* (New York: Fordham University Press, 2006), 117, 122, 134.

58. *Cong. Globe*, 42nd Cong., 2nd sess., 384, 3422 (1872).

59. *Cong. Globe*, 42nd Cong., 2nd sess., 434, 3193 (1872).

60. *Cong. Globe*, 42nd Cong., 2nd sess., 436, 3735 (1872).

61. *Cong. Globe*, 42nd Cong., 2nd sess., 3260 (1872).

62. On Edmunds's remarks on Catholics and Mormons, see Benjamin Justice, "The Blaine Game: Are Public Schools Inherently Anti-Catholic?" *Teachers College Record*

109, no. 9 (2007): 2197–98; Kelly Elizabeth Phipps, "Marriage and Redemption: Mormon Polygamy in the Congressional Imagination, 1862–1887," *Virginia Law Review* 95, no. 2 (2009): 435–87.

63. Representative John B. Storm (D-PA) and Senator Francis Blair (D-MO) quoted in *Cong. Globe*, 42nd Cong., 2nd sess., appendix, 569, 3425 (1872).

64. *Cong. Globe*, 42nd Cong., 2nd sess., 855, appendix, 353, 355 (1872). See also *Cong. Globe*, 42nd Cong., 2nd sess., 3124 (1872).

65. *Cong. Globe*, 42nd Cong., 2nd sess., appendix, 356, 855 (1872).

66. *Cong. Globe*, 42nd Cong., 2nd sess., 3425 (1872). See also remarks of Senators Orris S. Ferry (R-CT) and Eugene Casserly (D-CA), *Cong. Globe*, 42nd Cong., 2nd sess., 3422, 3251 (1872).

67. *Cong. Globe*, 42nd Cong., 2nd sess., 3424 (1872).

68. *Cong. Globe*, 42nd Cong., 2nd sess., appendix, 355 (1872).

69. On Ferry's Liberal Republican inclinations, see "Obituary: Senator Orris S. Ferry," *New York Times*, November 22, 1875, 4.

70. *Cong. Globe*, 42nd Cong., 2nd sess., 3422 (1872). See also Boreman's remarks, *Cong. Globe*, 42nd Cong., 2nd sess., 3422 (1872).

71. Joshua Paddison, *American Heathens: Religion, Race, and Reconstruction in California* (Berkeley: University of California Press, 2012), 17.

72. On freedpeople's retention of land in the Indian Territory after the Civil War, see Alaina E. Roberts, "A Different Forty Acres: Land, Kin, and Migration in the Late Nineteenth-Century West," *Journal of the Civil War Era* 10, no. 2 (2020): 213–32.

73. C. Joseph Genetin-Pilawa, *Crooked Paths to Allotment: The Fight over Federal Indian Policy After the Civil War* (Chapel Hill: University of North Carolina Press, 2012), 96.

74. *Cong. Globe*, 42nd Cong., 2nd sess., 3251–52 (1872).

75. *Cong. Globe*, 42nd Cong., 2nd sess., 3257 (1872).

76. Sara Ahmed describes this process wherein "the conversion of hate into love allows . . . groups to associate themselves with 'good feeling' and 'positive value'" (*The Cultural Politics of Emotion* [New York: Routledge, 2004], 123).

77. *Cong. Globe*, 42nd Cong., 2nd sess., 3258, 3727–35, 3737, 3738 (1872).

78. K. H. Wilson, *Reconstruction Desegregation Debate*, 22–23.

79. George Frisbie Hoar, *Autobiography of Seventy Years* (New York: Scribner's, 1903), 1:257. In Hoar's reflection, Sumner's emotions concerned a provision officially declaring education a part of Reconstruction policy. Sumner's contemporary and biographer Edward L. Pierce claimed that Sumner's remarks to Hoar concerned the failure to secure freedpeople's education (*Memoir and Letters of Charles Sumner* [Boston: Roberts, 1881], 4:317). Both accounts identify education as the cause of Sumner's discontent.

80. On the Panic of 1873 and its political implications, see Eric Foner, *Reconstruction: America's Unfinished Revolution, 1863–1877* (1988; New York: Perennial Classics, 2002), 512–24.

81. Democrats had regained control of Tennessee, Georgia, and Virginia; Alabama, Florida, North Carolina, and Texas still had Republican governors; and Republicans still controlled state governments in Arkansas, Louisiana, Mississippi, and South Carolina (Foner, *Reconstruction*, 539).

82. *Cong. Rec.*, 43rd Cong., 1st sess., 381 (1874).

83. K. H. Wilson, *Reconstruction Desegregation Debate*, 86–107.

84. *Cong. Rec.*, 43rd Cong., 1st sess., 377 (1874). Other Virginia Democrats sounded the same alarm, citing a *Richmond State Journal* editorial's insistence that "the attempt to combine the two races in the school will result *in the breaking up the schools altogether*. We recognize this fact as caused by prejudices and antipathies which we have no power to uproot." Both Representative Thomas Whitehead and Senator John W. Johnston referenced the editorial, (*Cong. Rec.*, 43rd Cong., 1st sess., 427, 4115), identifying the *Journal* as a Republican periodical reflective of the party's sentiments, though it clearly did not reflect the views of party members in Congress.

85. *Cong. Rec.*, 43rd Cong., 1st sess., 376–77 (1874).

86. Walter J. Fraser Jr., "William Henry Ruffner and the Establishment of Virginia's Public School System, 1870–1874," *Virginia Magazine of History and Biography* 79, no. 3 (1971): 263–64, 267–71; Dailey, *Before Jim Crow*, 29–30. Representative William Stowell (R-VA) directly confronted his fellow Virginians over this portrayal of the state's educational commitments (*Cong. Rec.*, 43rd Cong, 1st sess., 426 [1874]).

87. As Dailey notes, white Virginians rapidly reversed their views on public schooling once a system was in place. By early 1871, 73 of the state's 105 school districts were supported by local tax measures (*Before Jim Crow*, 25).

88. *Cong. Rec.*, 43rd Cong., 1st sess., 377 (1874).

89. See, e.g., Representative James H. Blount (D-GA) quoted in *Cong. Rec.*, 43rd Cong., 1st sess., 412 (1874).

90. Remark of Senator Thomas Norwood (D-GA), *Cong. Rec.*, 43rd Cong., 1st sess., 237 (1874).

91. Senator Augustus S. Merrimon (D-NC) quoted in *Cong. Rec.*, 43rd Cong., 1st sess., appendix, 316 (1874). See also remarks of Representatives John D. C. Atkins (D-TN), William B. Read (D-KY), and Ephraim K. Wilson (D-MD) and Senator Eli Saulsbury (D-DE), *Cong. Rec.*, 43rd Cong., 1st sess., 454, 343, 419, 4158–61 (1874).

92. *Cong. Rec.*, 43rd Cong., 1st sess., 405, 385, appendix 237, appendix, 318 (1874). See also remarks of Representatives John M. Bright (D-TN), William S. Herndon (D-TX), and Eppa Hunton (D-VA), *Cong. Rec.*, 43rd Cong., 1st sess., 415, 522, 119 (1874).

93. *Cong. Rec.*, 43rd Cong., 1st sess., 456, 426, appendix, 419 (1874).

94. Boutwell had previously argued against separating children based on religious sect, immoral or improper behavior, or economic class. See George S. Boutwell, *Thoughts on Educational Topics and Institutions* (Boston: Phillips, Sampson, 1859), 53, 70, 153–54, 160.

95. *Cong. Rec.*, 43rd Cong., 1st sess., 4116, 4169 (1874).

96. See remarks of Representatives C. B. Darrall (R-LA), Josiah T. Walls (R-FL), Richard Cain (R-SC), John Lynch (R-MS), Joseph Rainey (R-SC), *Cong. Rec.*, 43rd Cong., 1st sess., appendix, 477–80, 416, 901 (1874), 2nd sess., 943, 960 (1875).

97. *Cong. Rec.*, 43rd Cong., 1st sess., 4151, 4169, 4168 (1874).

98. *Cong. Rec.*, 43rd Cong., 1st sess., 4168 (1874).

99. Friedlander and Gerber, *Welcoming Ruin*, 99.

100. *Cong. Rec.*, 43rd Cong., 1st sess., 4153 (1874). The proposal was rejected 26–21.

101. *Dissociation* refers to the argumentative separation of two concepts previously presented as unified. More than a temporary compromise (e.g., setting aside part of a policy

for the sake of prudence), dissociation presents a more durable split that restructures the assumptions on which an argument was based. See Chaïm Perelman and Lucie Olbrechts-Tyteca, *The New Rhetoric: A Treatise on Argumentation* (Notre Dame, IN: University of Notre Dame Press, 1969), 411–15.

102. *Cong. Rec.*, 43rd Cong., 1st sess., 4172 (1874).

103. *Cong. Rec.*, 43rd Cong., 1st sess., 4172 (1874).

104. *Cong. Rec.*, 43rd Cong., 1st sess., 416, 417 (1874), 2nd sess., 960 (1875).

105. K. H. Wilson, *Reconstruction Desegregation Debate*, 86–107.

106. *Cong. Rec.*, 43rd Cong., 1st sess., 901 (1874).

107. Nicholas Guyatt, "'An Impossible Idea?': The Curious Career of Internal Colonization," *Journal of the Civil War Era* 4, no. 2 (2014): 234–63.

108. *Cong. Rec.*, 43rd Cong., 2nd sess., 1004 (1875). Representative James A. Garfield (R-OH) quoted the report when speaking before the House.

109. On parallels in postwar policy toward Native Americans and freedpeople, see Elliott West, "Reconstructing Race," *Western Historical Quarterly* 34, no. 1 (2003): 23.

110. *Cong. Rec.*, 43rd Cong., 2nd sess., 960 (1875).

111. As Lynch argued, many white policymakers seemed to believe that "the immoral, the ignorants and the degraded of their own race are the social equals of themselves and their families" by virtue of being white. By contrast, he recognized "hundreds of thousands of white people of both sexes whom I know to be the social inferiors of respectable and intelligent colored people" (*Cong. Rec.*, 43rd Cong., 2nd sess., 944 [1875]). Heather Cox Richardson contextualizes these comments within the wider schisms over class and respectability among Black people more generally (*The Death of Reconstruction: Race, Labor, and Politics in the Post–Civil War North, 1865–1901* [Cambridge: Harvard University Press, 2001], 133–34).

112. *Cong. Rec.*, 43rd Cong., 1st sess., 901 (1874).

113. Friedlander and Gerber, *Welcoming Ruin*, 488–98.

114. Representative Ellis H. Roberts concisely summarized these options (*Cong. Rec.*, 43rd Cong., 2nd sess., 980 [1875]).

115. William Preston Vaughn, "Separate and Unequal: The Civil Rights Act of 1875 and Defeat of the School Integration Clause," *Southwestern Social Science Quarterly* 48, no. 2 (1967): 146–54.

116. *Cong. Rec.*, 43rd Cong., 2nd sess., 981 (1875).

117. *Cong. Rec.*, 43rd Cong., 2nd sess., 981 (1875).

118. *Cong. Rec.*, 43rd Cong., 2nd sess., 1005 (1875).

119. Friedlander and Gerber, *Welcoming Ruin*, 553.

120. *Cong. Rec.*, 43rd Cong., 2nd sess., 1000, 1002 (1875).

121. Foner, *Reconstruction*, 556.

122. *Civil Rights Cases*, 109 US 3 (1883).

123. John Mercer Langston, "Equality Before the Law," in *Negro Orators and Their Orations*, ed. Carter G. Woodson (Washington, DC: Associated Publishers, 1925), 446.

124. Most legislators focused on questions of states' rights, Bible reading in schools, and the amendment's implications for church-state separation. See Steven K. Green, *The Bible, The School, and the Constitution: The Clash That Shaped Modern Church-State Doctrine* (New York: Oxford University Press, 2012), 216–21.

125. Edmunds grounded his defense of the Blaine amendment primarily in fears that Catholic elected officials would be bound by papal edict to defund secular public schools. See *Cong. Rec.*, 44th Cong., 1st sess., 5587–88 (1876).

CONCLUSION - SCHOOLING AND SENTIMENT

1. Charles Sumner, *The National Security and the National Faith; Guarantees for the National Freedman and the National Creditor: Speech of Hon. Charles Sumner at the Republican State Convention, in Worcester, September 14, 1865* (Boston: Wright & Potter, 1865), 18.

2. David W. Blight, *Race and Reunion: The Civil War in American Memory* (Cambridge: Belknap Press of Harvard University Press, 2001), 96.

3. On the religious and economic pressures that shaped Republican politics in the late 1860s and early 1870s, see Edward J. Blum, *Reforging the White Republic: Race, Religion, and American Nationalism, 1865–1898* (Baton Rouge: Louisiana State University Press, 2005), 87–119; Nancy Cohen, *The Reconstruction of American Liberalism, 1865–1914* (Chapel Hill: University of North Carolina Press, 2002), 61–85; Eric Foner, *Reconstruction: America's Unfinished Revolution, 1863–1877* (1988; New York: Perennial Classics, 2002), 512–63.

4. Upending history, the pamphlet described "a general flourishing condition of the public schools in the Southern States" except where Republican "carpet-baggers" had failed "to foster a public education" (Democratic National Committee, *The Campaign Text Book: Why The People Want a Change. The Republican Party Reviewed: Its Sins of Commission and Omission* [New York: Democratic National Committee, 1876], 254).

5. On white Virginians' initial resistance to common schooling before the state's system began to take shape in the 1870s, see Catherine A. Jones, *Intimate Reconstructions: Children in Postemancipation Virginia* (Charlottesville: University of Virginia Press, 2015), 159–61.

6. Gilbert C. Walker, "Letter of Governor Walker on the Public School System," *Richmond Whig*, October 4, 1870, 4.

7. Gilbert C. Walker, *Address of Gov. Gilbert C. Walker, at the Commencement of the Virginia Agricultural and Mechanical College, July 9, 1873* (Richmond, VA: Enquirer Book and Job Office, 1873), 6–7.

8. *Cong. Rec.*, 44th Cong., 1st sess., 3369 (1876).

9. *Cong. Rec.*, 44th Cong., 1st sess., 3370 (1876).

10. *Cong. Rec.*, 44th Cong., 1st sess., 5010 (1876).

11. Gordon B. McKinney, *Henry W. Blair's Campaign to Reform America: From the Civil War to the U.S. Senate* (Lexington: University Press of Kentucky, 2013), 89–90.

12. McKinney, *Henry W. Blair's Campaign*, 93; Hilary Green, *Educational Reconstruction: African American Schools in the Urban South, 1865–1890* (New York: Fordham University Press, 2016), 186–87.

13. Jeffery A. Jenkins and Justin Peck, "The Blair Education Bill: A Lost Opportunity in American Public Education," *Studies in American Political Development* 35, no. 1 (2021): 167.

14. Daniel Wallace Crofts, "The Blair Bill and the Elections Bill: The Congressional Aftermath to Reconstruction" (PhD diss., Yale University, 1968), 217.

15. As Nancy Beadie notes, Southern states provided "essentially equal" funding for Black education between 1870 and 1890 and did not implement literacy tests for voters until after the Blair Bill's failure—when it became certain that Black children would not receive the educational resources or a curriculum conducive to the formation of literacy ("The Federal Role in Education and the Rise of Social Science Research: Historical and Comparative Perspectives," *Review of Research in Education* 40 [2016]: 29–30).

16. *Cong. Rec.*, 44th Cong., 1st sess., 5455 (1876).

17. *Cong. Globe*, 42nd Cong., 2nd sess., 859–60 (1872).

18. Tracy L. Steffes, *School Society and State: A New Education to Govern Modern America* (Chicago: University of Chicago Press, 2012), 4. By the end of the nineteenth century, America's per-pupil investment in schooling exceeded that of most European countries, including Germany, the nation that (under the centralizing program of Prussia) so many Reconstruction-era members of Congress had cited as a model for the United States. See David Tyack, Thomas James, and Aaron Benavot, *Law and the Shaping of Public Education, 1785–1954* (Madison: University of Wisconsin Press, 1987), 53.

19. Citing several examples, Steffes notes that in the early twentieth century, states promoted educational changes by using "aid, standards, and supervision" in ways that could "prod, reward, and subtly shape local effort and to encourage local support for and identification with state policies" (Steffes, *School, Society, and State*, 85).

20. Department of Superintendence of the National Educational Association, *Education at the Centennial: Extracts from the Proceedings of the Department of Superintendence of the National Educational Association, at Its Meeting in Washington, January 27 and 28, 1875* (Washington, DC: Government Printing Office, 1875), 6–7.

21. Eugene F. Provenzo Jr., *Culture as Curriculum: Education and the International Expositions (1876–1904)* (New York: Lang, 2012), 33–34.

22. Elizabeth P. Peabody, "Impressions Made by the Centennial Kindergarten," *Kindergarten Messenger* 1, nos. 1–2 (1877): 6–10; Association for Childhood Education Kindergarten Centennial Committee, *The Kindergarten Centennial, 1837–1937* (Washington, DC: Association for Childhood Education, 1937), 9; James D. McCabe, *The Illustrated History of the Centennial Exhibition* (Philadelphia: National, 1876), 721.

23. Nina C. Vandewalker, *The Kindergarten in American Education* (New York: Macmillan, 1908), 18. *Frank Leslie's Historical Register of the Centennial Exposition* dedicated two columns of text to a quick gloss of dozens of US educational exhibits while providing a detailed page-long write-up and a two-page foldout illustration dedicated to the Kindergarten Cottage. See Frank H. Norton, ed., *Frank Leslie's Historical Register of the United States Centennial Exposition, 1876* (New York: Leslie's, 1876), 118, 158, 266–67. Likewise, J. S. Ingram's history of the exposition opined, "The various educational systems of the civilized world were well represented at the Centennial Exhibition, but none of them were, in our opinion, more instructive and entertaining than the Kindergarten . . . erected by the Women's Committee" (*The Centennial Exposition, Described and Illustrated* [Philadelphia: Hubbard, 1876], 714).

24. Stacey L. Smith, "Beyond North and South: Putting the West in the Civil War and Reconstruction," *Journal of the Civil War Era* 6, no. 4 (2016): 566–91.

25. On the fraught relationship between literacy and citizenship, see Amy J. Wan, *Producing Good Citizens: Literacy Training in Anxious Times* (Pittsburgh: University of Pittsburgh Press, 2014).

26. Kirk Branch, "'A Mockery in the Name of a Barrier': Literacy Test Debates in the Reconstruction Era Congress, 1864–1869," *Literacy in Composition Studies* 3, no. 2 (2015): 44–65.

27. For one example of how debates over literacy as a condition for citizenship unfolded, see Belinda A. Stillion Southard, "A Rhetoric of Epistemic Privilege: Elizabeth Cady Stanton, Harriot Stanton Blatch, and the Educated Vote," *Advances in the History of Rhetoric* 17, no. 2 (2014): 157–78.

28. Monroe held relatively egalitarian views on race and civil rights. He was a staunch abolitionist and a longtime professor at Oberlin College, one of the nation's only integrated universities before the Civil War. He consistently advocated for Black civil rights during Reconstruction. This background makes his comments all the more illuminating regarding how the colonial logics of education implicated race. See Catherine M. Rokicky, *James Monroe: Oberlin's Christian Statesman and Reformer, 1821–1898* (Kent, OH: Kent State University Press, 2002), 107–28.

29. James Monroe, "The National Government and Popular Education," *Ohio Educational Monthly* 16, no. 9 (1875): 357, 371.

30. Kyla Schuller, *The Biopolitics of Feeling: Race, Sex, and Science in the Nineteenth Century* (Durham, NC: Duke University Press, 2018), 207.

31. This was a common theme at the Lake Mohonk Conferences on the "Negro Question" attended by prominent white leaders in 1890 and 1891. See Mark Elliott, "The Lessons of Reconstruction: Debating Race and Imperialism in the 1890s," in *Remembering Reconstruction: Struggles over the Meaning of America's Most Turbulent Era*, ed. Carole Emberton and Bruce E. Baker (Baton Rouge: Louisiana State University Press, 2017), 139–72.

32. On the ideas underpinning colonial pedagogy, see James D. Anderson, *The Education of Blacks in the South, 1860–1935* (Chapel Hill: University of North Carolina Press, 1988), 33–78.

33. Ernest J. Wrage, "Public Address: A Study in Social and Intellectual History," *Quarterly Journal of Speech* 33, no. 4 (1947): 451–57.

34. For discussions of these perennial disciplinary concerns, see James Jasinski and Jennifer R. Mercieca, "Analyzing Constitutive Rhetorics: The Virginia and Kentucky Resolutions and the 'Principles of '98,'" in *The Handbook of Public Address*, ed. Shawn J. Parry-Giles and J. Michael Hogan (West Sussex, UK: Blackwell, 2010), 313–42; Mary E. Stuckey, "Jimmy Carter, Human Rights, and Instrumental Effects of Presidential Rhetoric," in *Handbook of Public Address*, ed. Parry-Giles and Hogan, 293–312.

35. See, e.g., Jamie Landau and Bethany Keeley-Jonker, "Conductor of Public Feelings: An Affective-Emotional Rhetorical Analysis of Obama's National Eulogy in Tucson," *Quarterly Journal of Speech* 104, no. 2 (2018): 166–88.

36. Jay Childers, "Reimagining Public Address," *Rhetoric & Public Affairs* 24, nos. 1–2 (2021): 405.

37. Christa J. Olson, *American Magnitude: Hemispheric Vision and Public Feeling in the United States* (Columbus: Ohio State University Press, 2021); Lisa M. Corrigan, *Black Feelings: Race and Affect in the Long Sixties* (Jackson: University Press of Mississippi, 2020).

38. *Cong. Rec.*, 43rd Cong., 2nd sess., 416 (1875).

39. *Cong. Globe*, 42nd Cong., 2nd sess., 594 (1872).

INDEX

References to illustrations are in **bold**.

abolition, 38, 92, 95, 187n52, 200n28
Adams, John, 135
affect, 10, 15, 18, 26, 31, 34, 36, 42, 62, 88, 90, 115, 158, 172n35, 174n60, 186n36
agency, 20, 85, 96, 148
Ahmed, Sara, 11–12, 15, 18, 62, 186n36, 195n76
Alabama, 120, 190n116, 195n81
Alcorn, James L., 129–30
alienation, 89, 117. *See also* estrangement
Allen, Danielle S., 10
Alvord, John W., 83, 90–91, 100, 103
American Missionary, 107
American Missionary Association (AMA), 25, 83–84, 87–89, 96, 107, 111, 189n91, 190n106
American Social Science Association, 66
Amnesty Act of 1872, 124–27, 132–33
Andersonville Prison, 84
Andrews, Sidney, 109
Antifederalists, 33–34, 124, 171n18
Arkansas, 21, 77, 195n81
Armstrong, Samuel Chapman, 100
Arnell, Samuel, 102–5, 108–9
Asen, Robert, 9, 11, 13
assessment, 62, 178n23; examinations, 62; public exhibitions, 58, 62
Atlantic Monthly, 50
atmosphere, 6, 12, 85, 109, 125
Aydelott, Benjamin Parham, 119

Balogh, Brian, 81, 110
Banks, Nathaniel P., 13, 38
Bardwell, J. P., 83

Barnard, Henry, 29, 59, 70–74, 88, 182n83
Bayard, Thomas, 74–75, 125, 128–30, 132, 135
Bayne, Thomas, 120
Beadie, Nancy, 170n1, 199n15
Beaman, Fernando, 94
Beecher, Catharine, 16, 88
Beecher, Henry Ward, 92–93, 121
Beecher, Lyman, 21
belonging, 7, 10–11, 18, 56, 152, 157
Benjamin, John F., 73
Berkeley, William, 41
Berlant, Lauren, 31
Biggs, Benjamin, 79
Bird, John T., 51–54
birthplace. *See* national origin
Bismarck, Otto von, 51
Black, Jason Edward, 175n94
Black activism, 26, 41, 89, 98, 114, 119–21, 144
Blaine, James G., 145
Blaine amendment, 145, 197nn124–25
Blair, Francis, 129
Blair, Henry W., 150, 183n115
Blair, William Henry, 27, 56
Blair Bill, 150, 183n115, 199n15
Blanding, J. B., 83
Blight, David W., 148
Bogy, Lewis V., 136
Boreman, Arthur I., 125
Boston, MA, 36–38, 93, 118–20, 172n34, 173n50, 192n25, 193n32
Boutwell, George S., 21, 134, 137–38, 196n94
Bright, John M., 78
Brooks, Charles, 38

Brooks, James, 102
Bureau of Education, 6–7, 13, 24–25, 44, 56, 57–82, 91, 104, 130, 141, 151–53, 157
Bureau of Refugees, Freedmen, and Abandoned Lands. *See* Freedmen's Bureau
Burke, Kenneth, 10, 164n35, 165n38
Burritt, Ruth, 153–54
Burrows, Julius C., 143
Butchart, Ronald E., 90, 109, 186n33
Butler, Benjamin, 134, 136, 143

Cain, Richard H., 134, 140–43
California, 46, 103, 131
Campbell, Alexander, 61, 65
Cardozo, Francis L., 113–15, 191n3
Carrington, Edward, 60
Casserly, Eugene, 131
Castiglia, Christopher, 20, 172n35
Census Bureau, 68–69, 71, 74
Centennial Exposition, 153, **154**, 199n23
Chanler, John W., 94–95
Charland, Maurice, 164n35
Chicago, IL, 182n80
Childers, Jay, 158
citizenship, 13, 15, 21, 27, 48, 53, 69, 82, 100, 105, 112, 118, 126, 155, 158
civil rights, 5, 11, 18, 28, 49, 65, 82, 114–16, 118, 126–27, 130, 133, 137, 139, 141–42, 144, 147–48, 194n57, 200n28
Civil Rights Act of 1866, 188n66
Civil Rights Act of 1875, 7, 26–27, 96, 114, 116, 133–45, 151, 157; Civil Rights Bill, 95, 112, 115–16, 124–26, 128–46, 148, 157; school clause, 115, 132, 134, 138–39, 142, 144–45
Civil War, 4–5, 13–14, 21, 30–31, 33, 36, 50, 121, 146, 149, 157
Clark, William T., 13
Cleveland, OH, 57, 65
Colfax, Schuyler, 23
colonization, 4, 91, 140, 175n94
Colored People's Convention, 41, 113
common schools, 15–17, 19–24, 26, 28, 29–33, 35–40, 43, 46–48, 51–52, 54–56, 57–59, 62–65, 67, 69, 78, 80–81, 85, 88–89, 114–17, 125–33, 135–37, 139, 141, 143–46, 147–49, 151–52, 158, 169n111, 187n52, 192n20; Minnesota, 75; New England, 35, 61, 118, 150; New York, 121; Ohio, 64; Pennsylvania, 72, 116, 168n99; South Carolina, 113; Southern, 3, 30; Virginia, 33
compulsory schooling, 15, 68, 76, 78, 174n71
Confederacy, 3, 23, 60, 68, 127
Congressional Globe, 8, 10
Congressional Record, 8, 10
Connecticut, 14, 29, 58, 73, 132
Corrigan, Lisa M., 9, 158
Cox, Jacob D., 4, 162n7
Cremin, Lawrence A., 169n111
criminality, 79
Critcher, John, 78
Cutler, Augustus, 149–50
Cvetkovich, Ann, 164n29

Dailey, Jane, 196n87
Dawes, Henry L., 80
Delaware, 74–76
Democrats, 6, 13, 24, 26, 32, 42–43, 45, 51, 53–54, 78–79, 81, 93, 98, 101–2, 106–7, 111, 115, 124–25, 128–29, 131, 133–38, 140, 142–43, 145, 148, 159, 168n99, 195n81, 196n84; Redeemers, 56, 142, 146; Southern, 23, 25, 32, 59, 78–79, 112, 134, 136, 139, 142–43, 145, 148–50, 183n115
Department of Agriculture, 72, 74
desegregation, 6, 18, 26, 37–38, 77, 112, 124–28, 132, 138, 151. *See also* integration; mingling; mixing; segregation
discrimination, 42, 144, 159. *See also* prejudice; racism
displacement, 25, 47, 55, 104
dissociation, 30, 77, 196–97n101
diversity, 14, 17, 29–31, 35, 55, 61, 89
Dockery, Oliver H., 7, 105
Dole, William P., 175n94
domesticity, 16, 22, 47, 89–90, 92, 94–95, 99, 106, 108, 110, 153. *See also* maternalism and motherhood

Donnelly, Ignatius, 22, 65–68, 70–71, 74, 102
Doolittle, James R., 101
Du Bois, W. E. B., 110
Dunnell, Mark H., 58, 65, 75–76
Durham, Milton J., 136
Dutton, W. S., 17

Eaton, John, Jr., 53, 57–59, 71, 73–75, 153
economy, 4, 16–17, 20, 25, 29, 34, 54, 81, 84, 133, 142, 145, 148, 157
Edisto Island, SC, 93
Edmunds, George F., 127–28, 131, 145, 198n125
Eliot, Thomas D., 84, 90, 93, 97–98, 100–101, 103–5, 108, 187n52
Eliot, William Greenleaf, 187n52
Elliott, Robert B., 42, 134, 140
emancipation, 4, 84, 86–87, 89, 101, 109, 131, 185n23, 187n52, 193n41
embarrassment, 25, 60, 68–69, 75, 77, 79, 153
emotions, 4–16, 18–24, 29, 31–32, 34–37, 39–41, 44–47, 49–51, 53–56, 58–62, 67, 70, 76, 80, 82, 84–94, 97, 100–101, 108–9, 111–12, 114–15, 117, 119–20, 125, 127–28, 132–33, 136, 138–39, 145, 147–53, 155, 157–59, 164nn30–32, 165n38, 174n67. *See also* feeling; sentiment; shame
emotions history, 158, 164n31
enfranchisement. *See* voting
Enoch, Jessica, 16
equality, 11, 17, 55, 77, 114, 118, 126, 134, 137, 140–41
estrangement, 7, 35, 46–47, 49, 56, 101, 154. *See also* alienation
exclusion, 14, 17, 19–20, 55, 82, 86, 103, 114, 117–20, 124, 141, 144, 150, 154–58

Farnsworth, John F., 72, 80
Faulkner, Caroline, 89
federalism, 13, 23, 30–31, 33–36, 40, 49, 51, 54, 80, 171n21
Feeley, Malcolm M., 30
feeling, 3–5, 7–22, 28, 29–56, 58, 89, 95, 105–9, 113, 116, 119–20, 125, 131, 133–44, 147–50, 152–55, 157–59, 164nn29–30; benevolent, 92–98; Black, 84–85, 90, 92–94, 99–100, 103, 157; collective, 9; common, 34, 46, 52, 59, 65, 85, 121, 126; estranged, 46; federal, 45, 47; fellow, 6, 14–16, 18, 21, 24, 27–28, 29, 31–33, 35, 37, 42, 45, 48, 52, 55, 59–60, 70, 82, 85–86, 98–99, 101, 105, 108–12, 113–16, 121, 125–28, 130, 132, 135, 137, 139–40, 142–43, 145–46, 149–50, 157–58; good, 27, 44, 60, 111–12, 125, 145, 147–60, 195n76; language of, 119, 133; maternal, 153; national, 10, 27, 33, 47, 50–51, 54, 58, 76, 85, 91, 96, 100, 118, 121, 125, 135, 143, 147; postwar, 85; public, 12–13, 18, 23, 30, 44–46, 54–56, 60, 63, 70, 80, 82, 109, 124–25, 129, 134, 137, 144, 148, 152, 155, 159; rhetoric of, 115, 124; social, 14; state, 54; sympathetic, 19, 121, 131; tranquil, 154; visceral, 120, 129, 138, 145, 157; white, 28, 132, 136, 157. *See also* emotions; sentiment; shame
Ferry, Orris S., 130–32
Fifteenth Amendment, 26, 46, 48, 50, 55, 82, 85, 103–4, 111, 127, 155, 157
Florida, 21, 77, 195n81
Foner, Eric, 90, 98
Fourteenth Amendment, 55, 125, 127, 144
Frank Leslie's Historical Register of the United States Centennial Exposition (Norton), **154**, 199n23
free labor system, 7, 16, 18, 84, 87–88, 91, 93, 95, 99
Freedmen's Aid Commission, 92
Freedmen's Bureau, 6–7, 25–26, 44, 47, 67, 73, 82, 83–112, 153, 188nn65–66, 189n85, 190n106, 190n116
freedpeople, 4, 6–7, 10, 16, 20, 25, 28, 39, 48, 59, 64–65, 67–70, 77–78, 82, 83–111, 113, 118, 124, 140–41, 147–48, 151, 157, 185n23, 186n33, 187n55, 188n65, 189n91, 195n79
Frelinghuysen, Frederick, 127, 138

Gardner, Charles W., 193n31
Garfield, James A., 22, 24–25, 58, 65–76, 81, 98, 111, 152
gender, 16, 20, 27, 47, 74, 85–88, 90, 108, 152–54, 192n20; men, 3, 28, 41, 48, 67, 77,

85–86, 89, 93, 95–96, 98–100, 107, 143, 152, 186n33; women, 16, 25, 47, 52, 82, 83–85, 88–90, 93–94, 96, 108–9, 111, 151, 153, 186n33, 188n55, 199n23
George Peabody's Fund for Southern Education, 110, 190n116
Georgia, 4, 78, 84, 94, 195n81
Germany, 50–52, 174n71, 199n18
Gewirtzman, Doni, 54
Giles, John Lawrence, 121, **122**
Grant, Ulysses S., 46, 52, 57, 104, 111, 131, 144
Green, Hilary, 190n116
Grenada, MS, 83
Grinnell, Josiah, 187n55
Guarantee Clause, 40, 42, 43, 150. *See also* republicanism

Harper's Magazine, 121
Harper's Weekly, 96, **97**, **123**
Harris, John T., 128–29, 134–36
Hartman, Saidiya, 88
Harwood, C. Anna, 83–84, 184nn1–2
Hayne, Henry E., 174n71
Hendricks, Thomas A., 73, 99, 102
Hoar, George Frisbie, 6–7, 22–24, 30, 32, 38, 44, 49–53, 55–56, 57, 75, 77–80, 105, 133, 159, 195n79
Hoar Bill, 31–32, 44–56, 79–81, 106, 110–11, 131
Hoffer, Williamjames Hull, 81
Hogan, David, 36
honor, 23, 25, 59–60, 66–67, 75–80
Howard, Oliver Otis, 84, 87, 91, 96, 103–9
Howard University, 106
Howe, Timothy, 138

identification, 10–11, 31, 35, 154, 164n35, 165n38, 199n19
identity, 10, 14, 26, 30, 144; American, 31, 35; communal, 132; group, 117–18; national, 9, 15, 36, 44–45, 52, 128, 147, 151, 158; political, 35–36, 51–52; racialized, 11
Illinois, 21, 52, 53, 64, 66–67, 72, 176n108, 180n48, 182n80
illiteracy, 46–48, 61, 64, 67, 69, 74, **74**, 76–80, 100, 150, 155–56, 183n115. *See also* literacy

immigrants, 25, 69, 82, 155; Catholic, 5, 17, 29, 31, 36; Chinese, 5, 20, 46, 131; European, 46; German, 118, 121; Irish, 118
immorality, 36, 47, 63, 78, 196n94, 197n111. *See also* morality
inclusion, 19–20, 82, 113, 126, 141, 147, 149, 151, 155, 157
Indiana, 21, 64, 66, 73, 178n25
Ingram, J. S., 199n23
"Instruction of Children in the Kindergarten Cottage, Under the Auspices of the Women's Department, The," **154**
integration, 11–12, 26–27, 78–79, 114, 117, 119–21, 124–26, 128–31, 134–40, 142–44, 192n25, 193n42, 200n28. *See also* desegregation; mingling; mixing; segregation
Iowa State Daily Register, 96

Jackson, Andrew, 29
Jasinski, James, 8–9, 33–34
Jefferson, Thomas, 33, 135
Jenckes, Thomas, 73
Jim Crow systems, 7, 27, 150, 155
Johnson, Andrew, 3, 39, 40, 71, 84, 90, 93, 95–96, 103, 108
Johnson, Jenell, 119–20
Johnston, John W., 196n84

Kellogg, Stephen W., 142–43
Kentucky, 77, 187n55
Keremidchieva, Zornitsa, 8
Kerr, Michael C., 32, 52, 79
Kersh, Rogan, 34
Knox, Samuel, 16
Koganzon, Rita, 16
Ku Klux Klan, 77, 102

LaCroix, Alison L., 171n21
Langston, John Mercer, 144
language, 5, 7–11, 21–22, 38, 40–42, 47–48, 60–64, 79, 91, 103, 106, 116, 119–20, 124, 131–33, 142–44, 154–55, 161n3 (intro.), 164n30, 172n30, 175n94, 176n108
Lash, Kurt T., 170n11
Lawrence, William, 105

Lawson, Melinda, 84
Lewis, Samuel, 63
Liberia, 4, 91, 140
Lincoln, Abraham, 3, 12, 18, 90, 108
literacy, 24, 27, 64, 71, 76, 81–82, 88, 141, 154–58, 199n15. *See also* illiteracy
localists, 24, 32, 37, 44–45, 51–56, 57–59, 68, 76, 79, 131, 152
Locke, John, 15
Lost Cause narratives, 7, 35, 150
Louisiana, 94, 121, 195n81
loyalty, 18–19, 43, 50, 54–56, 145
Lynch, John, 197n111

MacIntyre, Archibald T., 78
Madison, James, 33–35, 54, 80, 171n21, 172n30
Maine, 14, 21, 91
Maine Freedmen's Relief Society, 91
Mann, Horace, 14, 17, 29–30, 36–38, 44, 50, 56, 63, 80, 88, 114, 117–18, 137, 172n40, 173n50
"Map Showing the Illiteracy of the Aggregate Population," **156**
marginalized groups, 5, 49, 144, 158
marriage, 11, 38, 115, 136
Massachusetts, 15, 21, 29, 36–38, 40–41, 56, 57–58, 63, 69–70, 79–80, 93, 118–20, 135, 137, 174n71, 192n25
maternalism and motherhood, 16, 22, 84, 86, 88–89, 94, 96, 98, 105, 153. *See also* domesticity
McGuffey, William H., 62
McGuffey's New Fifth Eclectic Reader (McGuffey), 178n25
McKee, Samuel, 59
McNeely, Thompson, 32, 52–54, 56, 105–8, 176n108, 190n106
Memphis, TN, 96, **97**
Memphis Massacre, 96
Mexican Americans, 48, 67–68
Mexico, 5, 31, 47
Midwest, 16, 178n25
military, 25, 82, 85, 87, 91, 94, 97, 103–6, 110; campaigns, 5; camps, 86–87; Confederate, 27; education, 50; oversight, 40, 42, 82; protection, 13, 28, 94, 102–5; tactics, 50, 52; training, 52–53; Union, 124

Mills, Roger Q., 136
mingling, 17, 26, 112, 113–46, 151, 157, 192n20. *See also* desegregation; integration; mixing; segregation
Minnesota, 14, 21, 24, 58, 65, 75
missionaries, 6, 19, 25, 33, 46, 48, 64, 82, 84–88, 90–98, 102–3, 105–8, 110, 157
Mississippi, 83, 129, 195n81
mixing, 77, 117, 193n41. *See also* desegregation; integration; mingling; segregation
Mobile, AL, 190n116
Monroe, James, 155–56, 200n28
Montesquieu, Charles de Secondat, 33
"Moral and Political Chart of the World," **155**
morality, 39, 41, 61–62, 76–79, 107, 130, 138, 151, **155**, 157, 159, 171n18, 172n34. *See also* immorality
Morrill, Justin Smith, 80
Morrill Act, 56, 65, 75–76, 180n50
Morris, Robert, 118–19, 192n25
Moss, Hilary J., 19
Moulton, Samuel W., 58, 66–69

Nast, Thomas, 121, **123**, 124
National Association of School Superintendents, 66
national origin, 7, 26, 36, 69, 74, 79, 114, 117, 121, 124, 128, 139, 154
national school system, 6, 13, 24–25, 44, 50–51, 54, 57, 65, 68–69, 75, 105, 150, 159
National Teachers' Association, 57, 65
nationalism, 17, 36–38, 84
Native Americans, 5, 19, 20, 31, 34–35, 46–48, 60, 64, 77, 131, 140, 175n94, 180n50; Cherokee, 131; Chickasaw, 131; Choctaw, 131; Ho Chunk (Winnebago), 47–48; Omaha, 48; Pueblo, 48; Wyandot, 64
New England, 10, 15–16, 19, 21, 23–26, 29–32, 35, 40, 42, 52–53, 57–60, 63, 65, 76, 78–82, 114, 118, 146, 150
New Hampshire, 21, 183n115
New Mexico, 47

New Orleans, LA, 94, 137
New Orleans Tribune, 121
New York state, 69, 121
Newman, Louise Michele, 89
North, 6, 12, 19, 21, 23, 26, 28, 29, 35, 39, 41–43, 45–46, 49–50, 55, 60, 67, 69, 77, 79, 82, 83–85, 87–91, 94, 96, 98–103, 108, 111, 115, 125, 145–46, 148, 150, 175n88, 185n23, 186n33, 188n55, 189n85, 193n42
North Carolina, 7, 120, 195n81
Northeast, 29, 37
Northwest, 56, 58–66, 72, 76, 80, 178n23, 180n48
Northwest Ordinance, 60–61, 63
Norton, Frank H., **154**
Norwood, Thomas, 136

Ohio, 4, 21, 24, 57, 62–65, 69, 72, 76, 99, 103, 119, 155, 178n25
Ohio Educational Monthly, 62, **62**
Olson, Christa J., 158
Ore, Ersula J., 10
"Our Common Schools as They Are and as They May Be," 123

patriarchy, 25, 85, 89, 91, 98, 109
Peabody Fund, 110, 190n116
Pennsylvania, 10, 20, 46, 48, 69, 72, 116, 153
Perce, Legrand, 25, 59, 75–77
Perce Bill, 60, 75–82, 111, 149, 159, 183n115
Pestalozzi, Johann, 15
Petersburg, IL, 53
Philadelphia, PA, 22, 153
Pierce, Edward L., 88, 195n79
Pike, Frederick, 68
Pius IX (pope), 128
Pollard, Edward, 35
Pomeroy, Theodore M., 71
Port Royal, SC, 88
prejudice, 4, 13, 17, 24, 26, 70, 90–91, 109, 113–21, 126–31, 133–43, 145, 147, 159, 193n32, 196n84. *See also* discrimination; racism
pride, 3, 58, 60–66, 69–70, 75–82, 141, 151, 153
Prosser, William F., 13, 31–32, 45–53, 55, 154

Prussia, 36–38, 41, 50–51, 63, 76, 172n40, 173n45, 199n18
public address, 7–13, 158

race, 5, 7–8, 10–11, 13–14, 17–20, 22–27, 30–31, 41, 46, 48–49, 54–56, 64–65, 67, 69–70, 74–75, 77–79, 81, 84–87, 93, 95, 101, 104, 112, 114–30, 133–42, 144–45, 148, 154, 157–58, 193n41, 196n84, 197n111, 200n28; Black, 3–5, 10–11, 13, 19, 24, 26–28, 31, 33, 37–38, 41–43, 46, 48–49, 54–56, 64, 67, 70, 77–78, 82, 84–86, 88–96, 98–104, 106–12, 114–16, 118–21, 124–29, 131, 133–36, 138–45, 147–50, 153, 155, 157, 162n7, 168n91, 180n48, 186n33, 188n55, 189n85, 190n116, 191n3, 192n25, 193n32, 193n42, 197n111, 199n15, 200n28, 200n31; white, 3–6, 11–12, 14, 17, 19–21, 24–26, 28, 31, 34–35, 41–43, 45, 47, 49, 54–56, 59–60, 64–70, **74**, 77–78, 82, 83–84, 86–89, 91, 93–96, 98–101, 103, 107–12, 113–16, 118–21, 124–32, 134–36, 138–43, 145–46, 148–53, 155, 157–58, 162n7, 168n91, 185n23, 186n33, 189n85, 193n32, 197n111, 200n31
racial hierarchies, 5, 19, 55, 64, 89, 111, 116, 124, 126, 129, 140–41, 148, 155, 157
racism, 6–7, 12, 24, 54, 59, 64, 66, 84, 91–92, 96, 115, 119–20, 124, 133, 136, 142, 148–49. *See also* discrimination; prejudice
Rainey, Joseph H., 27–28, 77–78, 134, 139–40
Randall, Samuel J., 68
Randolph, Theodore F., 152
Readers (McGuffey), 62
reconciliation, restoration, and Southern readmission, 7, 13, 26–27, 32, 39–40, 44, 50, 60, 79, 81, 98, 112, 115, 126, 130, 133–35, 139, 144–46, 147–60
Reconstruction, 4–6, 11–15, 17, 20–24, 26–28, 30, 32–33, 38–46, 50, 54, 58, 60, 65–66, 70–71, 80–81, 90, 95–96, 100, 105, 110–12, 115–16, 120–25, 133, 144, 147–48, 150–59, 163n14, 194n57, 195n79, 199n18, 200n28
Reconstruction (Giles), 121, **122**

Reconstruction Acts, 32, 38–44, 49, 80, 85–86, 98–100, 120
Reconstruction Amendments, 81, 146, 148. *See also specific amendments*
religion, 5, 7, 14, 16–17, 19–20, 22, 26–27, 29–30, 32–37, 46, 48, 52, 58, 61–63, 69–70, 84, 86–88, 107–8, 114, 117, 121, 124, 128, 130, 139, 145, 148, 154, 162n10, 196n94, 197n124; Catholic, 5, 17, 20, 29, 31, 36, 46, 63, 107, 114, 118, 121, 124, 128, 139, 145, 162n10, 198n125; Christian, 34, 92–98, 108, 171n18; Disciples of Christ, 61, 65–66; Episcopalian, 124; Methodist, 84, 121; Mormon, 5, 31, 46, 128; Protestant, 5, 17, 19, 45, 47, 50, 61–62, 64, 69, 84, 87–88, 92, 118, 128, 145, 190n106; Puritan, 14–15; Quaker, 34; Second Great Awakening, 58, 61
Report of the Commissioner of Education Made to the Secretary of the Interior for the Year 1870, 74
republicanism, 17, 33, 39–40, 42–43, 49, 61, 80, 112, 114, 134
Republicans, 3–7, 25–26, 31, 33, 38, 41–42, 44–46, 49–51, 53–56, 71, 75, 79, 81–82, 84–85, 87, 90, 92–93, 95, 98–102, 106–10, 112, 115, 117, 120–21, 124–25, 128, 130–31, 133–40, 142–45, 147–49, 155, 157, 162n10, 175n80, 176n112, 195n81, 196n84, 198n4; Liberal, 12, 124–25, 130, 133, 194n57; moderate, 6, 39, 44, 81, 98, 115, 126; New Departure, 50–51; Northern, 23, 136, 183n115; Radical, 5, 11–13, 17, 23–24, 26, 28, 30, 32, 39–40, 42–46, 54, 57–58, 71–72, 98–99, 101–3, 114–16, 124–30, 133, 135, 148–49, 152, 159
resources, 8, 11, 14, 50, 70, 72, 87, 92, 97, 141–42, 146, 199n15
rhetoric, 7–23, 25–28, 39, 63, 65, 69, 75, 77, 85, 91, 96, 105, 112, 114–21, 124, 130, 139, 143, 147–58, 162n10, 164n35, 175n80
Rice, Jenny Edbauer, 9
Richardson, Heather Cox, 99, 197n111
Richmond State Journal, 196n84

Rickoff, Andrew Jackson, 65
Roberts v. City of Boston (1850), 38, 118, 120, 124, 126
Rogers, Andrew J., 68
Rogers, Anthony, 107–8
Rosenwein, Barbara, 10, 164n31
Rousseau, Jean-Jacques, 15
Rubin, Edward, 30
Ruffner, William H., 134–35
Rush, Benjamin, 16, 33
Ryan, Susan M., 89

Sargent, Aaron, 138–39, 143
Sawyer, Frederick A., 75
Sawyer, Philetus, 73
"Scenes in Memphis, Tennessee, During the Riot," **97**
"School Government" (Slocomb), **62**
school journals, 24, 63, 65
school punishments, 17, 37, 58, 61–62, 114, 173n45
Schuller, Kyla, 18, 88, 186n27
Schurz, Carl, 3–5, 12, 50, 125
Scott, James C., 181n59
Scribner, Campbell F., 29
secession, 35, 42, 67, 148
segregation, 7, 64, 79, 81, 113–15, 118, 120–21, 126–28, 130–31, 135, 138, 142, 145, 148, 168n91, 183n115. *See also* desegregation; integration; mingling; mixing
Segur, Carrie, 83, 184n2
Senter, DeWitt, 42
sentiment, 4–6, 10, 13–17, 21, 24–25, 27, 29, 31–38, 45–54, 61, 65, 80, 82, 85, 91, 95, 102, 104, 109, 114, 118, 120–21, 126–28, 133–37, 140, 143–44, 147–60, 162n10, 164n30, 196n84. *See also* emotions; feeling; shame
sex, 11, 26, 115, 120, 136, 193n41
shame, 12, 14, 22, 24–25, 56, 58–82, 103, 109, 141, 151–54, 157. *See also* emotions; feeling; sentiment
Shanklin, George S., 95
Shaw, Lemuel, 120

Sherman, John, 127, 150
slavery, 4, 28, 30–31, 35–36, 39, 41, 43, 46, 54, 64, 67, 73, 76–77, 84, 87–88, 92–93, 127, 131, 149
Slocomb, William, **62**
Smith, Adam, 14–15
Smith School, 118, 192n25
social class, 7, 16, 20, 22, 26, 29, 36–37, 52, 69, 114, 117–18, 133, 137, 139, 148, 196n94, 197n111; lower, 59, 68–69, 72, 77–78, 136, 145; upper, 6, 31, 35, 39, 41, 43, 77, 111, 145, 152, 157, 159
South, 3–7, 12–13, 20–21, 23–26, 28, 29–56, 59–60, 66–69, 75–82, 84–86, 88–102, 106–12, 113–16, 120–21, 124–27, 129, 131, 133–40, 142–46, 147–51, 153–54, 156, 159, 162n7, 185n23, 186n33, 188n66, 198n4, 199n15
South Carolina, 4, 10, 27, 41–42, 88, 93, 113, 120, 140–41, 195n81
spaces, 16–17, 31, 35, 47, 84; classroom, 19, 84, 107; domestic, 16, 25–26, 47, 82, 84–86, 88–89, 91, 108, 151, 153–54; educational, 94; emotional, 117; feminine, 25; intimate, 94; maternal, 96; physical, 11, 113; pluralistic, 144; public, 11, 124; sacred, 26; sanctuary, 16; segregated, 7; separate, 157; social, 11
State Convention of the Colored Citizens of Ohio, 64, 119
Statistical Atlas of the United States Based on the Results of the Ninth Census (Walker), **156**
statistics, 63, 66–69, 71–73, 75–79, 141, 152–54, 183n115
Steffes, Tracy L., 152, 199n19
Stephens, Alexander H., 101, 133, 140
Stevens, Thaddeus, 71–72
Stewart, William M., 75, 138
Stiles, Joseph, 4
Storm, John B., 78–79
Stowe, Calvin E., 63, 117–18
Stowell, William, 136, 196n86
suffrage. *See* voting
Summers, Mark Wahlgren, 102

Sumner, Charles, 23–24, 26, 30–33, 38–44, 49, 54–56, 57, 79, 94, 100, 112, 114, 116, 118–20, 124–30, 132–33, 137–39, 142–43, 147, 159, 173n50, 174n67, 175n80, 192n25, 194n57, 195n79
Supplementary Civil Rights Bill, 125–26, 130–33
sympathy, 15–16, 18–19, 26, 40, 48–49, 55, 91, 113, 118–21, 124–27, 131–32, 134–35, 137, 140, 148, 157, 159–60

taxpayer-funded education, 6–7, 12, 21, 30, 32, 40–42, 58, 64, 81, 104–5, 115, 145, 148, 151
teachers, 6, 12, 15–16, 20–21, 25–26, 29, 36–37, 44, 46–47, 52–53, 58, 62–66, 73, 77, 82–86, 88–103, 106–11, 117–19, 128, 141, 143, 153–55, 186n33, 188n55, 190n106
Tennessee, 42–43, 46, 73, 77–78, 94, **97**, 103, 195n81
Texas, 195n81
Thirteenth Amendment, 4, 92, 106, 127, 131, 144
Townsend, Washington, 76, 78
Trumbull, Lyman, 44, 84, 92–93

unequal schooling, 19, 27, 31, 37, 49, 64, 135, 150
Union, 3–4, 15, 23–27, 45, 50
Union Leagues (Loyal Leagues), 102, 189n85
University of Virginia, 135
Utah Territory, 5, 46

Vermont, 193n32
violence, 3, 28, 36, 39, 48, 83, 91–92, 94, 96–100, 102, 124–25, 133, 147, 159
Virginia, 4, 33, 41–44, 120, 135–37, 145, 149, 195n81, 196n84, 196nn86–87
visceral rhetoric, 26, 112, 115–17, 119–20, 139
voting, 26, 42, 46, 49, 67, 82, 86, 95, 98–105, 107–8, 111, 124, 155, 157, 199n15

Walker, Francis A., **156**
Walker, Gilbert C., 43, 149, 175n80
Walls, Josiah T., 139–40, 159

Washburne, Elihu B., 96
Washington, DC, 66, 72, 127
Washington, George, 33–34
Waud, Alfred R., **97**
Weikle-Mills, Courtney A., 15
West, 5, 19–21, 24–25, 30, 45–48, 55, 98, 103, 114, 145, 154, 162n10, 187n52
Western Freedmen's Aid Commission, 87
Western Reserve Eclectic Institute, 65
westward expansion, 5, 31, 45
Whig Party, 20, 168n99
White, Emerson E., 66
white supremacy, 67, 77, 96, 111, 121, 125, 133, 140–41, 149, 151
Whitehead, Thomas, 196n84
whiteness, 64, 149, 155, 158
Wickersham, James Pyle, 20–21, 116–17, 153
Willey, Waitman T., 93
Williams, Charles G., 143
Wilson, Ephraim K., 137
Wilson, Henry, 43, 50–51, 92–94, 103
Wilson, Kirt, 11, 114, 124
Wolf, George, 168n99
Wood, Fernando, 106–7, 190n106
Woodbridge, William Channing, **155**
Woodbridge's School Atlas (Woodbridge), **155**
Woods, Michael E., 15, 35
Woodward, George W., 102
Wrage, Ernest J., 158

Yao, Xine, 14
Young, Brigham, 128

Zaeske, Susan, 77

ABOUT THE AUTHOR

Photograph by Christie Clancy

MICHAEL J. STEUDEMAN is assistant professor of rhetoric at Penn State University. He researches how policymakers in the United States invoke education as a way to sidestep, reframe, or obfuscate debates over an array of social issues. He is editor of *Teaching Demagoguery and Democracy: Rhetorical Pedagogy in Polarized Times*. His work has appeared in journals including the *Quarterly Journal of Speech*, the *Rhetoric Society Quarterly*, and the *History of Education Quarterly*.

www.ingramcontent.com/pod-product-compliance
Lightning Source LLC
Chambersburg PA
CBHW022015220426
43663CB00007B/1087